# Woman of Letters

*Virginia Woolf, 1939*

# Woman of Letters
# A Life of Virginia Woolf

PHYLLIS ROSE

NEW YORK
OXFORD UNIVERSITY PRESS
1978

Library of Congress Cataloging in Publication Data
Rose, Phyllis, 1942–
  Woman of letters: a life of Virginia Woolf.

  Includes index.
  1. Woolf, Virginia Stephen, 1882–1941.   2. Authors,
English—20th century—Biography.   I. Title.
PR6045.072Z867     823'.9'12     77-16489
ISBN 0-19-502370-6

*For*

ELI & MINNIE P. DAVIDOFF
RICHARD DAVIDOFF
SUSAN D. GILBERT

# Preface

*Let me state that without my notes Shade's text simply has no human reality at all since the human reality of such a poem as his (being too skittish and too reticent for an autobiographical work), with the omission of many pithy lines carelessly rejected by him, has to depend entirely on the reality of the author and his surroundings, attachments and so forth, a reality that only my notes can provide. To this statement my dear poet would probably not have subscribed, but, for better or worse, it is the commentator who has the last word.*

Nabokov, *Pale Fire*

In beginning this book, which aims to place Virginia Woolf's works in a biographical context, I think for caution of Nabokov, whose brilliant mockery of such an endeavor serves as my epigraph. In trying to provide the "human reality" of a work of art, the commentator may impose upon it his or her own vision, turning, for example as in *Pale Fire*, a low-keyed nature poem into an epic about the exile of a Baltic king. To try to make connections between a writer's experience and his or her art is to risk transporting our own bees to other people's bonnets. Richard Ellmann, perhaps the best of contemporary literary biographers, acknowledges the risk when he uses the phrase "biographical speculations" to describe his work.

In setting itself the task of exploring what is variously called the "inner life" or the "imaginative world" of creative artists, contemporary biographical criticism may be seen—unsympathetically—as trying to create for itself an artificially workable gray area between the facts of a writer's life and his fictions. But in fact it is moving toward the recognition that a life is as much a work of fiction—of guiding narrative structures—as novels and poems, and that the task of literary biography is to explore this fiction.

The metaphors may vary—you can be at a fork or a crossroad in life, you can be like Dante in the middle of life's pathway, lost in a forest—but the need to shape expectations about experience does not: past, present, and future would be an unassimilable, perhaps an unlivable blur unless we projected upon it a structure of meaning to sift out certain moments as significant, some experiences as crucial. Each of us, influenced perhaps by one ideology or another, generates his or her own symbolic landscape, with its individual twists and curves, so that one persons's fork in the road—to take a crude example, the fork between family and career—is no fork at all to another, but a two-lane highway, and one person's state of liberation is another's state of chaos and disintegration.

The highly personal configuration of significance by which a person views his experience I would call his personal mythology. Only autobiographers are forced to reveal their personal mythologies, and even some of them manage to avoid doing it, but Virginia Woolf's personal mythology, the set of stories she made up about her own experience, informs her correspondence, her memoirs, and many of her essays, as well as her novels. So in the parts of this book which deal exclusively with biographical material, I have been guided by what Woolf herself found significant, the myths she generated about her own experience.

My first two chapters, for example, rely heavily on memoirs Woolf wrote at various times which can be put together to form a more or less chronological coverage of her life until the first World War.* The narrative structure of these memoirs, which I follow and elucidate, seems to me more significant than any particular facts they reveal. Indeed, the details vary; there are inconsistencies. Woolf cannot resist telling a good story, or, on the next go round, telling it even better. At the end of one essay she describes how her half-brother, George Duckworth, entered her room one night to plague her with embraces. The light was out, she was almost asleep, and he told her not to turn the light on. In her next essay she recalls that episode again, only now she is in bed reading *Marius the Epicurean* when Duckworth comes in, and he turns the light out—a trivial change, perhaps, but the effect is more sinister. These chapters present the leading figures and events in the myth of her youth, material which served as the basis of much of her fiction. The focus of succeeding chapters will alternate between her life and her novels, seeking points of fruitful connection between them.

Books on Virginia Woolf tend to be of two kinds. Studies of her novels, even very recent ones, concentrate on their

* Published as *Moments of Being*, ed. Jeanne Schulkind (Sussex: The University Press, 1976).

form and technique. Emphasizing the autonomy of the text, eschewing context, they concern themselves with point of view, with "modes of subjectivity," with the way in which the novels' forms are generated by Woolf's interest in the subjective nature of life, rather than by traditional elements of plot and character. These formalist approaches have generally sustained the image of Virginia Woolf that was her own worst fear, that of the artist encased in the bubble of her own art. Her novels emerge from such studies as fictionalized meditations on Self and Other, Time and Flux, rather like Woolf's own parody of Mr. Ramsay discoursing on "subject and object and the nature of reality."

On the other hand, recent years have produced a flood of biographical information about the Bloomsbury group, led off by the publication of Leonard Woolf's autobiography. Michael Holroyd's work on Lytton Strachey should be mentioned here, Quentin Bell's urbane and masterful biography of Virginia Woolf, and Nigel Nicolson's *Portrait of a Marriage.** Quentin Bell defined the task he set for himself as historical—to record the facts of his aunt's life. The interest of the other books is partly historical, partly sociological. Although Holroyd has chapters on Strachey's works, his absence of perspective on them shows that his interest is really elsewhere, and his biography has aptly been described as a monument in the history of gay liberation rather than of literature. The Nicolson book, in addition to its unembarrassed presentation of female homosexuality, constitutes an extended—and provocative—argument for open marriage. Bloomsbury seems to be serving a contemporary audience as

---

* Quentin Bell, *Virginia Woolf: A Biography*, 2 vols. (London: The Hogarth Press, 1972); Michael Holroyd, *Lytton Strachey: A Critical Biography* (New York: Holt, Rinehart and Winston, 1968); Nigel Nicolson, *Portrait of a Marriage* (New York: Atheneum, 1973); Leonard Woolf, *Autobiography*, 5 vols. (London: The Hogarth Press, 1960–70). The Nicolsons were not really "Bloomsbury," but, outside of scholarly circles, the distinction has seemed a fine one, especially from this side of the Atlantic. More recently, The Hogarth Press in London and Harcourt Brace Jovanovich in New York have begun to publish, in yearly installments, Virginia Woolf's complete diary and correspondence.

a historical touchstone in the examination of its own sexual revolution, and while this may be valuable, it is a long way from literature.

This new spurt of biography has done little to revise the damaging image of Virginia Woolf for which E. M. Forster formulated a phrase in 1941: the Invalid Lady of Bloomsbury. Indeed this image has been reinforced. Leonard Woolf revealed in *Beginning Again* details of his wife's mental illness and his own efforts to cope with her problem. Quentin Bell tells about her sexual exploitation in childhood by her half-brother George Duckworth and about her later frigidity.*

Bell's biography will no doubt remain the definitive source of information about Woolf—and deservedly. All the more reason, however, that its bias should be clearly defined. Bell says little about Woolf's novels, and his willingness to describe her mental disturbances and ultimate suicide combined with an unwillingness to treat in the context of biography what was in fact the center of her life, her writing, creates the impression of a singularly unhealthy existence. Leonard Woolf emerges as the hero of his wife's life and a martyr to her insanity. Bell made use of Virginia Woolf's unpublished memoirs, journals, and correspondence in constructing his history of her life, but his exclusion of her essays and novels as evidence of her development left it to others to explore the ways in which Woolf's life fed her fiction and in which her fiction may illuminate aspects of her life. And so I have returned to the original sources used by Bell, but I employ them in a rather different way, as evidence of myth rather than fact.

In uniting a study of Woolf's life with a study of her works, I want to redress the biographical emphasis on her illness and suicide by showing the extent to which she took her life into her own hands. It is true that from one point of

* "A Sketch of the Past," her most extensive and revealing memoir, which implicates both her half-brothers in sexual abuse, was not available to Quentin Bell until after his book was completed.

view, her biography is an allegory of how not to live; she was intermittently insane and ended by drowning herself. But the fact that Van Gogh cut off his ear or that Woolf drowned in the Ouse, while undeniably part of the drama, is as little the point of the drama as the fact that Hamlet dies in a swordfight at the end of Shakespeare's play. In fact, the greater temptation these days is to assume that suicide is a proof of genius and to revere as "more creative" writers who have been neurotic on a spectacular scale. I think it unfortunate in more ways than one that some of the leading women writers of our century—one thinks of Plath and Sexton as well as Woolf—have killed themselves. Erica Jong calls this the "head-in-the-oven" school of women writers, and like her, I would prefer to see less emphasis on despair, more on resilience in the literary history of women.

Despite her illness, despite restrictions on her activity, Virginia Woolf was immensely productive. To say nothing of her novels, her literary criticism and essays, by themselves, constitute a major achievement. She was the most ingratiating and in some ways the most sophisticated spokeswoman that feminism has ever had. And in her journals, only a small part of which have been published in *A Writer's Diary*, she explored her life as it passed with a seriousness and sustained acuteness unmatched by any woman except Anaïs Nin, whose diaries are clearly her central work. A claim to reputation, slim but valid (look after all at the attention paid Horace Walpole), could also be based on her delightful and extensive correspondence.

Such creative achievement is a rare thing; in a woman— for reasons Woolf herself explored—it is even rarer, and to examine her life is to examine the dynamics of a miracle. Few of us may match her achievement, but to some extent, the problems of achievement for a woman are typical, so that the dynamics of a miracle may possibly shed some light on other lives.

Like everyone else, however, Virginia Woolf was unlike

everyone else. It would be easier for me, and in some ways more pleasant, to portray her completely as a feminist heroine, the victim of social and cultural forces which every woman who sets high standards for herself in a society like ours must face, and to this extent a model for us all. But the danger exists of overly normalizing a unique and complicated person. Born with unusual talent as well as an inherited tendency to madness, with a distinguished man of letters for her father and a charismatic woman, a great beauty, for her mother, she had extraordinary opportunities in childhood, but was also subjected to extraordinary pressures. To erase the squiggles of her life in order to make it conform to a clear and typical trajectory would be, at the very least, untruthful.

In this study I want also to readjust the critical perspective on Woolf's art, for I see in her novels not meditations on philosophical themes but personal treatments of vital and immediate problems of identity. Her concern with the position of women, intertwined as it is with her sense of herself, informs the novels, which tend to state contrasting impulses toward issues of selfhood: the urge to be a maternal Mrs. Ramsay, for example, and the urge to reject her in favor of independence and achievement; the urge to affirm life by creating social bonds like Mrs. Dalloway, and the urge to despair in isolation like Septimus Warren Smith. To see her as a novelist deeply concerned with social and cultural reality requires that one appreciate the feminist perspective in her books, taking "feminist" to refer to a political consciousness which began with reasoning, to borrow a phrase from E. L. Doctorow, from her own hurt feelings. I view Woolf's feminism as the crux of her emotional as well as her intellectual life. It is also the key to revising the image of her as an isolated and somewhat precious technician.

In one of those fascinating shifts which suggest how closely aesthetic judgments are linked to other kinds of awareness, we are currently witnessing a thorough revaluation of Virginia Woolf. In the past, she was considered for the most part an elegant but finally a minor writer; she is well on the way to becoming major. Though her literary achievement can sustain this surge of scrutiny, what inspired it, I believe, was her feminism, which found in the contemporary spread of feminist consciousness a receptive audience.

Certainly in my own case the path of interest led to the novels from an initial, strong response to *A Room of One's Own* and certain passages in *A Writer's Diary*, like this one, which reflects upon feminine identity:

> Father's birthday. He would have been 96, 96, yes, today; and could have been 96, like other people one has known: but mercifully was not. His life would have entirely ended mine. What would have happened? No writing; no books;—inconceivable.

This entry, written in 1928, astonished me when I read it for the first time in 1971. Its frank confrontation of a possible conflict between a woman's achievements and the lives of her loved ones seemed more daringly to the point than anything being written about women at that time, and although, since then, the theme has been sufficiently worked over, Woolf's statement of it remains fresh and direct.

Woolf's feminism expresses itself most tellingly in her essays and diary as a concern with the psychological effects of social structures, with the internalization of patriarchal authority even after the actual authority has weakened. She is particularly sensitive to shadowy internal prohibitions and emotional phantoms, like the one she imagines standing behind her as she wrote her first review, telling her not to deal harshly with a book by a man. Without minimizing social and cultural problems, Woolf suggests the extent to which the struggle for liberation is going on inside. Her novels, reread after *A Writer's Diary* and *A Room of One's Own*, seemed continued revelations of the same concerns. At that point Woolf ceased in my mind to be an impersonal generator of elegant works of fiction and became a larger and more interesting figure—practitioner of an art which conceals art, elegant, to be sure, but more importantly the author of works written in passion which do not boast of their passion, and, indeed, often try to hide it. Although her novels can stand alone, their full emotional resonance only emerges when they are seen in a wider context, the context of Woolf's experience and of her beliefs.

Virginia Woolf's talent, spreading from a core of strength and vulnerability, of self-containment and resentment, of charm and anger, is so variously expressed that to consider her achievement as a novelist is not enough, and so, largely in token of the breadth of her accomplishment (and of my admiration), I call her in the title of this book a woman of letters. I also intend some ironies in that title, but they are not directed at Virginia Woolf. *Woman of Letters* was written in sympathy, by which I do not mean that it was written always in agreement with or approval of its subject; I mean that my goal throughout has been imaginative understanding of a figure who, as the years pass, seems less remote and less aloof, but whose deepest concerns—her art and her feminism—remain to be fully explored.

*Middletown, Connecticut*                                    P.R.
*November, 1977*

# Acknowledgments

If I were to articulate fully my gratitude to the people who have helped me in the writing of this book, I should vex everyone but myself and perhaps the recipients of my thanks. So I shall be spare and merely beg those of you named here to believe in the warmth of my gratitude.

My colleagues at Wesleyan University have sustained and enlightened me for many years. One could ask little more of an intellectual community. I would like particularly to thank Professors Joseph W. Reed, Jr., Carol B. Ohmann, Richard Ohmann, and Jeffrey Butler for meticulous help with the manuscript, David Schorr and Danny Dries for their friendship, and the President and Trustees of the university for the allocation of funds in support of research.

I am grateful to Mark Rose of the University of California at Santa Barbara for early encouragement and help, to Mary Price of *The Yale Review* for her contributions as both editor and photographer, and most of all to Quentin Bell, for his seminal biography of Woolf, for his kind permission to quote from Woolf's unpublished writings, and—in general—for wisdom and generosity which defy catalogue. James Raimes and Stephanie Golden of Oxford University Press helped bring this book through the stage so difficult for Virginia Woolf. My gratitude to them is enormous, as is my appreciation of their talents.

To the Henry W. and Albert A. Berg Collection of the New York Public Library, Astor, Lenox and Tilden Foundations, I am indebted for allowing me to quote from unpublished manuscripts of Virginia Woolf in their possession. The staff of the Berg Collection has been enormously helpful, and I want especially to thank Dr. Lola Szladits, curator of the collection. For assistance in research, my thanks are also due to the staff of the Humanities Research Center of the University of Texas, the staff of the King's College Library, Cambridge, and the staff of the University of Sussex Library, especially Mrs. Bet Inglis.

To the National Endowment for the Humanities I am indebted for a fellowship in 1973–74 which enabled me to do much of my research, and to Harcourt Brace Jovanovich, the American publisher of the works of Virginia and Leonard Woolf, for permission to quote from published writings.

Perhaps by the time this is published, my son, Teddy Rose, will be old enough to recognize his name in print and to read the word "THANKS" which I write here for him, in small recompense for the vivacity that brackets my day.

# Contents

# Illustrations

# Woman of Letters

# St. Ives
# and Kensington

Her earliest memory was of red and purple flowers on a black dress. She was sitting on her mother's lap, returning from St. Ives, in Cornwall. Then, the sound of waves breaking on the beach as she lay in the nursery.

She was Adeline Virginia Stephen, third child, second daughter of Leslie and Julia Stephen, born 25 January 1882. She shared the nursery with her older sister and brother, Vanessa and Thoby, and later with her brother Adrian, born a year after she was. Since each of her parents had been married before and widowed, it was a household crowded with children: Leslie's daughter, Laura, who would turn out to be retarded, and Julia's children, George, Stella, and Gerald Duckworth, who were twelve, thirteen, and fourteen when Virginia was born.

Her parents were solid members of upper-middle-class late-Victorian society, not rich, but well-to-do and well connected. Leslie Stephen was an intellectual, but not a bohemian. He observed the bourgeois pieties. Tea was served formally in the afternoon, great men like Henry James were entertained with dignity, and in the evening one dressed for dinner. Neither the informal lifestyle of intellectuals today nor their modest birth rate had come to prevail, so that the quantity of emotion generated by so many people living in the same house was kept in check by strict rules of behavior. It is hard to over-emphasize the repressive force of the world Virginia Woolf was born into.

On the other hand, it was an extremely literate, verbal, and articulate world. Reading and writing were the center of Leslie Stephen's life. Giving up the quiet life of a don at Cambridge because of religious doubt, Stephen had moved to London in his mid-thirties and had begun turning out literary journalism with the characteristic energy of the great Victorians. As editor of *The Cornhill Magazine,* he worked with the leading writers of his time, maintaining his own output all the while. His monumental *History of English Thought in the Eighteenth Century* thrust him to the summit of English literary life, and, more or less as respite from his serious labors, he contributed to the English Men of Letters Series volumes on Pope, Swift, Johnson, George Eliot, and Hobbes. In 1882, the year Virginia was born, he resigned as editor of the *Cornhill* and undertook the production of the *Dictionary of National Biography,* that vast collection of biographical essays of which he himself wrote 378. For the next ten years, this enormous project of writing and editing was being conducted in, was to some extent dominating, the house in which Virginia Woolf was growing up. By the time

Stephen was forced to abandon it, worn out by the writing, the working over of copy, the correcting of proofs, leaving it to someone else to push on through Q, R, and S to Z, he had established himself as the leading man of letters of England, the successor to Matthew Arnold,[1] and had imprinted on the mind of his youngest daughter a heroic impression of literary activity.

Naturally, her father's friends were writers, too: George Meredith, Henry James, J. A. Symonds, John Morley, and James Russell Lowell, a frequent visitor to the Stephen house in the early eighties, when he was American ambassador to the Court of St. James. He was also Virginia's godfather. Such men, along with many bores, no doubt (for even as children the Stephens made such distinctions), would gather in the drawing room. Less palpably, a great Victorian novelist haunted the house in the person of Laura Stephen, for her mother Minny, Leslie's first wife, had been one of Thackeray's daughters. His other daughter, the children's aunt, Anny Ritchie, was a popular novelist in her own right. For the young Virginia Woolf, all this was enabling. It doesn't hurt a writer to be born into a family where writing is a normal human activity.

If there was a family tradition of Talent, there was also a family tradition of Beauty. Julia Stephen's mother was one of seven sisters, the Pattles, six of whom were famous for their looks. The seventh, Julia Margaret Cameron, the photographer, was to become famous for her talent. The breathtaking beauty of the Pattles (it has not dated, as beauty can do) may be seen in Mrs. Cameron's photographs of Julia Stephen, the magnificent structure of her face highlighted against and seeming to emerge from the dark like a crescent moon.

Virginia inherited this beauty, but from early on her relationship to it (for her beauty seems, as she talks of it, a thing detached from her) was complex and difficult. She could not simply accept it or rest easy with it. Another of her

*Virginia Woolf's mother, Julia, photographed by Julia Margaret Cameron circa 1867, when she was Mrs. Herbert Duckworth.*

early memories focuses on the looking-glass in the hall at the house in St. Ives. She was six or seven, and already she could scarcely bring herself to look in the mirror. Why? She offers explanations: she was a tomboy, and it violated the tomboy code. More searchingly, she says that something in her made her reject whatever in herself gave her pleasure. Her paternal grandfather, Sir James, smoked a cigar, liked it, and so threw it away, vowing never to smoke another. She treasures that example of the puritanical streak, the strain of spartan asceticism, which she thinks she inherited from her father, which made her shy and self-conscious when she looked in a mirror, and which kept her from taking pleasure in her beauty.[2] One may think that at her birth some malicious fairy gave Virginia the distressing compulsion to see dualities. Beauty and talent are not necessarily immiscible, but Virginia seems to have perceived them as such and from the earliest of ages to have chosen to enroll herself under the standard of talent.

What she called "looking-glass shame" lasted all her life, making everything to do with dressing her body painful and sometimes terrifying. She hated shopping, being fitted for clothes, wearing a new outfit. She could hardly bear to be photographed. She enjoyed beauty intensely but it had to be beauty of nature—of a nature outside of herself; anything connected with her body carried a burden of shame.

Partially, confusedly, she associates a sordid childhood episode with this "looking-glass shame." When she was six or seven, again at Talland House in Cornwall, her handsome, eighteen-year-old half-brother, Gerald Duckworth, placed her on a ledge outside the dining room and explored her body as she sat there. She said in later years she could recall the feel of his hand going lower and lower and hoping he would stop. She stiffened and wriggled as his hand approached her private parts and went on to explore them, too. Her feelings? Resentment, dislike, and shame, a shame she didn't later understand. Why, she wondered, should she have felt shame at the age of six? She concluded that certain parts of the body must not be touched, that it is wrong to allow them to be touched, and that this feeling is instinctive, inherited at birth.

Her memoirs present the story of Gerald's assault as confirming a sexual reticence already established rather than traumatically provoking it. With the experience she associates a dream: she is staring into the mirror when a hideous face, the face of an animal, appears over her shoulder, the very face of sex. When Woolf writes about sex in her novels, the elements present in this childhood episode are usually repeated—male advances as aggression and exploitation, the woman's chief response a fear of violation and a desire not to be touched, the shame and disgust represented by an animal. The animal, that curiously Victorian image, suggests that at least some of her disgust is culturally conditioned. Ladylike Kensington had bred reticence, a reluctance to deal with things of the body, which Virginia Woolf was later to acknowledge as the chief flaw of her writing, as it was the chief distortion and diminishment of her life.[3]

One thing that makes us pause at this remembrance is that, by Woolf's account, something so similar happened to her later. Some time after her mother's death in 1895, probably when she was twenty, her other half-brother, George Duckworth, began making advances which seemed to her distinctly sexual.[4] Her description of these events is vague: George kissed her, George embraced her, George leapt upon her in bed. He was a sloppily emotional sort of man, particularly maudlin about family ties, but he was also the soul of propriety, a believer in dressing for dinner, a social climber. His physical gestures seemed to him, no doubt, proper expressions of family feeling, but not to Virginia. Although she never accused him of anything more than ambiguously erotic gestures, never, that is, accused him of actually raping her, she regarded his behavior as sexually criminal and called him (with relish) her "seducing half-brother."

Gerald's sexual tampering left nowhere near the same residue of bad feeling that George's did, and George Duckworth, not Gerald, came to symbolize sexual perfidy to Virginia. Throughout her adult life, with some intervals of pity, benign contempt, and even, occasionally, mild affection, she regarded George as a nasty creature and talked of him spitefully to her friends. In her memoirs, George is a fully developed character, a villain, albeit faintly comic, whereas Gerald is rarely mentioned. He is a Duckworth, which is to say well-dressed, good-looking, largely philistine; but in contrast to George's frenetic pursuit of social success, Gerald seems to have gone about his business quietly and with self-restraint, never bullying Virginia and Vanessa as George did. He set up a publishing house and was, in fact, the publisher of Virginia's first two novels. She never, so far as I can tell, mentioned the incident on the slab outside the dining room of Talland House until quite late in her life, in "A Sketch of the Past," which she wrote in 1939–40, and in a letter to Ethel Smyth of 1941.

Her mother, who holds her in her lap in her earliest memory, continues to dominate Virginia's memories of childhood, whether in her own person or in her more diffused embodiment in the landscape of St. Ives. Of the family's two houses, Virginia vastly preferred Talland House at St. Ives, where the entire menage relocated for the summer, to the gloomy town house at 22 Hyde Park Gate, Kensington. As with most children, the country made a deeper impression on her than the city. Twice-daily walks in Kensington Gardens could not compare to sailing, digging, and scrambling over rocks at the beach, or playing in the gardens of the house overlooking the bay and the Godrivy lighthouse. Still, there is more to it than a simple preference for country over city. Most of Virginia's early memories are of St. Ives, warm and sensual memories, full of light and color, and the place is intimately connected in her imagination with her mother, who was the altarpiece, the center of the cathedral space of her childhood.

She recalled her mother's rings, one diamond, one emerald, one opal, and the twisted silver bracelets James Russell Lowell had given her, which tinkled as she walked, remembered particularly when she came into the nursery to say goodnight, her hand shading a candle. Very early she became aware, through servants and visitors, that her mother was considered very beautiful.

Julia Jackson Duckworth, when she married Leslie Stephen in 1878, was a young widow of astonishing beauty, and, by all accounts, a remarkable person. Her beauty made people think of Greek goddesses and the Elgin marbles; her character made them think of madonnas and saints. She had three children by her first marriage and four more with Leslie, and she was, it would seem, a splendid mother. According to Leslie's reverential account of her, to love was her essence, and all her energies were spent in caring for other people. She possessed instinctively the art of soothing, of ministering to needs almost unspoken, and naturally enough people were always falling in love with her. In a backhanded tribute to Leslie Stephen after his death, George Meredith told Virginia Woolf, "He was the one man to my knowledge worthy to have married your mother."

Julia Stephen had spent much time in her youth at Little Holland House, the home of her aunt, Mrs. Prinsep, a Pattle sister who had married a retired Indian official and who turned her home into a gathering place for artists. G. F. Watts was given a studio at Little Holland House, and the Prinseps also cared for Burne-Jones occasionally. Tennyson might turn up for croquet on Sunday afternoons. It was a hothouse of aestheticism, where, according to Ellen Terry, another habituée, all the men were gifted and all the women were graceful.[5] The women, scorning the crinolines of the day, walked about in Venetian draperies and offered strawberries and cream to artists they were taught to revere. Julia Jackson was used to admiration: Woolner, the sculptor, and Holman Hunt, the painter, are said to have proposed to her when she was in her teens. She chose to marry instead a man with no pretensions to art or intellectuality, the handsome, wealthy, and respectable barrister Herbert Duckworth, by whom she had three children and with whom she was exquisitely happy, until one day, reaching up to pluck her a fig, he burst an abscess and died.

What was Julia besides beautiful? Quick, direct, practical, amusing, says Virginia. She liked simplicity, disliked affectation. She struck people as a combination of madonna and woman of the world. With no waste motion, she managed the business of a large household. Something of a matchmaker, she liked bringing people together. Virginia uses metaphors of weaving and connection in describing her. She supported the fabric of their lives, but living on such an extended surface, she had no time to concentrate on any one of them, unless they were ill, or unless, perhaps, it was Adrian, her youngest and favorite child.

From very early, verbal facility was Virginia's principal weapon in the nursery battle for place and for identity. She used it to hold her own against an older sister and brother who had been close before she arrived on the scene, and it was also her chief way of winning the approval of adults, who liked her because she made them laugh more than the other children. In 1891, the children, with Virginia as chief writer, began producing a family newsletter, the *Hyde Park Gate News*. Vanessa remembers, as typical of her sister's sensitivity to the good opinion of adults, a particular day when they laid a copy of the paper on the table next to their mother's sofa while she was at dinner and then crept into another room to watch her response. As they looked, Virginia trembling with excitement, they could see their mother's lamplit figure sitting near the fire, their father on the other side, both reading. Then Mrs. Stephen saw the paper, picked it up, began to read. Virginia and Vanessa listened greedily for comment. "Rather clever, I think," she said. Without seeming much excited, she put the paper back down, but this was, according to Vanessa, enough to thrill Virginia.[6] What is striking is how Leslie Stephen fades into the background and this scene about the need for approval is dominated by Julia.

Virginia presents her childhood as radiantly happy, merry, lively, filled with people, and the center of it all was Julia. When Julia died in 1895—worn out, some said, by her demanding husband and family cares—the joyful days were over. A palpable black pall seemed to settle over the family. The children had to wear mourning clothes. Even their small pleasures were curtailed. Their greatest pleasure, the house at St. Ives, where they had spent thirteen summers, had to be given up, because Leslie associated it too painfully with his dead wife. A regime of sorrow, solemnity, and heavy emotion was enjoined upon them by the grief-struck widower and a wailing chorus of female relations. It was unnatural for children, and they resented it almost as much as they were pained by their mother's death. "The shrouded, cautious, dulled life took the place of all the chatter and laughter of the summer. There were no more parties; no more young men and women laughing. No more flashing visions of white summer dresses and hansoms dashing off to private views and dinner parties, none of that natural life and gaiety which my mother had created." No more of those "snatched moments that were so amusing and for some reason so soothing and yet exciting when one ran downstairs to dinner arm in arm with mother; or chose the jewels she was to wear. There was none of that pride when one said something that amused her."[7] Leslie presided over the replacement of gaiety and laughter by foolish sentimentality, hypocritical solemnity, and all the conventions of sorrow. They had lost, in a way, not one parent but two, for their father in his assertive and coercive grief had suddenly become hateful.

Woolf's memoirs shape her life before the move to Bloomsbury in 1904 as a two-act drama with a brief entr'acte. The long first-act idyll of childhood happiness, starring her mother, ends with her mother's death. In the entr'acte, spanning the years from 1895 to 1897, Stella Duckworth, Virginia's half-sister, inherits Julia's place, running the household and trying to wrest it from despair. Stella, almost as beautiful as her mother, shared her mother's early preference for gentlemen over artists and intellectuals, and she fell in love with a simple, honest, affectionate, well-dressed young solicitor named Jack Hills. Jack brought some of the healthy openness of country life to the Kensington household. It was he, for example, who much later explained sex, in a relaxed and humorous way, to Virginia. Incredibly innocent, she had thought that all men loved only one woman, as her father did, and were "dishonourable" if "unchaste," as much as women were. Jack was a breath of fresh air in Virginia's book-centered world.

The marriage of Stella and Jack, which seemed so good and so natural, was taken as a personal blow by Leslie Stephen. Virginia was to say later that if only her father could have said "I am jealous" rather than "You are selfish," the whole family atmosphere would have been lightened. But he chose to take the tack that Stella, in marrying, was selfishly abandoning him, although she was moving only three doors away and he was to enjoy daily visits. In an atmosphere of pain and gloom he consented to the marriage, a marriage which opened up vistas of renewed joy to Vanessa and Virginia. Stella, married, would launch them on the sea of life, love, and womanhood. But Stella returned from her honeymoon suffering from the infection of which, a brief three months after her wedding, she was to die. So the entr'acte, promising a happy ending, closed with a tragedy which recapitulates the tragedy at the end of Act I.

In describing this period (1895–97), Virginia barely touches upon the fact that her mother's death was followed by her first mental breakdown, but Stella's death forced her to recall the earlier one and to feel consciously, perhaps for the first time, its full impact.

> Anyone whether fifteen or not, whether sensitive or not, must have felt something very acute, merely from the pressure of circumstance. My mother's death had

*Julia Stephen and her daughter Stella Duckworth, circa 1894.*

been a latent sorrow. How at thirteen would one feel it fully? But Stella's death two years later fell upon a different substance. . . . The glooms, the morbidity, the shut bedrooms, the giving up of St. Ives, the black clothes—all this had found my mind and made it apprehensive: made it I suppose unnaturally responsive to Stella's happiness and the promise it held out for us and for her—when once more, unbelievably, catastrophically, I remember saying to myself, this impossible thing has happened: as if it were unnatural, against the law, horrible, as a treachery, a betrayal,—the fact of death. The blow, the second blow of death struck on me; tremulous, creased, sitting with my wings still stuck together on the broken chrysalis.[8]


This double blow conditioned her to perceive happiness and beauty as a fragile fabric containing a much more substantial world of chaos and pain, explosive, always threatening to break out. If she connected her mother's death with the demands of marriage, Stella's death so soon after her wedding must have confirmed the yoking of the ideas of death and sex.

Contrasts had dominated her childhood: the beauty of the Pattles and the talent of the Stephens, the self-absorbed energy of her father versus her mother's diffused concern for others, restricted London winters and golden summers at St. Ives, nondescript days of cotton-wool well-being and periodic outbreaks of violence. Three miniature epiphanies prefigured the double blows of death, moments when a hidden enemy emerged from the haze of daily life and startled her consciousness. First, she and her brother Thoby were having a fight when, suddenly overwhelmed by her own powerlessness, Virginia dropped her fists and let Thoby beat her. Second, she heard that a man who had stayed with them at St. Ives had killed himself. Third—and this is the odd element in this series of memories—she perceived a flower rooted in the earth. The discrepancy between flower and earth seemed to bother her as had the suicide against a background of placid contentment, until she recognized that "that is the whole," earth and flower.[9] So fundamentally was the world divided into the threatening and the non-threatening that even a flower could be disturbing unless you recognized that it emerged naturally from the mothering earth and was a part of it. Virginia connects her deepest impulse as a writer with this attempt to see the intruding, destructive, assertive elements of life as a part of a whole. Constructing such "wholes" would be her equivalent of sexual activity.

Even before the blows began to fall, she had been fearful. In the nursery at night, she would check to see if the fire was low. She dreaded its burning after they had gone to bed, frightened of the flickering shadow on the wall. Adrian, on the other hand, who shared the nursery with her, liked the flickering flame-light. To compromise, the nurse would put a towel over the fender, muting the shadows. (In *To the Lighthouse* the shadows cast by the night light on a boar's skull nailed to the wall terrify Cam, but James cannot go to sleep without a light and will not let the skull be touched. Mrs. Ramsay, the peacemaker, wraps her shawl around the skull, softening the shadow, so Cam sees mountains and bird's nests and gardens instead of the face of death.) Tempering the wind to the shorn lamb, Woolf's art, too, softens the harsh angularities of fact by placing them in a context of affective perception. Even a puddle of water must be seen in connection to something else, placed into a context, or it becomes unbearable. Rigid boundaries between perceived and perceiver, rigid boundaries between one part of reality and another are abhorrent to her. *The Waves*, her most ambitious novel, seeks to portray six individuals as aspects of one being; seeking continuity is her hallmark as a writer.

Her mother's death, reinforced by Stella's death two years later, was the cataclysmic disruption of her childhood, its major discontinuity, the blow from the hidden enemy which made everything else seem insubstantial. It was decades before she could fit this violence into an artistic whole. In the meantime, until she was forty-four, she was haunted by her mother. She could see her, hear her, imagine her responses as she went about her day. Invisible presences like that of her mother, she writes, tug us this way and that in daily life, luring us one way, deflecting us into different paths, yet how seldom are they described. Woolf, lover of memoirs, says that most memoirs and biographies, in ignoring such invisible presences, describe the fish, but not the stream which holds them in place.[10] Her mother was the current of her life. She was obsessed by her "unhealthily," as she says in her diary, until she finished *To the Lighthouse,* and then the obsession ceased—she no longer heard her voice or saw her. "I suppose that I did for myself what psychoanalysts do for their patients. I expressed some very long felt and deeply felt emotion. And in expressing it I explained it and then laid it to rest."[11]

"A Sketch of the Past," the memoir in which Woolf describes her early childhood, is of extraordinary interest, not only because it was written by a connoisseur of memoirs, adept at the art, and a reader of Proust, who enjoyed the chance to savor the interactions of past and present, of memory and consciousness, but also because it was written late in her life by a recent reader of Freud, one who had at least a passing knowledge of the theory of psychoanalysis.[12] Free association only loosely linked to chronology provides the structure for the essay, so that she begins—as I have done—not with her background and birth but with her first and most important memories, and if, as self-analysis, "A Sketch of the Past" is the merest beginning, still it is a beginning.

If we step back and adopt a more analytic view of her recollections, what strikes us first is their well-bred, repressed, but unmistakable eroticism. She remembers a time of "raptures" and "ecstasies," of intense shame about her body which suggests an intense awareness of her body. Woolf herself found the clue to the identity of these opposites when she thought of her grandfather, who enjoyed his cigar and so threw it away. Sensitive to pleasure, she prohibited it to herself, or sanitized its source by acknowledging only her responses to nature and impersonal things. In her first recollection she sits on her mother's lap; in the second, the maternal presence is the sea and the rhythmic sound of the waves and of the acorn on the window shade being drawn by the wind across the floor which lulls her to sleep. This displacement onto nature of the sources of her childhood pleasures is the next striking feature of her memoirs. Her third early memory provides an even better example of this. It is a highly sensual remembrance of the garden at St. Ives—bees murmuring, flowers in bloom—fairly bursting with fertility. "It still makes me feel warm; as if everything were ripe; humming; sunny; smelling so many smells at once; and all making a whole that even now makes me stop—as I stopped then going down to the beach."[13] Later in "A Sketch of the Past" she wonders, without answering her own question, why she should remember the hum of bees as she walked to the beach and forget being thrown naked into the sea by her father, an event brought to mind only because it was mentioned in the memoirs of a St. Ives acquaintance. Woolf goes out of her way in "A Sketch of the Past" to prove that she was frigid from birth, telling about Gerald Duckworth's exploration of her and her response to it to assert the myth of her congenital asexuality. She protests, one feels, rather too strongly, and the sensual texture of her recollections belies her point. This was not an anaesthetic childhood.

In the second act of the drama, which opens after Stella's death in 1897 when Virginia is fifteen years old, Leslie Stephen emerges as a full-fledged villain and the heroine's role is thrust upon Vanessa. The pattern had been set earlier, of course. In their afternoon walks at St. Ives, one of the children had always to accompany their father. Julia was too concerned with his pleasure and his health and seemed, to her children, willing to sacrifice them on the altar of his needs. How much better for everyone if he could have taken his walks alone and overworked if he chose to, but instead this "legacy of dependence" survived Julia and became a terrible burden for her daughters—one of whom, at least, couldn't help noticing that Julia, so concerned about her husband's health, had died of fatigue at forty-nine while cancer found it very hard to kill Sir Leslie at seventy-two.

When Vanessa took over from Stella the running of the household, she had to endure not merely his screams and rages, his sighs and groans, at the weekly presentation of the account books, but the demand to satisfy all his emotional needs, needs for flattery, sympathy, and consolation. His daughters witnessed histrionics and attitudinizing such as his friends would never have believed possible in him, for such scenes were saved for women. With men, he was rational and analytical. Women, creatures of emotion as the Victorian myth had it, were for Leslie emotional wastebaskets. Afraid of having failed as a writer and thinker, he could not confess his failure to men, so he turned to his daughters for reassurance. Virginia Woolf would come to think of egotism as an exclusively masculine trait, and when one glimpses the monumental egotism of the principal man of her childhood, it seems less implausible.

Woolf's family experience reinforced the Victorian polarity of the intuitive sympathy of women and the rational, analytic understanding of men. In Virginia's opinion, Leslie was unrelentingly, repellently analytical, and underdeveloped emotionally. Give him an idea to analyze, let us say the philosophy of Hobbes, and he was clear, concise, shrewd: a splendid example of the Cambridge analytic spirit. But give him a character to discuss and he was cruder than a child. Virginia attributed this to Cambridge, whose overemphasis on intellection she found crippling. Leslie so ignored, disguised, covered up, suppressed his own emotions during his life, that by the age of sixty-five he was completely isolated, with no conception of what he felt himself or what others felt. The powerful example of her father planted in her mind the notion that men were emotional cripples, having sacrificed feeling to thought, a perception which has come to many but which few have stated as strongly as Woolf. Part of her defense against the prestige of an education she could not have would be to say that the education was sterile and draining.

To his two remaining daughters Leslie Stephen seemed a Bluebeard, a devourer of women. They remembered how he had tasked Stella's fragile strength, made her few months of joy bitter and difficult, and had not seemed unhappy enough after her death. He was more vigorous than any of them, and now it seemed he was going to make Vanessa his next victim. No woman of character could listen to him carry on without getting angry. Vanessa got angry but fought him in silence. They made him the type of everything they hated. He was a tyrant, a monster of selfishness. Writing later, Virgina could say that she had been extremely harsh and to some extent unjust—but not altogether so.

Vanessa was well suited for her central role. With a great deal of the beauty and much of the character of her mother and half-sister, she was thought worthy to carry on their tradition, and in their morbid state, "haunted by great ghosts," the Stephen children told themselves that to be like Julia or like Stella was to "achieve the height of human perfection." Everyone turned to Vanessa. Enormous demands were made on her, and she moved like a young queen weighted down by the pomp of her ceremonial robes. "It was, in a sense, so easy to be what was expected, with such models before her, but also it was so hard to be herself."[14] She was acclaimed by all as the inheritor of all womanly virtues, yet she managed to keep something of herself intact: she mounted her bicycle and went off every day to study art.

There were, of course, other men in the household in those unhappy years from 1897 to 1904. Virginia's favorite was her brother Thoby, a year and a half older than she. He was not outstandingly clever, but he liked people, got along well with them, and took the lead out of a kind of natural ascendancy. Virginia's favorite image of him was from the St. Ives days, steering their sailboat around the point as he strained to keep the sails from flapping. During London winters, they argued about Shakespeare, and she was an eager listener to his stories about school, with no experience of her own with which to cap his. She imagines he found her a sheltered little creature, studying Greek and writing essays for only herself in her room at the top of the house at Hyde Park Gate, while he wrote essays for prizes at Trinity. When he went to Cambridge she missed him and envied him his freedom. She pictured him sitting of an evening by the fire with Lytton Strachey, smoking a pipe, carrying on fascinating discussions denied her in her solitary Kensington study. He was the man of the world—the intellectual world she longed for—while she was the immured maiden.

She defined herself by contrasts, and if Leslie Stephen was an eminent Victorian remnant against whom the more up-to-date daughters longed to rebel, if Thoby enjoyed a masculine freedom which Virginia envied, the Duckworths represented a conventional society which she loathed, but whose power over her was in some ways more real, more insidious than Leslie's melodramatic tyranny.

Up in her room, Virginia could spend the mornings reading, writing, translating Greek, but towards four-thirty she had to transform herself into a well-bred young lady and participate in the rites of polite society, dressing up and chatting at the tea table in the proper Victorian manner. The ability to make small talk and to respond in the manner spoken to did not come naturally to Virginia and Vanessa, but they had learned it from their mother. Rereading some of her early reviews, she would blame their politeness, their lack of bite, on her tea-table training. Her father trained her, in reading books, to state her reactions clearly and candidly, but the lesson of the tea table was precisely the reverse—to flatter, to sympathize, to console.

At seven-thirty the young ladies changed clothes again and scrubbed their necks and arms, for at eight they had to enter the drawing room in evening dress, arms and neck bare. Down Virginia came in a green dress—made of curtain fabric, partly to save money, partly for the adventure of it—to face George Duckworth in black tie and evening jacket, sitting in a chair by the fire with all the lights in the room up. He inspected her dress, he looked her up and down as he might have a horse, and then a look of sullen disapproval came over his face, a disapproval not merely aesthetic, for he recognized hints of more serious insurrection, moral and social. He told her to go and rip the dress up.

That he was thirty-six and she was twenty, that he had a thousand pounds a year and she had fifty made it difficult to disobey George. But there was more to it—he made her feel like an outsider, a tramp or gypsy peering into the tent in which the spectacular Victorian circus was in full swing. Virginia and Vanessa had a good view of the show and could see all the acrobats, George among them, jumping through hoops, winning themselves headmasterships, judgeships, cabinet posts, but they were not allowed to take part. She was amused, cool, detached, but still George, with the force of wealth, tradition, and power behind him, was not to be defied.

George made even Leslie look a little better, for the Duckworth suppression of natural feeling was in the service of nothing more than propriety, polite appearances. The old man, upstairs in his study, now deaf and completely cut off, devoted himself to the life of the mind. George ruled a world of convention in the drawing room, and no one cared less for convention than Leslie Stephen. Virginia would leave the gossip in the drawing room to return a book to the library, find her father there absorbed in a book, becoming only slowly aware of her presence, and feel a flash of love for this unworldly, lonely old man.

George was the perfect social being, eagerly trying to please, buying umbrellas for the servants at Christmas, giving Virginia a looking-glass to encourage her vanity, calling cabs in the rain, attending funerals, remembering aunts' birthdays, sending turtle soup to the afflicted—a kind of male Mrs. Dalloway. His style more than anything else offended Virginia, and the way he insisted on imposing his philistinism on his sisters. Why would he insist on dragging them with him on his relentless climb up the social ladder? Handsome, rich, private secretary to Austen Chamberlain, he had London society before him. "He believed that aristocratic society was possessed of all the virtues and the graces. He believed that his family had been entrusted to his care. He believed that it was his sacred duty—and when he reached that point his emotions overcame him; he began to sob; flung himself on his knees; seized Vanessa in his arms; implored her in the name of her mother, of her grandmother, by all that was sacred in the female sex and holy in the traditions of our family to accept Lady Arthur Russell's invitation to dinner, and to spend the weekend with the Chamberlains at Highbury."[15] Vanessa did not want to go out to be bored by young men in the Foreign Office and condescended to by ladies with titles. Every morning the post brought new invitations for Mr. Duckworth and Miss Stephen, and every evening they fought.

When Vanessa refused finally to accompany George, he turned his attentions to Virginia, who was not as resolute in her opposition to society as Vanessa. For Virginia it had charms—glamor, brightly lit rooms, beautiful clothes. But she was not a social success. She was not asked to dance, hid, was discovered, was given by a kindly peeress a piece of cake. On the evening that epitomized for Virginia the whole disastrous social enterprise, George took her to dine with Lady Carnarvon and her sister, and Virginia proceeded to shock them by talking of Plato. Later, before leaving for the theater, Virginia heard George and Lady Carnarvon kissing passionately, and yet, on the principle that one might do such things but never talk about them, Lady Carnavon felt obliged to lead her little group away from the play when it turned out to be a racy French comedy. Afterwards, she could not even bring herself to mention the distressing episode at the theater. In the cab, she took Virginia's hand and said in a tremulous voice, "I do hope, Miss Stephen, that the evening has not tired you very much." Bloomsbury's social radicalism was to consist not so much in novel and shocking behavior as in talking openly about the things people had been doing all along in private.

The account of her evening out with George ends with a vignette intended to be offhandedly shocking: Virginia has taken off her white satin dress, her long white gloves, her white silk stockings and is lying in bed, almost asleep, when the door opens stealthily, and George, telling her not to be frightened and not to turn on the light, flings himself onto the bed and takes her in his arms. "Yes, the old ladies of Kensington and Belgravia never knew that George Duckworth was not only father and mother, brother and sister to those poor Stephen girls; he was their lover also."[16] George's behavior was of a piece with the larger Victorian coverup, the disguising of all real emotion in a veil of propriety, sentimentality, and polite conversation. Elsewhere Virginia might blame George's disgusting advances for warping her sexuality, but in the context of her memoirs, the affair is presented as the final and most grotesque example of the cleavage between appearances and reality which so distressed her about the world of fashion.

This is the view of polite society one gets when Virginia, in her later memoirs, is developing the myth of a repressed, constricted childhood, a kind of imprisonment in Kensington, which ends when the ogre dies, the spell is broken, and the enchanted maidens are freed to live in Bloomsbury. But she has another myth of society, developed in her diaries of the time and one which will inform *Mrs. Dalloway:* society is a heroic endeavor, social life a holding action against chaos and despair. This view enables Virginia to watch with some delight the social game which otherwise caused her such

*Virginia Woolf as an adolescent, contemplated by George Duck-worth, her half-brother.*

pain. "Major so and so laughs as though he hadn't a care in the world; we know he can't pay his butcher's bill. Mrs. Thingamagig is more amusing than ever tonight—didn't she lose an only son in the war?"[17] A moralist, she writes, might find this artificial and conclude that society is hollow and heartless, but the other side is this—doesn't Mrs. Thingamagig do better making the world laugh than by sitting home crying over her sorrows? To be a social success one has to have the courage of a hero. There is a certain amount of irony in all this, yet a residue of sincerity remains: Mrs. Thingamagig, transformed, filled out, sobered up, and elevated to the nobility, will become Lady Bexborough whom Mrs. Dalloway so admires, who opens a bazaar still holding the telegram announcing her son's death in World War I.

In mapping the social landscape of Virginia's youth, one must mention, too, the world of artists to which she was allied because of her mother's Little Holland House connections. After leaving Lady Carnarvon that scandalous evening, she and George continued on to a party at the Holman Hunts', where the painter sipped cocoa and discoursed to his admiring guests on the symbolism of *The Light of the World*. Virginia felt no more at home in the world of artists than she did in the world of fashion and high society, and she was keenly aware before she was twenty that there was nothing in Philistia to equal the snobbery of Bohemia. "I am always impressed," she wrote mockingly in her 1903 diary, "by the splendid superiority of these artist men and women over their Philistine brethren. They are so thoroughly convinced that mankind is divided into two classes, one of which wears amber beads and low evening collars—while the other follows the fashion. Each thanks God it is not the other—but the artist is the more intolerant."[18]

In Virginia's personal myth of liberation, the world of art could be as much of a threat as the world of bourgeois conventionality. Later she would write a little play called *Freshwater*, to be acted by members of the family at a family party. Intended as a joke, this comic sketch of life at the home of her great-aunt, Mrs. Cameron, features Tennyson always reading "Maud" and complaining about the prevalence of sibilants in the titles of Watts' paintings, Watts turning his wife into a model of Modesty trampled on by Mammon, Mrs. Cameron always about to leave for Ceylon but in the meantime using her cook as a model for Guinevere, and Ellen Terry, Watts' wife, sick of being given perfect white roses instead of kisses, sick of Art, a lusty young woman married to an old man. "Nothing ever changes in this house," she says. "Somebody's always asleep. Lord Tennyson is always reading Maud. The cook is always being photographed. The Camerons are always starting for India. I'm always sitting to Signor." Out of this atmosphere of stifling, didactic aestheticism, out of this enchanted sleeping-beauty world, Ellen Terry escapes, running off (disguised as a boy) with Edward Gordon Craig to 46 Gordon Square, Bloomsbury, precisely where the Stephen sisters went when they left Hyde Park Gate.[19]

Bloomsbury makes no sense in Woolf's personal mythology without 22 Hyde Park Gate preceding it. In telling the story of her own life, when she comes to the Bloomsbury years, she doubles back and describes again the house in Kensington from which in 1904 she and Vanessa freed themselves. In the symbolic landscape of her youth, it is the principal monument, embodying the claustrophobia of Victorian family life. This tall half-brick, half-stucco structure, covered with vines, so close to its neighbor you could see Mrs. Redgrave across the way washing her neck, generated gloom and darkness. Eleven people between the ages of eight and sixty were thrown together inside, waited upon by seven servants. Three families dwelt there—Stephens, Duckworths, and the retarded girl Laura. You never knew, Virginia says, if you would stumble across Herbert Duckworth's barrister's wig, Leslie's discarded clergyman's collar, or sheets of drawings by Thackeray.[20]

If ages and families were conflated at 22 Hyde Park Gate, everything else presents itself to Virginia's recollection as rigidly segregated. It was a house divided. The drawing room was divided by black folding doors, on one side of which (when Julia was still alive) ladies would tell dark and troubled stories about husbands accidentally poisoned or discovered in bed with the maid, while on the other side the men discussed India and botany. Even when the sexes converged, their roles were clearly defined, and when Leslie got irritated and with the privilege of an elderly masculine eccentric groaned "Oh Gibbs, what a bore you are!" his wife would throw a pretty young woman his way to charm him back to good humor, just as Mrs. Ramsay uses Minta Doyle to keep her husband happy. Mrs. Stephen's favorite for this purpose was Kitty Lushington (later Kitty Maxse). "Kitty wants to tell you," she would say to Leslie, "how much she loved your lecture."

Virginia's only refuge from family life was her own room, which so strongly suggested to her a symbol of psychic space that it deserves some attention. It had been the night nursery, shared with Vanessa, until 1897 when Stella married, freeing her room for Vanessa. The nursery was done over (at George Duckworth's expense) into a more grown-up space for Virginia, a combination bedroom and sitting room. On one side was her bed, flanked by the washstand and the looking-glass. On the other side was the wicker chair in which she read, a writing table inherited from Stella, made by the St. Ives carpenter and stained green and brown with a leaf pattern by Stella herself, and, on top of it, her Greek lexicon, always open—also, inkpots and manuscript books in which she was constantly working. This "literary" side of the room contained Virginia's icons of selfhood, and it was to this side that she escaped, reading in the hours between tea and dinner, writing whenever she could. She began keeping journals in her teens, sporadic notations of events, but by 1903 her diary consisted of a series of attempts to write fully modeled essays. In these notebooks, too, she practiced descriptive writing. Already she was training herself to be a writer, finding in writing a happier reality, an alternative to family life.

In the other half of her room not much went on. She remembers herself listening to traffic, to dance music, to cats wawling, as she waited for Vanessa to come home. She makes a great deal of the division of the room into writing part and sleeping part, as though they were in conflict and represented a conflict in herself:

> Which would I describe first—the living side or the sleeping side? They could be described separately. Yet they were always running together. And how they fought each other: how often I was in a rage and in ecstasy, torn between all the different forces that entered that room, whether one calls them the living side or the sleeping side. . . . But I was thinking, feeling, living there two lives that the two parts of the room symbolize with the intensity which the butterfly or moth feels when with sticky tremulous legs and antennae it pushes out of its chrysalis and emerges; waits beside the broken shell for a moment; damp; its legs still creased; its eyes dazzled; incapable of flight.[21]

She is one-half well-bred young lady, a body to be dressed up and put on display for the marriage market, and one-half intellectual, a mind to be nourished and trained. Life at Hyde Park Gate was, for the most part, focused on preparing her for marriage and a social role. Furtively, in her own room, she carried on her insurrectionary labors of the mind, engaged, in a small but determined way, in overturning the established order of things. Her pleasures in life were almost all to come from being a mind—her miseries from having that mind housed in a body.

# 2

# Bloomsbury

46 Gordon Square, Bloomsbury, looks out on a miniature gem of a park, romantically lush and asymmetrical. Gordon Square, Virginia says in her memoirs, may not in fact have been the most beautiful of the Bloomsbury squares but in October 1904 it seemed "the most beautiful, the most exciting, the most romantic place in the world."[1] Inside the house, light and air and white walls replaced the dark Morris wallpapers and rich red gloom of 22 Hyde Park Gate. The credit for releasing the Stephen children from their Kensington enchantment should go largely to Vanessa. Virginia had had an-

other mental breakdown shortly after her father's death, and while she was recuperating, Vanessa had wound up their affairs at the old house and installed them in the new one. Before and after the move, Kensington—as represented by Violet Dickinson, Virginia's good friend, by Kitty Maxse, Vanessa's society mentor, and by assorted female relatives—disapproved. Young girls should not live alone with no better chaperones than their brothers. Bloomsbury was not a fashionable neighborhood. But this did not bother the Stephen girls; it was to turn their backs on Kensington that they moved to the other side of London.

The rigid social regime was destroyed. Gone were the white satin and seed pearls. No more dressing for dinner. The Stephen sisters went out to lectures and to bookstores; they met new people, had people in; above all, they talked, for Thoby's university friends began to come round, and when masculine Cambridge met feminine Kensington, what we have come to call the Bloomsbury group was born.

To appreciate what the masculine component of Bloomsbury meant to Virginia, we must leave her for a moment, while we imagine what she had been missing in the years she was educated at home. Biographies and autobiographies of men who were at Cambridge at the turn of the century testify to its impact on them. Keynes and Bertrand Russell come immediately to mind, but Leonard Woolf's encomium might have particular relevance. Most of the ties in life that made him what he was, he writes in his autobiography, were ambivalent: he loved his family but hated them too, he was proud of being Jewish but also ashamed, he felt affection for St. Paul's but detested its ugliness and philistinism. His loyalty to Trinity College and Cambridge, however, was different from all the others, "more intimate, profound, unalloyed." He delighted utterly in the physical, intellectual, and spiritual beauty of Cambridge, its sense of being impregnated with history, the civilized life it afforded, the opportunities for friendship and good talk. To convey the nature of the university's claims on a man's affections, he quotes a letter from Desmond MacCarthy. The scene is a Trinity dinner which MacCarthy attends as the guest of Mc-Taggart, the philosopher. At first he does not enjoy himself: he must eat too much and drink too much and the talk is mediocre.

> Then the Master got up, holding his glass of wine in both hands and swaying solemnly from side to side in a way that was in itself a benediction, proposed the guests in a speech of admirable blandness and effortlessness and nothingness and as I listened I felt the glamour of success. How fine it is that the college should send out men who become ministers and judges and bishops and how very gratifying it would be to come down as the bigwig of the evening and make a most splendid speech in reply—all this sublimated by the rosy mist of port. . . .
>
> Then McT and Theodore and I went to the reception at the Lodge. The Master stood at the top of the stairs and welcomed us—received us, wrapped us round with romantic ceremonial hospitality. He was the Master of Trinity—the leaders of their generations were there—I was a brilliant young man—it was an Occasion.
>
> Then we went to Jackson's at home. You know the scene—clouds of tobacco smoke, a roar of conversation—dozens of whist tables with lighted candles on each—clay pipes—boxes of cigars, a piano and someone singing God knows what. . . . Then songs with choruses—school songs, the various representatives of different schools gathering round the piano in turn and shouting with defiant patriotism—then music hall songs. . . . Then came the event of the evening for me. I got on the sofa with Strachey and had a good talk. . . . We talked for a long time about the Society, angels, brothers, and embryos—and felt as tho' we were getting things clear—at least I did—and we agreed.[2]

Leonard Woolf went up to Cambridge in 1899 and stayed there for five years. It was a golden moment in the university's history, with three philosophers, Alfred North White-head, G. E. Moore, and Bertrand Russell, dominating and energizing the younger generation. Woolf's close friends were Thoby Stephen, Lytton Strachey, Saxon Sydney-Turner, and to a lesser extent Clive Bell, who eventually married Vanessa. Later John Maynard Keynes joined this circle, and more particularly, joined the secret and select discussion society, The Apostles (the "Society" MacCarthy refers to in his letter), which was dedicated to "the pursuit of truth with absolute devotion and unreserve by a group of intimate friends, who were perfectly frank with each other"[3] and which represented a Cambridge within Cambridge, an inner circle of male culture and civilization.

I focus attention on Virginia Woolf's relationship to an institution she never attended because some books on Bloomsbury[4] assume that Cambridge filtered down to her through contact with her brother's friends—as though the heady draught of Moore's intellect, bottled in Cambridge, was carried to London by Strachey and the rest and there greedily swallowed by Virginia, giving direction and intellectual substance to her work. The model presupposes the passive female, taking on attitudes and ideas from the men around her. The real process, I would suggest, is more interesting and more complex.

Virginia Woolf's vision of Cambridge is inseparable from the experience of exclusion. Alongside of MacCarthy's letter to Leonard Woolf, describing a Cambridge evening and the sense of well-being it inspired, we must place Virginia Woolf's description of "Oxbridge" in *A Room of One's Own*, for, significantly, the male university is the setting she chooses for her musings on women and their difficulties in writing fiction. The lawn is magnificent, an eloquent testimony to years of care; a beadle chases her off—it is only for Fellows. The library attracts her like a magnet but she is refused admittance, for ladies must have letters of introduction. The physical splendor of Oxbridge bears witness to the importance of the young men it nurtures, but to Virginia it says merely, "You are a person of no importance. Bring me a letter from a man and we will let you in to visit." MacCarthy's easy assurance that he was a "brilliant young man" was denied to her. Perhaps that is one reason why MacCarthy, who was a genius, all his friends agreed, never did justice—also in his friends' opinion—to his potential, whereas Virginia Woolf was impelled to achieve what she did. He was one of the elect without trying, whereas she had to prove herself, to the world at large and more importantly to herself. Then, too, the distinction and originality of her art is that it emerges from a sense of weakness rather than of strength: she proceeds tentatively, abjuring the strong authority of the Victorian novelist, delicately capturing the transient splendors of the physical world, the wavering movements of the mental life. Her exclusion from the university made her realize the liabilities and the benefits of being a woman, and in coming to terms with her exclusion, she came to terms with her own identity.

Her resentment needs some explanation, for like Dickens' reaction to his brief time in the blacking factory, its strength and duration seem uncalled for by the simple facts of the case. Other young men have had to work at a young age to support their families, even some who wanted to be writers; many young women have not gone to college. Woolf fared better than most, for her education, although interrupted occasionally by illness, was largely in the hands of her father. From her mid-teens, he allowed her the freedom of his excellent library and discussed with her whatever she read, training her in the fearless, accurate, and pithy expression of her responses to books. "Freedom of that sort," she wrote in a conciliatory mood in later years, referring to her hours in her father's library, "was worth thousands of cigarettes."[5] Yet after his death she began to smoke: her image of the intellectual life was tobacco-smoky. We may envy Woolf her freedom from schedule, her individual attention, her tutor, her chance to direct her own growth. She, however, envied her brother his freedom from the restrictive social world of Kensington and his chance to immerse himself wholly in the intellectual life. As for her, the very arrangement of her day made it clear that social accomplishments were at least as important as intellectual accomplishments. She could study in the morning, but in the afternoon she was expected to entertain visitors and preside over the tea table; the experiences of the afternoon must have somewhat counteracted the morning's training in candor.

She also envied Thoby's chance to participate in that intellectual camaraderie, that open-ended discussion with friends, which may well be a more important part of a university education than anything that goes on in the classroom. Vanessa was at art school, frequently, and in any case, her interests were different. "I don't get anybody to argue with me now, and feel the want," Virginia wrote Thoby in 1903. "I have to delve from books, painfully and all alone, what you get every evening sitting over your fire and smoking your pipe with Strachey etc. No wonder my knowledge is but scant."[6] The conviction that she was badly educated stayed with her to some extent throughout her life, affecting her self-esteem, and this, rather than any actual deficiency in knowledge or training, was the significant result of her mode of education. As she imagined Thoby smoking his pipe with Strachey and discussing Shakespeare, she later imagined Jacob Flanders walking down a London street with Timothy Durrant, all civilizations at their feet, and bestowing their greatest approval, confident of the importance of their choice, upon the Greeks. Virginia might read Greek better than her brother, better than Jacob Flanders, but that splendid communion of intellects, the continuum of male culture through the centuries, was closed to her. Cambridge was transformed into a symbol of privilege and intellectual authority, more important because it withheld its embrace than for what it could concretely give, and since Cambridge was a family tradition, and Thoby Stephen by no means the first male of his line to go there—Leslie had been for years a don at Trinity Hall—making some small allowance for metaphor we may say that the embrace withheld by the university was a father's embrace.

Leslie, whose dedication to intellect she aspired to copy, seemed to thrust her back into the feminine seclusion of a tea-party world, pointing the path to achievement, then shutting the door in her face. While her brothers were free to make lives for themselves, her life seemed significant only insofar as she could minister to the needs of men, chiefly those of her father. In *Three Guineas* she describes feelingly the sacrifice of women to their brothers' careers: women must scrimp so Arthur's Education Fund may swell. Her brothers went to Cambridge; she had to stay home. Feelings do not always examine evidence or obey the laws of logic. In fairness to Leslie Stephen it should be said that no evidence shows she ever tried to go to Cambridge but was prevented by him from doing so. Because so much of her youth was spent in illness, she probably could not have passed the exams for Newnham or Girton. Had she been admitted, perhaps he would have let her go.

As it was, however, Cambridge lured and frustrated that part of her which passionately desired achievement. In her metaphorical imagination it became more than the sum of its parts of books, dons, and evenings of good talk. It was freedom. For a while it is true that she was not deprived of books at Hyde Park Gate, she was deprived of something more important for a writer, experience of the world. In *A Room of One's Own* she contrasts Tolstoy, living with this gypsy and that countess, making love, fighting wars, seeing life, with George Eliot, secluding herself apologetically in The Priory because she was living with a man she was not really married to. Would Tolstoy have written *War and Peace*, she wonders, if he had had to live at The Priory?

*Virginia Woolf and her father, Leslie Stephen, circa 1900.*

Woolf saw her life in terms of symbolic locales, as a series of moves from one neighborhood to another, each embodying a spirit or phase of personal growth: from St. Ives to Kensington, from Kensington to Bloomsbury. The move to Bloomsbury meant social and intellectual freedom. Now, when Thoby, Strachey, and the rest continued the discussions they had enjoyed as undergraduates, she could join in. It was exhilarating. The young men would come in and fold themselves up on sofas. Conversation was allowed to languish in a fashion unthinkable at Hyde Park Gate. One had to speak with caution, for the standard of what was worth saying was high, but once they got going on some abstract idea like truth or beauty or good, they could go on, talking deliberately, fascinatingly, with difficult but interesting silences, sometimes until three in the morning. "From

such discussions," Virginia wrote, "Vanessa and I got probably much the same pleasure that undergraduates get when
they meet friends of their own for the first time."[7]

But Duncan Grant, who has left the most vivid account
of those early days of Bloomsbury, insists that Virginia and
Vanessa Stephen did not merely absorb what Thoby's friends
had to say: "These Apostolic young men found to their
amazement that they could be shocked by the boldness and
skepticism of two young women."[8] Included now in the circle of discussion which had been closed to her while Thoby
was at Cambridge, Virginia Stephen resisted the role of aco-
lyte. G. E. Moore was not her God, the *Principia Ethica* not
her Bible: she did not even read the book until August 1908,
and then, with restraint and irony, she pronounced Moore
"humane in spite of his desire to know the truth."[9] The style
of conversation which Moore fostered, pregnant and sincere
silences punctuated by sincere attempts to articulate one's
feelings, she regarded with amusement. Rather than adopting the style and values of the Cambridge men, she seems to
have defined herself against them, insisting on the value of a
distinctively "feminine" and even untutored approach to
life: "They sit silent, absolutely silent, all the time," she
writes Violet Dickinson in 1905, describing the visit of two
Cambridge graduates. "Occasionally they escape into a
corner and chuckle over a Latin joke. Perhaps they are falling in love with Nessa; who knows? It would be a silent and
very learned process. However I don't think they are robust
enough to feel very much. Oh women are my line and not
these inanimate creatures!"[10]

The charm of early Bloomsbury for Virginia was not
merely that she could unrestrictedly use her mind but also
that nothing else except her mind mattered. These young
men, having no manners in the Kensington sense, didn't notice clothes or looks. What a simplification of life, to have to
worry not about how you appeared but only about how you
made your point. It was all refreshingly abstract, intellec-

tual, and the threatening cloud of love and marriage which hung so heavy over her father's house was gone. "It seemed incredible that any of these young men should want to marry us or that we should marry them. Secretly I felt that marriage was a very low down affair, but that if one practised it, one practised it . . . with young men who had been in the Eton Eleven and dressed for dinner."[11] Thoby's friends were reassuringly unpresentable, and it seemed that the idyll of abstract argument, with no dressing for dinner, could go on forever.

Vanessa disagreed. She thought they would all marry, a fate which Virginia could perceive only as a "horrible necessity" threatening rudely to snatch them apart just as they had achieved freedom and happiness. But Vanessa was right, and the Bloomsbury idyll was ended by Vanessa's marriage, in 1907, to Clive Bell. At about this time—one cannot be so precise, of course, but the date will serve as well as any to mark a turning point—what had been a latent irony about the intellectual pretensions of men became something more clearly and more frequently articulated, a new way of perceiving her life. If before this the autobiographical "plot" had been the myth of liberation, the story of the immured maiden freed at last from bourgeois captivity, now the elements recombine and take shape as a concern with two ways of knowing which are at war. At its least biased, this dualistic myth presents masculine and feminine traits as very different but both valuable; at its most biased, it opposes masculine sterility to feminine creativity. In formulating this myth, largely in reaction to the masculine exclusivity of her brothers' friends, Virginia began to create a more positive and distinctive sense of herself.

When in 1905 some of Thoby's friends had published a volume of verse called, with characteristic pomposity, *Euphrosyne*, Virginia had secretly wondered if as many of the poems were destined for immortality as Thoby said, and she wrote a parody review of the book which reveals some of the myths about her experience which she had evolved to cope with her exclusion from the charmed circle. She begins by mentioning the superior education of the authors: if such trash is the best that men with university degrees can produce, then perhaps "there is much to be said . . . for that respectable custom which allows the daughter to educate herself at home, while the brother is educated by others abroad."[12] Beneath the irony is a serious attempt to readjust perspective. The prison of home is not really a prison but a sanctuary, where a woman may be free not from the contamination of sex, as her parents intended, but from the greater blot of intellectual pretentiousness. Throughout the review the university appears as a source of contamination: to escape its influence a stroke of luck. The university years are supposed to be the best years of the men's lives, yet they emerge from them "pale, preoccupied, & silent," and "the things they once found pleasing please them no longer." The university has taught them not to respond to life enthusiastically but to withhold response. It has sapped their emotions. Worst of all it has turned them into snobs. "They admire . . . the works of minor French poets, & crown certain English authors with the epithets 'supreme' and 'astounding'; but if the public show signs of appreciating the same things they dextrously transfer their praise to some more obscure head." The young men cannot bear, she says, to agree with the common herd and like to meet on Sundays, when they imagine the rest of the world respectfully on its knees, to congratulate themselves on the works "unprinted as yet, 'unprintable' they proudly give you to understand" which they have written. The implication is clear: women, whose lot is disadvantage, cannot presume to be such snobs.

In 1925 when Woolf came to publish the essays and reviews she had been writing for many years, she called the volume *The Common Reader*, recalling with approval Samuel Johnson's genial and democratic sentiment: "I rejoice to concur with the common reader; for by the common sense of

readers uncorrupted by literary prejudices, after all the refinements of subtilty and the dogmatism of learning, must be
decided all claim to poetical honours."[13] Her persona for
criticism, uniting all the essays, is that of a woman, neither
professional critic nor scholar, moderately informed, who is
modestly, earnestly trying to illuminate life through the
reading of books. It can be seen as a defiantly feminine response to the male domination of criticism, anti-authori-
tarian, abjuring omniscience,[14] and as an ironic turning to
account of her own lack of advantages, an extension of her
tactics in the *Euphrosyne* review. Whereas the authors of
*Euphrosyne* "transfer their praise to some more obscure
head" if the public shows signs of agreeing with them, the
common reader rejoices in carrying the public along with
her.

When she wrote the *Euphrosyne* review Virginia Stephen
was twenty-four and just beginning the long effort to establish herself as a writer. What, she may have asked herself,
did she have to offer the world? Her brother's friends were so
incontestably clever, so much better educated than she.
What could she do that they couldn't do better? In this spoof,
she asserts with pluck and wit her sense of her own worth.
What has kept her from those magic realms of tobacco smoke
and good talk will also carry her high: the fact that she can
speak as a woman. The classic charges leveled in later years
against Bloomsbury writing, including Woolf's, that it was
bloodlessly intellectual and lacking vitality and contact with
life, she here levels against many of her Bloomsbury friends.
The *Euphrosyne* review suggests the nature of her conscious
response to the challenge of the clever young men—she turns
her defensiveness about being a woman and her sense of inadequacy into something positive, the basis for a distinctive
sense of herself.

By 1909 Virginia had begun writing *The Voyage Out,* and
Mr. Pepper, if a bit extreme, is representative of a little gal-
lery of desiccated scholars in that novel. Helen Ambrose

wonders if Pepper has ever been in love, and of course, he hasn't, he couldn't—"His heart's a piece of old shoe leather."[15] Commenting on the novel in its early stages, Clive Bell objected to the clear-cut contrast between the male and female characters and the glorification of the women at the expense of the men. He found this "didactic, not to say priggish."

> Our views about men & women are doubtless quite different, and the difference does'nt matter much; but to draw such sharp & marked contrasts between the subtle, sensitive, tactful, gracious, delicately perceptive, & perspicacious women, & the obtuse, vulgar, blind, florid, rude, tactless, emphatic, indelicate, vain, tyrannical, stupid men, is not only rather absurd, but rather bad art, I think.[16]

His comments on the manuscript were careful and extensive, and many of them Woolf acknowledged in her reply to be just, but at this one she stood her ground.

> Your objection, that my prejudice against men makes me didactic "not to say priggish," has not quite the same force with me [as his other criticisms]; I don't remember what I said that suggests the remark; I daresay it came out without my knowledge: but I will bear it in mind. I never meant to preach, & agree that like God, one should'nt. Possibly, for psychological reasons which seem to me very interesting, a man, in the present state of the world, is not a very good judge of his sex; and a "creation" may seem to him "didactic."[17]

The bias which Bell saw as didacticism and which Woolf claimed was truth to nature, we may view as a strategic psychological maneuver. To value women, even at the expense of undervaluing men, is, when one is a woman in a society which gives all power and prestige to men, a first step towards valuing oneself. Later the inflexible schema could be modified. In writing her father's obituary, for example, she would emphasize that his love of clear thinking and his hatred of sentimentality and gush did not necessarily mean he was cold and unemotional.[18] But in her early years there was urgent work to do building up the fabric of her self-esteem. Like housing thrown together to meet an immediate need, the structure was rather crude. Refinements, subtleties, could be added later (certainly they are in *To the Light-house*). For the moment it was enough to see value in her own sex, deprived of Oxbridge though they were.

Sex made the difference between early Bloomsbury and later Bloomsbury. After Vanessa's marriage, conversation at Gordon Square no longer focused exclusively on the nature of the good and other chaste subjects. Virginia describes the momentous evening, probably in 1908, which initiated frank talk about sex amongst the friends. She and Vanessa were sitting quietly in the drawing room of Gordon Square when "suddenly the door opened and the long and sinister figure of Mr. Lytton Strachey stood on the threshold." She sets the scene perfectly, for it was a threshold experience, the crossing of a frontier. The long and sinister figure "pointed his finger at a stain on Vanessa's white dress."

> "Semen?" he said.
> Can one really say it? I thought and we burst out laughing. With that one word all barriers of reticence and reserve went down. A flood of the sacred fluid seemed to overwhelm us. Sex permeated our conversation. The word bugger was never far from our lips. We discussed copulation with the same excitement and openness that we had discussed the nature of good. It is strange to think how reticent, how reserved we had been and for how long.[19]

To become aware of sex, however, was to become aware that most of the young men in her circle were not sexually attracted by her. She had known from reading Plato that there were buggers (the word she insisted on using) in ancient Greece, and she had guessed there were buggers at Cambridge, but it never crossed her mind that there might be buggers sitting in her drawing room at Gordon Square. It had never struck her that the abstractness and simplicity which were so great a relief after Kensington resulted from the lack of physical interest, on the part of the majority of young men she saw, in women. To talk about sex meant, largely, that Vanessa and Virginia could listen—the one sympathetically, the other laughingly—to stories about "the loves of the buggers." If she had been excluded intellectually at Kensington, now she was excluded sexually.

The gatherings went on at Fitzroy Square, where Virginia moved with Adrian after Vanessa's marriage, but now Virginia was less than ecstatic. The silence she had respected began to bore her. "They sat round mostly silent," she writes to Vanessa, describing a typical evening, "and I wished for any woman—and you would have been a miracle. I talked to Frankie [Francis Birrell] and Keynes most of the time. But it was desperate work."[20] Why should such gifted people be so barren? Why was it all so negative?

She discovered that there were parts of her personality which she could not express in the young men's company— an effervescence, a playfulness of the imagination. It was tedious always to have to be clever, always to seek earnestly for truth. Couldn't truths be found at a leap, on a wave of intoxication? The society of buggers, she writes, has advantages for a woman. One can be simple and honest and at ease. But one can't fizz up like champagne. To fizz like champagne she fled the dim discretion of Fitzroy Square gatherings to the strange house, all "lustre and illusion," in Bedford Square, "that extraordinary whirlpool where such odd sticks and straws were brought momentarily together" where Lady Ottoline Morrell held sway.[21]

After granite, this was the rainbow—a drawing room full

of people, pale yellow and pink brocades, tassles, scents, pomegranates, pugs, potpourri, and Ottoline sweeping down on you in a white shawl with scarlet flowers on it, bearing you out of the large crowded room to a smaller nook where she could ply you with intimate questions. This aristocrat, disaffected with her class, who sought the company of artists and writers, provided Virginia with relief from the masculine exclusivity of Bloomsbury, what Noel Annan has called "the homosexual conspiracy."[22] Although there was a great difference between Ottoline's magical gatherings of writers and artists and the formal dances where one met young men from the Foreign Office, Virginia's enthusiastic response to Bedford Square represented something of a return to the feminine social activity of the Kensington years. She had worked so hard to get away from the lit-up drawing rooms and well-dressed festivities imposed upon her by George Duckworth that it took a while for her to realize how much a part of her liked them.

A sense of the romantic luster of great hostesses was to stay with Virginia throughout her life. From Sybil Colefax, too, in later years, she would get that heady feeling of champagne, an intoxication peculiarly feminine. In contrast, no party of intellectuals ever sent her, as she put it, "flying down the Farringdon Road." "I have dined with H. G. Wells to meet Bernard Shaw, Arnold Bennett, and Granville Barker, and I have only felt like an old washerwoman toiling step by step up a steep and endless staircase."[23] Fittingly, her memoir on "Old Bloomsbury" ends with Ottoline Morrell and the ensuing—and final—memoir in *Moments of Being,* titled "Am I a Snob?," describes her fondness for aristocratic ladies.

Virginia invited people to Fitzroy Square that Vanessa would never have dreamed of asking to her home in Gordon Square—society women, mostly. And Virginia's attraction to Bedford Square represented an impulse her sister did not share. One of her earliest stories, poorly written but revealing, describes two young ladies brought up to do nothing but appear well at teas and evening parties, with the goal of making good marriages. They encounter two other sisters living a much more independent and open life in Bloomsbury. It is, as Quentin Bell says, as though the Stephen sisters of 1903 had gone to pay a call on the Stephen sisters of 1906.[24] But one can say more about the manuscript. It reveals a deep split in allegiance which persisted in Virginia even after 1906. "What did she really want, [Phyllis] asked herself? What was she fit for? to criticize both worlds and feel that neither gave her what she needed." Just as she was not wholly satisfied by Kensington, Virginia was not wholly satisfied by Gordon Square, Bloomsbury, something I think it was difficult for her Gordon Square friends to understand.

With a few exceptions, the mythic period of Woolf's life was over by World War I; that is, the personal experiences which formed the basis of her novels derive largely from the first thirty years of her life. In *The Voyage Out* one can see a fictionalized transformation of her liberation from Kensington and her traumatic encounter with the young men of Bloomsbury. In *Mrs. Dalloway* she explores, among other things, her ambivalence about the world of the Duckworths and mythologizes some of her responses to the great hostesses in her life, of whom Lady Ottoline Morrell was the first. In *To the Lighthouse* she returns imaginatively to St. Ives, resurrecting her parents, exploring her involvement with them, and questioning at last the myth of sexual duality developed partly through her experience of her father and mother, partly in reaction to the masculinity of early Bloomsbury. The outspoken feminism of her later years is not a change of direction but an intensification and a clarification of attitudes developed early in her life and in response to early experiences.

# 3

# The Voyage Out

Virginia Woolf spent seven years writing *The Voyage Out*. She began it when she was twenty-five, just after her sister's marriage. She was still working on it in 1912 when she married Leonard Woolf. At the same time she was writing reviews for *The Times Literary Supplement* and establishing herself as a journalist. These were the years of her young adulthood, and not surprisingly the novel traces a young woman's approach to maturity. From the time of its publication *The Voyage Out* has never lacked admirers. Reviewers in 1915 were enthusiastic. Readers today continue to enjoy it, although

no one is likely to argue that it is her masterpiece. It is more
uneven than Woolf's later works, and its charms are the
charms of a first novel, that is, it projects the voice of a person coming to grips with her own experience. At about the
time she began *The Voyage Out,* Woolf described herself to
Strachey as "a painstaking woman," wishing to express
"some of the perplexities of her sex, in plain English."[1] The
book is animated by her effort to explore her own experience
and through it to work to some more general illumination of
the perplexities of her sex. At times she doesn't succeed and
falls into gratuitous autobiography; at times, she tries too
hard to elevate her modest experience into something more
exciting. But when she succeeds, when autobiographical impulse and the form of her narrative fit together comfortably,
*The Voyage Out* is as moving as the greatest of Woolf's later
works.

At the start of the novel, Rachel Vinrace is twenty-four
and quite astonishingly ignorant. Her mother having died
when she was eleven (Julia Stephen died when Virginia was
thirteen), she has been brought up by maiden aunts at Richmond with excessive care first for her health and then for
what "it seems almost crude to call her morals."[2] Her reading was censored, and although friends might have told her a
few facts of life, she has had few friends her own age. Her
aunts' house in Richmond and the park where they walk are
sheltered spots which seem disconnected from the outside
world. The "sheltered gardens" of Richmond figure in Rachel's mind throughout the book as emblems of the protective, stifling enclosure from which she breaks out by voyag-
ing to South America in the company of Helen Ambrose,
another aunt, but very different from the maiden aunts of
Richmond.

Life on shipboard is somewhat like life at Hyde Park
Gate, for although Rachel's father owns the ship (called, of
all things, the *Euphrosyne!*), he presides over it remotely; his
only contact with her is his unspoken demand that she act as

hostess at table. In that role Rachel is as uncomfortable and as inept as Virginia Stephen felt she had been in a similar role. At the first meal she serves soup to her uncle in such a way as to make him mutter, just loud enough for her to hear, that she isn't, alas, like her mother (something people were continually telling Virginia). Rachel copes with her difficult position by retreating from it and burying herself in her own cabin with her piano. "It was far better to play the piano and forget all the rest" (36). And later, when they arrive at Santa Marina and move into a villa, Helen promises Rachel "a room cut off from the rest of the house, large, private—a room in which she could play, read, think, defy the world, a fortress as well as a sanctuary" (123). We recall the importance to Virginia of her own transformed nursery at the top of her father's house and notice that she is aware of the ambivalence of Rachel's room: "a fortress as well as a sanctuary," it fosters her independence and imaginative freedom, yet it cuts her off even further from the outside world and any real contact with experience.

Rachel Vinrace, that wispy amalgam of ineptness, shyness, and innocence, represents an odd portrait of the artist. But then, it is a portrait of the artist as a young lady and not as a young man. Here are no signs of genius. She is alienated, but this alienation is a sign not of her superior perceptions, as it would be, for example, in *Sons and Lovers*, but of her insecurity. This is an ordinary girl, notable only for her extraordinary ignorance. Her art (playing the piano) does not redeem her, but is presented as a kind of retreat. Think of her alongside the heroines of other novels of development and the contrast is striking. Emma Woodhouse, for one, is only too confident when we first encounter her. Her education is a process of humbling, of learning that she is not as important or as infallible as she thinks. And with Isabel Archer the question is, how will she dispose of herself? There is never any doubt about the worth of what is to be disposed. Even Dorothea Brooke, the most self-effacing of heroines, values the self she wants so passionately to surrender to some noble cause. Only Rachel steps out so timidly to encounter the world of experience—she hardly flings herself into it, but, cautiously testing the temperature of the water, immerses herself bit by bit, half wanting to retreat to her room, to play the piano and stay dry. The world lies all before her, as it lay before Isabel Archer, but having crossed the ocean and come to the wild shores at the edge of the jungle, who or what emerges to meet her? Savages, gods, evil, deception? No, she encounters two young men who have just come down from Cambridge.

Part of the interest of *The Voyage Out* is that it explores with such rigor the issues raised by Woolf's limited experience. Rachel is the product of the kind of education given to women in the nineteenth century—indulgent, patronizing, demanding no serious work, designed to keep her free from contamination. The result is a profound and even dangerous ignorance, dangerous because a kiss can produce nightmares, dangerous because the thought of sex is associated with thoughts of death, dangerous because sickness comes to seem a sort of integrity. The two great realities of Rachel's life, as she says in an earlier version, are her fear of men and her mother's death.

There were some ten drafts of *The Voyage Out* (as compared to Woolf's usual three for later novels), and as she wrote and rewrote the book over the years Woolf changed the portrait of Rachel, eliminating some gratuitous self-description.[3] In an earlier version Rachel is even closer to Virginia Stephen as the world saw her in her early twenties. She comes frankly from Kensington; Richmond and the maiden aunts have not yet been invented as images of her seclusion. She may be ignorant of sex, but she has read a lot—even *Religio Medici*. She is more sure of herself, talks more, stands up for herself more, and although she is aloof, one does not know—as Duncan Grant did not know about Virginia—whether her aloofness proceeds from shyness, as is surely the case with her final incarnation, or from fierceness. Certainly she is more judgmental than the ultimate Rachel who seems content with people if they do not hurt her.

These modifications sharpen the focus of the novel. In the earlier version, because she starts out relatively strong and self-confident, Rachel grows imperceptibly. The movement from innocence to maturity is clarified by making Rachel more clearly ignorant at the start. So *Religio Medici* is dropped. The detail is confusing and unnecessary unless one were committed to strict autobiography, to capturing that odd mixture of bookish sophistication and worldly innocence which typified Virginia Woolf's youth. Mrs. Vinrace's death, to take another example, is mentioned again and again in one earlier version, but all it serves to tell us is how important Julia Stephen's death was to Virginia—it is not worked into the novel in anything more than a tantalizing way. The over-insistence on it disappears in the revisions, although the fact that Rachel's mother has died remains. As for the most important change, the fading of Rachel's tough public posture, one must speculate that the fierceness masked and simultaneously muddied what Woolf felt to be the essence of Rachel and what interested her in the character, her vulnerability. The net effect of the changes is to create a Rachel who more forcefully embodies one side of Virginia Woolf. The world saw her as a mixture of shyness and fierceness; she chose to emphasize the shyness—the dreamy, withdrawn, secluded part of her own personality.

Rachel's shipmates on the voyage out strike one as coming attractions for future Woolf novels, for in addition to Ridley and Helen Ambrose, the crusty scholar and his forthright, maternal, intuitive wife, who anticipate the Ramsays of *To the Lighthouse*, among them also are Mr. and Mrs. Richard Dalloway, the very Dalloways Virginia Woolf would write about more fully and from a slightly different perspective in 1925. Their appearance in *The Voyage Out* is odd. They board the ship after the voyage has begun, leave it before it is finished. Stylish and worldly inhabitants of the upper crust of London society, they are vividly realized characters, and Clive Bell, reading the novel in manuscript in 1909, said, "Surely the Dalloways must appear again."[4] But they do not. The world of polite Mayfair society and political power from which the Dalloways emerge was the one in which George Duckworth moved, in which Virginia felt herself a failure. Although she professed to despise this world, simultaneously it fascinated her, and I think the Dalloways' disconnected appearance in *The Voyage Out* is partly a tribute to this fascination. But they flutter still on the periphery of her imagination; she is not yet ready to transfigure that part of her experience into fiction. Before he disappears, however, Richard Dalloway has one important action to perform. Against all probabilities of plot he has been dragged out of Mayfair to give Rachel Vinrace her first kiss.

It was George Duckworth, the Mayfair swell who insisted on fine clothes, polite conversation, and the importance of titles, who introduced Virginia Woolf to sex with his fondlings and gropings. Whether George's attentions were the cause or merely the confirmation of Woolf's aversion to sex, there are still similarities between her introduction to sexuality and Rachel Vinrace's. Both erotic pursuers inhabit the same social milieu. Both are inappropriate lovers, Dalloway because he is married, George because he is her brother. Both represent power, Dalloway political power (he has been in Parliament), George the sheer power of money. The picture she is trying to create in the Dalloway episode in her polite, chaste fashion is of male lust so strong it expresses itself despite all restraints:

> "You tempt me," he said. The tone of his voice was terrifying. He seemed choked in fight. They were both trembling (85).

But if Dalloway is trembling from the effort to control himself, Rachel is trembling from shock and from a feeling of powerlessness in the face of this "assault." In earlier versions this is more explicit: "I felt weak you see," she says, describing the encounter to Helen afterward; "I felt he could do what he chose with me."

Compared to the story of George's (and Gerald's) incestuous exploitation of Virginia, Richard Dalloway's kiss seems small beer, a spontaneous, almost innocent gesture: the ship lurches as they chat in her room, Rachel falls forward, Richard takes her in his arms and kisses her. But Rachel reacts strongly, seized by "a strange exaltation." "Life seemed to hold infinite possibilities she had never guessed at" (85). This is her daytime reaction; her nighttime reaction is equally strong, but negative. She has a horrifying dream of being trapped in a damp vault with a deformed man whose face is that of an animal. The dream suggests once more Woolf's fixation on rooms, enclosed spaces, as images not only of her situation but of herself. In this dream the space is a tunnel which turns into a vault, and its likeness to the female body need not be elaborated. The horror, however, does not lie in being trapped in that damp space but in being trapped in it *with* someone, a deformed brute of a man. All that night Rachel "felt herself pursued, so that she got up and actually locked her door." "All night long barbarian men harassed the ship; they came scuffling down the passages, and stopped to snuffle at her door" (86). The response seems inappropriate to the event, and however it may have been with Duckworth and his sister, it seems that Dalloway with Rachel has merely activated a fear of violation and a deep anxiety about sex.

Dalloway may be, like George, a thoroughgoing bounder, a Victorian wolf in Savile Row clothing, but he is not directly blamed for provoking Rachel's horror. The novel insists that in part, at any rate, his kiss suggests the richness of life, the "infinite possibilities" that have been heretofore closed to Rachel. Helen Ambrose pins the blame for Rachel's terror on her sheltered upbringing, for which her father is responsible. "Helen could hardly restrain herself from saying out loud what she thought of a man who brought up his daughter so that at the age of twenty-four she scarcely knew that men desired women and was terrified by a kiss" (90). Rachel is kept ignorant to protect her from sex; the paradoxical result, of course, is that sex is so much more overwhelmingly a threat when she finds out about it.

To appreciate the kiss episode and Helen's subsequent explanation of the facts of life to Rachel requires something of a leap of the imagination, for the assumptions about sex are so thoroughly Victorian. Even Helen's view of sex—and she is supposed to be advanced—may strike us as odd:

> "You oughtn't to be frightened," she said. "It's the most natural thing in the world. Men will want to kiss you, just as they'll want to marry you. The pity is to get things out of proportion. It's like noticing the noises people make when they eat, or men spitting; or, in short, any small thing that gets on one's nerves" (91).

We are back in a world where sex is a minor irritation that women must occasionally and in a ladylike fashion tolerate to satisfy the insatiable desires of men. Men are creatures of lust who pursue; women have no desires but must submit. After Helen's explanation of sex, Rachel thinks immediately of the prostitutes in Piccadilly, seeing no distinction between Dalloway's kiss and the purchase of a woman by a man—it all amounts to the same thing. Her conclusion? "It *is* terrifying—it *is* disgusting" (91). "So that's why I can't walk alone!"

> By this new light she saw her life for the first time a creeping hedged-in thing, driven cautiously between high walls, here turned aside, there plunged in darkness, made dull and crippled for ever—her life that was the only chance she had—a thousand words and actions became plain to her.
>
> "Because men are brutes! I hate men!" she exclaimed (91–92).

Rachel's fear and resentment of men and her disgust with sex
are, if anything, muted in the published version of *The
Voyage Out*, perhaps because Woolf felt this also was too peculiar to herself, but it is still an important part of Rachel's
character. "O how I hate it—how I hate it!" she exclaims in
an early draft, seeing Susan Warrington and her fiancé roll
about on the grass in an embrace. Later this is softened to a
tight-lipped, "I don't like that," and beside her she has a
young man who does not lecture her on birds and bees or ad-
vise her to pay no mind to unpleasant things, but who tells
her sympathetically that he can remember a time when he
didn't like it himself.

For the first part of the book, Helen Ambrose seems destined
to be her niece's mentor, guiding her out of ignorance and
into the broad world of experience. We are told that under
Helen's influence Rachel begins to change and grow and that
three months with her in Santa Marina make up in large
part for all that "time spent . . . in sheltered gardens." She
becomes "less shy" and "less serious" and begins to listen to
conversations as though she might contradict what was
being said. This development in Rachel recalls the change
that took place in Woolf's life when she and her sister and
brothers moved to Bloomsbury and broke with the stifling
life of their relatives, when she stopped making tea talk at
her father's table and began holding court with Vanessa instead. Helen's educational tool, like Bloomsbury's, is talk,
free, frank and open talk about everything, and the description of Helen's powerful and liberating effect on Rachel may
well be Woolf's tribute to the influence on her of her sister,
who possessed the same kind of easy and gracious but tough-
mindedly candid way of talking with men that distinguishes
Helen Ambrose. Clive Bell found Helen such a sympathetic
portrait of his wife that he said reading the book would
make Vanessa believe in herself.[5] But soon after their establishment at Santa Marina, Helen diminishes in signifi-

cance for Rachel and her place is taken by two Cambridge graduates on vacation, Terence Hewet and St. John Hirst.

It may seem odd for our heroine to journey all the way from England to South America to find herself a young man from Cambridge; it becomes less odd if we consider Rachel's pilgrimage as a fictionalized presentation of Virginia Woolf's own "journey" from Hyde Park Gate to Bloomsbury. The exotic setting, the adventurous voyage, are superimposed on the novel, not intrinsic—Clive Bell had told her she was trying too much to write like other people, and he was right. Mostly, she was trying to write like Conrad, to some extent like E. M. Forster, whose first three novels had appeared by 1908 when Woolf was just beginning *The Voyage Out*. The journey motif does not really suit and henceforth she will not use it; her most exotic setting after this is the Hebrides of *To the Lighthouse*, and even that, as we know, is really Cornwall by another name.

The mid-section of *The Voyage Out* turns on Rachel's response to the challenge of Hewet and St. John Hirst, just as Woolf's life at the time of writing the novel centered on coming to terms with those notable products of Cambridge, her brother's friends. When Rachel meets Hewet and Hirst, *The Voyage Out* finds its direction, becoming in a thoughtful, controlled way a novel about the challenges to feminine identity. Vanessa, on whom Helen is based, is put off—like the Dalloway-Duckworth world—for fictional treatment later, when, conflated with Julia Stephen, she re-emerges as Mrs. Ramsay. Perhaps in writing of her sister Woolf touches on issues so deep she isn't yet prepared to handle them. At any rate *The Voyage Out* is not Vanessa's book. It becomes the book of Virginia and the clever young men—even more specifically, the book of Virginia and Lytton Strachey.

In *The Voyage Out* Strachey is transformed into St. John Hirst, a vivid character, some might even say caricature, very intelligent and very ugly, who uses his intelligence as a weapon in social encounters to cover his insecurity, as Strachey apparently did until the success of *Eminent Victorians* let him feel secure enough to be charming. Hirst is given to outrageous remarks like "There never will be more than five people in the world worth talking to," but only Rachel, who is intimidated by him, remains unaware that his wit is a kind of defense and that he desperately wants affection. Being ugly is the great reality of his life, being clever the great facade. He is a Gibbon-lover, devoted to reason and polished style, mannered, ungainly, decidedly misogynous.

Tweedledee to this eccentric Tweedledum, Terence Hewet suffers by contrast and appears rather colorless, if not, indeed, diaphanous. He seems unformed, like Rachel herself, a person more in potentia than in actuality. For Hewet there is no obvious Bloomsbury model. He is sensitive, perceptive, sociable, down-to-earth, and eminently sane; and as opposed to Hirst, he likes women, though he approaches them with something of the spirit of scientific curiosity with which Darwin approached beetles. He is going to be a novelist and wants to write a novel about silence, about the things people don't say, an aspiration which has frequently been taken as identical to Woolf's own. There is "something of a woman in him" (247), as various Santa Marinites notice. The question posed by the structure of the novel and articulated by Helen Ambrose is, which of these two young men will educate Rachel?

One scene in particular captures the nature of Hirst's relationship with Rachel and dramatizes, I would suggest, the challenge Strachey presented to Woolf and her response. Their first important meeting takes place at a dance in honor of Susan Warrington's engagement, the occasion suggesting a celebration of the compatibility of men and women, but proving, in Rachel's experience, exactly the opposite. She and Hirst try dancing, but "instead of fitting into each other their bones seemed to jut out in angles making smooth turning an impossibility" (179). When they talk, her platitudes alternate with his silences until, determined to ingratiate himself (for Hewet has taunted him with being unable to get on with women), Hirst brings up the subject he loves best, books. As Helen was scandalized that Rachel had reached the age of twenty-four without being kissed, Hirst is scandalized that she has reached twenty-four without reading Gibbon, and the question in his mind is not what Gibbon can do for her, but whether she is up to Gibbon.

> "Mon Dieu!" he exclaimed, throwing out his hands. "You must begin tomorrow. I shall send you my copy. What I want to know is—" he looked at her critically. "You see, the problem is, can one really talk to you? Have you got a mind, or are you like the rest of your sex? You seem to me absurdly young compared with men of your age."
> Rachel looked at him but said nothing.
> "About Gibbon," he continued. 'D'you think you'll be able to appreciate him? He's the test, of course. It's awfully difficult to tell about women," he continued, "how much, I mean, is due to lack of training, and how much is native incapacity. I don't see myself why you shouldn't understand—only I suppose you've led an absurd life until now—you've just walked in a crocodile, I suppose, with your hair down your back" (181).

From its opening mannered French exclamation (Strachey was fond of larding his conversation with French phrases) to its concluding jibe about walking in a crocodile (that is, as girls in school walk, by twos in a file), this monologue, with its unanswerable questions—"Have you got a mind or are you like the rest of your sex?"—is brilliantly done; insult follows challenge so swiftly that the passage reads like a series of slaps in the face. In an earlier version of this scene, Hirst and Rachel exchange one-liners, and the effect is of her deflecting his attack, standing up to him by evasion. Woolf reworked it to bring out more strongly that Hirst's speech is a massive assault on Rachel's self-esteem in the face of which she can say nothing, can in no way defend herself, since the insidious thing is that much of what he suggests is true—she has more or less walked in a crocodile, although it was not her fault. She finds this detail particularly "unjust and horrible" and Hirst's cool assumption of the "superiority of his nature and experience" not merely "galling but terrible—as if a gate had clanged in her face." Eventually, "with the best will in the world," Hirst becomes aware that he and she are not getting on well and resolves to leave her.

> "I'd like awfully to lend you books," he said, buttoning his gloves and rising from his seat. "We shall meet again. I'm going to leave you now."
> He got up and left her.
> Rachel looked round. She felt herself surrounded, like a child at a party, by the faces of strangers all hostile to her, with hooked noses and sneering indifferent eyes. She was by a window, she pushed it open with a jerk, and stepped into the garden. Her eyes swam with tears of rage.
> "Damn that man!" she exclaimed. . . . "Damn his insolence!" (181).

Hirst's offer to lend books is well-meant but seems condescending and merely reinforces his assertion of superiority and her sense of exclusion: the books are his to lend. And then he leaves her. The Dickensian image of the child in a world of powerful and menacing adults suggests her feeling of insecurity and exclusion: power is not hers.

I am reminded here of another woman writer's initial encounter with a man of great learning and intellectual prestige—Anaïs Nin's panicked reaction to Edmund Wilson.

> . . . Wilson arrogant, sure of himself. Even in his empty house I had the feeling he was born in the English tradition of letters, nourished by libraries, formulas, and classical scholarship.

I ran away, and the only reason I consented to see him again was that when I left he ran out to get me a taxi, and because my leaving was so precipitate he felt it was a desertion and shouted a most untypical cry: "Don't desert me. Don't leave me alone."

The next day I had a cold. Edmund Wilson sent flowers, and a set of Jane Austen, with a note. He was hoping I would learn how to write a novel from reading her!

But I am not an imitator of past styles.

Meanwhile, he reread *Winter of Artifice*, and when I was well he came to see me.

His face was red and flushed from weather or from drink. . . . He was so directly affected by the book that he stood in the middle of the studio and blurted out: "You realize, of course, that the father is right, in *Winter of Artifice*, and the daughter completely in the wrong."

"Yes, of course, you would feel that. You identify with the father, the classicist, and you imagine we have the same conflict."[6]

It is peculiarly apt that Wilson, who tells Nin, " 'I would love to be married to you, and I would teach you to write,' " comes with Jane Austen in hand as Hirst, also a lover of classical style, comes with Gibbon: Jane Austen seems to be a man's idea of what a woman writer should be. More fluid, more romantic writers like Woolf and Nin naturally resent having Jane Austen held up to them as a model. Wilson, at any rate, bears down on Nin with all the weight of "libraries, formulas, and classical scholarship" behind him, and Nin, trained in psychoanalysis, feels that in fleeing from him she flees "the full tyranny of the father." She sees in Wilson a man "whose will would bend mine, ignore my aspirations, beliefs, deprive me of my liberty, threaten my development." The prestige of his learning subdues her, as Hirst subdues Rachel, making her feel she is back in childhood with the gate shut. "Faced with Edmund Wilson, I felt myself as ado-

lescent. Why? I don't know. But there it was. I felt without
authority, vulnerable, stripped of power."[7]

Nin hints that her way of dealing with the threat Wilson
posed was to seduce him and abandon him, thereby asserting
in a very feminine way her power over him. For obvious
reasons this subtle sexual ploy was not available to Woolf.
Even if Strachey had not been homosexual, thereby compli-
cating enormously the threat of his masculine authority, she
was hardly sophisticated enough in matters of sex to have
imagined it. Rachel's response in *The Voyage Out* is to escape
from sex altogether. She walks into the garden to be alone,
retreating into herself and her imagination as Woolf did in
her private nook in the precincts of her father's house, and
she fantasizes about having absolute power in a sexless
world. "She would be a Persian princess far from civilization, riding her horse upon the mountains alone, and making
her women sing to her in the evening, far from all this, from
the strife of men and women" (181).

Just at this point the other young Englishman turns up,
and we move abruptly from the world of private fantasy to
the world of social reality as Rachel reveals her conclusions
about the incompatibility of the sexes—"It's no good; we
should live separate; we cannot understand each other; we
only bring out what's worst." Hewet brushes this aside, "for
such generalizations bored him and seemed to him generally
untrue," and since he does not want Hirst's rudeness to influence Rachel's view of life and sex, he tries to explain it as
merely an awkward person's attempt to be nice.

> ". . . You see, Miss Vinrace, you must make allow-
> ances for Hirst. He's lived all his life in front of a look-
> ing-glass, in a beautiful panelled room, hung with Jap-
> anese prints and lovely old chairs and tables, just one
> splash of colour, you know, in the right place . . . and
> there he sits hour after hour with his toes on the fender,
> talking about philosophy and God and his liver and his

heart and the hearts of his friends. They're all broken. You can't expect him to be at his best in a ballroom. He wants a cosy, smoky, masculine place, where he can stretch his legs out, and only speak when he has something to say. For myself, I find it rather dreary. But I do respect it. They're all so much in earnest. They do take the serious things very seriously" (183).

Hewet places Hirst in perspective with a satirical sketch of the mixture of aestheticism, hypochondria, and earnest philosophical style typical of Cambridge at the turn of the century. "Cosy, smoky, masculine" though it is, this world seems in Hewet's presentation as much a prison, or ivory tower, if you will, as Rachel's aunts' more feminine prison in Richmond, and Rachel is so satisfied with Hewet's explanation that her grudge against Hirst begins to evaporate and her respect revives.

> "They are really very clever then?" she asked.
> "Of course they are. So far as brains go I think it's true what he said the other day; they're the cleverest people in England. But—you ought to take him in hand," he added. "There's a great deal more in him than's ever been got at. He wants someone to laugh at him. . . . The idea of Hirst telling you that you've had no experiences! Poor old Hirst!" (183–84).

From Rachel's initial rage and embittered sense of inadequacy to the emergence of an amused equanimity, with Hewet's help, this sequence recalls Virginia's own response to the challenge posed by her brother's clever friends, and particularly by Strachey, the most imposing of them. Terence's description of the ingrown world of Cambridge resembles Woolf's own in the *Euphrosyne* review, and his assumption that cleverness can be arid and wants a bit of laughing at is hers as well. From this point on in the novel, it is never in doubt who will educate Rachel. The sequence ends with the couple dancing: "They clasped hands and swept off magnificently into the great swirling pool."

In considering a novel in which three major characters—Helen, Hirst, and Rachel—have actual models, it is natural to wonder who played the role in Virginia Woolf's emotional development that Hewet plays in Rachel's. Is Hewet based on someone in particular? Jack Hills, Stella Duckworth's husband, easy-going and out-of-doorsy, is a possibility. Clive Bell is even more likely, for in 1909 Virginia was interested enough in him as a subject for fiction to jot down a few pages of notes about his background and character.[8] Bell, like Hewet, was jovial and sociable. His father, like Hewet's, was a fox-hunting squire, and because of his country background, he seemed less exclusively intellectual than most of Thoby Stephen's friends. While Strachey worried about his liver, Bell liked to hunt. Moreover, and most importantly, in this largely homosexual society, he was enthusiastically heterosexual. He engaged his sister-in-law in an intense flirtation beginning around February 1908, when Vanessa gave birth to their first son. If this flirtation served Virginia as a balm for her hurt feelings about her treatment by the Bloomsbury homosexuals, then the spirit in which she turned to her brother-in-law is much like the spirit in which Rachel turns at the dance from Hirst, who has in fact abandoned her, to waltz off with Hewet.[9]

But understanding and support are what Terence offers Rachel, not flirtation, not passion. He pursues women in a quasi-scientific spirit of inquiry, rather than with relish, and in the course of various conversations makes Rachel feel "at once singular and under observation," which is quite a different thing from making her feel singular and cherished. He is aware of the effect that a male-dominated social structure has on women's sense of themselves, how everything is arranged, for example, to support St. John's sense of his own importance, how scarcely a day goes by without a discussion of St. John's career. " 'But St. John's sister. . . . No one takes her seriously, poor dear. She feeds the rabbits' " (253). His perspective anticipates Woolf's own as expressed in the "Shakespeare's sister" section of *A Room of One's Own* and the "Arthur's Education Fund" segment of *Three Guineas*. We are hardly surprised later on to encounter Terence making notes for a novel under the heading "Women." " 'Lack of self-confidence at the base of most serious faults,' " he writes, articulating another Woolfian perception, and he wonders if " 'Dislike of own sex traditional, or founded in fact?' " (357). The kind of interest in women Terence displays, the kind of questions he asks, would be unusual for a man, but seem a natural part of the process of self-discovery and self-definition that intelligent, self-conscious women go through. Consider Terence female, and his questions lose their priggishness and patronizing tone: they reveal a somewhat self-alienated woman coming to terms with her own femininity. I am suggesting that the future author of a novel about silence, who has "something of the woman in him," is as much an aspect of his creator's self as Rachel Vinrace, and many of his conversations and encounters with Rachel, notably the one we examined before, in which Terence boosts Rachel's self-esteem after she has been insulted by Hirst at the dance, are best read as dialogues of self and soul, the down-to-earth, positive, and willed side of Virginia Woolf talking to the more dreamy, withdrawn, and vulnerable part of her nature.

Changes in the various drafts of *The Voyage Out* which clarify the portrait of Rachel as timid and vulnerable are balanced by added passages which serve to bring Terence out more strongly and to present him as concerned and positive about Rachel's experience. In as late a version as the 1912 holograph Rachel is still ambivalent about her Richmond seclusion. For example, when Terence pities St. John's sister for feeding rabbits all her life, Rachel replies, " 'I've fed rabbits for twenty-four years, . . . and its full of mar-

vels.' " "And its full of marvels" is crossed out, and the reply
as it appears in the published version is no longer defiant,
but wistful. To find the marvel in feeding rabbits becomes
Terence's function. He listens enthralled to Rachel's dispar-
aging accounts of her limited life with her maiden aunts. His
fascination is a useful expository device, of course, but more
than that, it represents Woolf's own hope that her experience, such as it was, a woman's experience, the experience of
life in houses and not on the broad thoroughfares, really has
some interest.

Considering the two young lovers as split projections of
Virginia Woolf helps to explain some oddities of *The Voyage
Out*. Chiefly, the dramatic presentation of sex in this novel,
so concerned on the thematic level with sexuality, must be
described as unconvincing, or perhaps more charitably,
rather too indirect.[10] Partly this flaw proceeds from Woolf's
lifelong reticence about treating sex frankly in fiction. But
what would the "honest truth" be about Rachel's feelings for
Terence? That her body desired his body, that she quickened
and tingled as they walked together in the jungle? Or that
she felt, simply, nothing? My own guess is nothing. The tepid
Terence is more a position paper than a character. He is sympathetic and reassuring about Rachel's femininity whereas
she herself is a mass of ignorance and fears, and the process
she engages in with him is not so much falling in love as it is
self-affirmation.[11]

Rachel's choice of Hewet over Hirst as her "educator" and
later her husband suggests the same kind of willed commitment to normality that the decision to marry Leonard Woolf
and the earlier flirtation with Clive Bell represented in
Virginia's life. Rachel, in turning from the fascinating but
disdainful Hirst, also turns from self-deprecation towards a
union which boosts her self-esteem: the issue is not so much
sexual passion as her acceptance of herself as a woman. For
Rachel as for Woolf, marriage represents a plunge into real-

ity, the wide river of experience; we sense in the novel the excitement of a withdrawn young person discovering that the ordinary adventures of life are open to her. But no sooner do Rachel and Terence start planning the wedding than she contracts a fever, connected presumably with the jungle voyage on which they declare their mutual love, and she rather precipitously dies. The jungle and the sick room dominate the end of the book, a strong contrast, the one setting so exotic with its snakes and palms and tropical colors, the other with its rumpled sheets and water jugs so familiar.

The trip upriver to see the sights of the jungle is as extraneous to the plot of the novel as the Dalloways' appearance on the *Euphrosyne:* it has been undertaken out of a whim, inspired and organized by Mrs. Flushing. The party consists of Hewet, Hirst, Helen, Rachel, and the Flushings. We can speculate that Woolf hoped through this episode to suggest a penetration to a kind of reality beyond the ordinary, to lay the groundwork for Rachel's sudden death (jungle fever), and to provide the properly torrid setting for the young lovers' declaration of feeling. The jungle setting, the symbolic journey upriver in burning heat through dense vegetation, has to suggest, as James Naremore notes, the sexual passion Terence and Rachel feel for each other, and it cannot do it. "They seemed to be driving into the heart of the night, for the trees closed in front of them, and they could hear all round them the rustling of leaves" (325). The country gets "wilder and wilder" as they move up the river on their small boat. "The trees and the undergrowth seemed to be strangling each other near the ground in a multitudinous wrestle; while here and there a splendid tree towered high above the swarm, shaking its thin green umbrellas lightly in the upper air" (327).

If the Dalloways' appearance represented gratuitous autobiography, here we encounter gratuitous fiction, a straining after heightened effect. The most revealing commentary on the jungle scenes of *The Voyage Out* was made indirectly by Woolf herself in 1909. In "Memoirs of a Novelist," a piece rejected by *Cornhill*, she describes an imaginary lady novelist who takes up writing at thirty-six, and, because she finds it indecent to describe what she has seen (though one of her brothers led an odd life and her father was interesting material), she invents Arabian lovers and sets them on the banks of the Orinoco. "The scenery was tropical because one gets effects quicker there than in England."[12] Pages are spent describing "mountains that looked like ramparts of clouds, save for the deep ravines that cleft their sides, and the diamond cascades that went leaping and flashing, now golden, now purple, as they entered the shade of the pine forests," and so on—Woolf's parody of lush descriptive writing is splendid—but when the imaginary novelist has to face her lovers, she stammers and blushes and her fluent pen dries up.

The scene in which the lovers in *The Voyage Out* declare their love is eerily silent—the few words Terence utters are echoed by Rachel, giving the effect of someone talking to himself in a cavernous room:

> . . . "We are happy together." He did not seem to be speaking or she to be hearing.
>
> "Very happy," she answered.
>
> They continued to walk for some time in silence. Their steps unconsciously quickened.
>
> "We love each other," Terence said.
>
> "We love each other," she repeated.
>
> The silence was then broken by their voices which joined in tones of strange unfamiliar sound which formed no words. Faster and faster they walked; simultaneously they stopped, clasped each other in their arms, then, releasing themselves, dropped to the earth. They sat side by side. Sounds stood out from the background making a bridge across their silence; they heard the swish of the trees and some beast croaking in a remote world.
>
> "We love each other," Terence repeated, searching her face (332).

This is certainly an improvement on Woolf's earlier version of the same encounter:

> He stopped; the moments seemed to Rachel as messengers approaching.
> "You know that I love you," he whispered. The messenger had arrived.[13]

Nevertheless the final version bears the same marks of straining as the earlier one. Such a scene must have seemed necessary to Woolf, but in writing it she was working against the grain of her experience. Sexual passion does not appear to have been part of her emotional repertoire.

The sick room scenes, in contrast, have enormous power. Here Woolf touches on her own experience and conveys a much greater illusion of reality than in the jungle scenes, for she knew well the dismaying and tedious agony of standing by as someone gradually and relentlessly dies an unexpected and untimely death. If we think Rachel's death hard on the heels of her engagement melodramatic, what is one to think about Stella Duckworth, Virginia's half-sister, who returned from her honeymoon suffering from the infection of which three months later, she died? She was twenty-eight. She was buried next to her mother, who had died only two years before. I have already quoted Virginia Woolf's description of the effect this double blow had on her. Dazed, tremulous, she began to see all happiness as perilously fragile, with destruction waiting to explode. In this section of *The Voyage Out*, she touches on that frightening abyss, and Terence learns, as young Virginia had learned, never again to feel secure, never to believe in the stability of life "or forget what depths of pain lie beneath small happiness" (421). Absurdly, irrelevantly, he quarrels with Hirst about whether the Portsmouth Road is macadamized where it passes Hindhead, just as Thoby and Adrian had argued while Vanessa lay dangerously sick in Greece in 1906.[14] But Vanessa, although she returned to England ill of that fever contracted in Greece, did not die of it. Thoby also returned sick, with typhoid, and he died. Unskilled writers often end with a death, and Rachel's death may, as a result, strike us at first as cheap and easy. But Virginia Woolf, by day after day of waiting for the smallest signs of improvement in an inevitably deteriorating patient, by the experience of learning that the unthinkable could happen and then happen again, by watching her brother and her half-sister, in their twenties, follow their mother to the cemetery, had earned her ending.

She knew death well from the outside, madness from the inside, and to portray Rachel's fevered delirium she had only to recreate the dislocations of her own mind in the two bouts of illness she had already suffered when she began to write *The Voyage Out*. She conveys superbly the weird visual distortions produced by Rachel's fever, the rapid changes of perception of temperature, the heightened sensitivity to all touch, as the sick girl grows by the day more and more cut off from any reality outside of her tormented body and brain.

On this day indeed Rachel was conscious of what went on round her. She had come to the surface of the dark, sticky pool, and a wave seemed to bear her up and down on it; she had ceased to have any will of her own; she lay on the top of the wave conscious of some pain, but chiefly of weakness. The wave was replaced by the side of a mountain. Her body became a drift of melting snow, above which her knees rose in huge peaked mountains of bare bone. It was true that she saw Helen and saw her room, but everything had become very pale and semitransparent. Sometimes she could see through the wall in front of her. Sometimes when Helen went away she seemed to go so far that Rachel's eyes could hardly follow her. The room had an odd power of expanding, and though she pushed her voice out as far as possible until sometimes it became a bird and flew away, she thought it doubtful whether it ever reached the person she was talking to. There were immense intervals or chasms . . .

between one moment and the next; it sometimes took Helen an hour to raise her arm, pausing long between each jerky movement, and pour out the medicine. . . . But for long spaces of time she would merely lie conscious of her body floating on the top of her bed and her mind driven to some remote corner of her body, or escaped and gone flitting around the room. All sights were something of an effort, but the sight of Terence was the greatest effort, because he forced her to join mind to body in the desire to remember something. She did not wish to remember; it troubled her when people disturbed her loneliness; she wished to be alone. She wished for nothing else in the world (423–24).

In her sickness Rachel is utterly alone and untouchable, her feverish brain inside the fortress-sanctuary of the sick room, the ultimately impregnable space. Her mind, delirious as it is, is her only reality, and she wants no more—she does not want Terence to force her to consciousness, invading her solitude. Woolf's descriptions of the phantasmagoric riot of Rachel's sick brain are, to my mind, the best writing in *The Voyage Out*, and I want to suggest why this might be so. It is not just that she has had the experience of delirium and knows it well but that she is convinced it is interesting. She needn't strain to heighten it. In madness she had transcended the limitations of a housebound young lady's experience, and she valued this about it. In *A Room of One's Own* she would envy Tolstoy for having made love and seen wars all over Europe. How can a woman, whose youth has been protected, whose experience has been so confined, write novels with the scope of *War and Peace?* But if Virginia Woolf was prevented from having the flamboyant adventures of a Tolstoy, in madness she found her own unique adventure.

Rachel's illness inevitably seems connected with her engagement to Terence—she withdraws into herself as she always does when threatened, but now in a final and ghastly fashion; her purity and integrity are preserved through death. She dreams again, in slightly different form, the horrifying dream which followed Richard Dalloway's kiss, and in this context, again, the dream suggests a fear of violation to which her delirious illness, her immersion in the fantasia of the unconscious, represents a response and a solution: it is the ultimate room of her own, a reality into which no one else can enter. Terence, always optimistic, finds with Rachel dead a more perfect, more "complete union" than they ever had when she was alive (431), and Woolf herself seems to have had a Shelleyan notion of the dead becoming part of a great life flow and therefore accessible to the living; but Terence's anguished cry of "Rachel, Rachel!" as he struggles to get back to her and perceives she is lost (432) is much more convincing. The extraordinary power of the sick room scenes must be taken into account when considering the issues of identity this novel raises. It endorses marriage, intimacy, but its emotional message, its hidden message, is the primacy of the self. The room is Woolf's space, richest when she is alone in it.

Exclusion from Cambridge focused for Virginia Woolf all the liabilities of being a woman: being restricted, being dependent, being considered inferior. To her credit she accepted this as a challenge and not as a fate. We have seen how she responded to this challenge in the early Bloomsbury years, asserting her difference and her worth. *The Voyage Out* reflects this: worked and reworked over the course of years, this extraordinary first novel served as a proving ground both for Woolf's fictional art and for her personal identity. In it she speaks as a woman, confronting what seems to her the essential fact of a woman's life, limited experience, and she offers the hope that there may be a voyage out. The novel reveals that for a woman of her temperament the real danger is not to accept the fate that would seem to be imposed on her—that is, to submit, to be passive and masochistic in her relations with men—but to desire independence so fiercely, to fear so strongly the loss of her painfully acquired identity, that any intimacy becomes impossible. The ending suggests Woolf's fearfulness about the future and her disbelief in the endurance, in the ordinary world of marriage, of the character we have watched being formed in the course of the novel. "But won't it be awful," she asked Violet Dickinson after accepting Leonard, "if . . . my character, which promised so well, finally rots in marriage?"[15]

# 4

# Lytton Strachey
# and Leonard Woolf

In 1909 Lytton Strachey proposed marriage to
Virginia Stephen. It seems that even as the words
were coming out of his mouth, "the arch-bugger of
Bloomsbury," as Quentin Bell calls him,[1] saw the
impossibility of such a marriage, and by the next
day had succeeded in disentangling himself.
Virginia had been most tactful. She had said she really did not love him anyway. Yet when other men
proposed to her, she would reply that Strachey was
the only person she could marry. He had, to begin
with, all the prestige accruing to the friends of beloved older brothers, and among Thoby's friends he

was acknowledged to be the most distinguished—an Apostle (as Thoby himself was not), a member of a family with a tradition of intellectual achievement as extraordinary as the Stephens' own. As Bloomsbury coalesced, Strachey, by force of intelligence and personality, dominated the group.

His manner was pre-eminently rational, fitfully witty. He was extremely clever, with a mind both "naturally and cultivatedly Voltairean."[2] Always in love with some young man or other, full of despair or ecstasy about his latest *amour*, he was never, according to Leonard Woolf, wholly serious about such matters. There was a great deal of posing, of tongue-in-cheek histrionics in Strachey's affairs, and Leonard Woolf doubted whether in fact he had any strong passions. Self-conscious gesture, as behooved a spiritual son of Oscar Wilde, was strong in Strachey's presentation of himself to his friends.

In the early years of their relationship, Virginia Woolf imagined him variously as "an oriental potentate, in a flowered dressing gown," full of passion, style, and immorality, and as a "kind of Venetian prince, in sky blue tights, lying on [his] back in an orchard, or balancing an exquisite leg in the air."[3] (Until Vita Sackville-West entered her life much later, no one inspired in Virginia such exotic fantasies as Strachey did.) All Bloomsbury agreed that the correspondence between its two literary luminaries was too stiff and self-conscious to be interesting, but from the way Virginia imagines roles for Lytton and defines herself against them we learn a great deal. If he praises the eighteenth century, she defends the nineteenth as "hotter in the head." If he praises Jane Austen, she replies that Austen might have learned something from Anne Radcliffe. If he is an Oriental potentate, she is a humble, plain-speaking Englishwoman.

Quentin Bell has exploded the notion of a monolithic Bloomsbury group.[4] There were no doctrines to subscribe to, no theories one had to uphold—this was merely a loose group of friends. The relationship between Woolf and Strachey supports this, because, certainly for Virginia, what the two did not have in common was more important than what they did. Friends give support. They also supply, as in this case, healthy rivalry. In later years Virginia would compare her sales to Lytton's and get depressed. With the publication of *Eminent Victorians* in 1918 and *Queen Victoria* in 1921 he seemed to have outdistanced her, for she did not enjoy great acclaim until the publication of *Mrs. Dalloway* and *The Common Reader* in 1925. But the difference between them was consciously delineated (classic vs. romantic) and playfully manipulated, so when Strachey wrote and said that he did not like *Mrs. Dalloway*, Woolf, usually so sensitive to criticism, was by no means devastated. "It's odd that when Clive and the others (several of them) say it is a masterpiece, I am not much exalted; when Lytton picks holes, I get back into my working fighting mood."[5]

The story of their sexual opposition is rather darker, for Strachey's homosexuality, which was so much a part of his self-definition, was decidedly misogynist. Many of the Bloomsbury homosexuals—Keynes and Duncan Grant are cases in point—later married or had liaisons with women; there was no biological obligation in their youthful preference for men. From the middle of the nineteenth century, there had been, according to Noel Annan, a "cult" of homosexuality among the British upper classes, centered in Cambridge.[6] E. M. Forster's novel *Maurice*, written in 1913 though not published until after Forster's death, conveys the platonic, Greek spirit of attachments between university men at the turn of the century and their anti-female bias. Maurice's utter lack of respect for his mother and sisters, as much as anything else, sends him into the arms of Clive, and it appears that Clive, who initiated the relationship, never really wanted Maurice's body—only his soul. In an afterword Forster discusses the influence on him of Edward Carpenter's notions of idealized friendship. It seems that such lofty unions could only be achieved by men. Not all homosexuals dislike women, of course, but Forster's do, and the combination of their educational advantages—their university education—and their misogynist homosexuality does not seem haphazard. Where men enjoy status and prestige at the expense of women (ancient Athens, Oxbridge), only men seem worthy of being loved, and homosexuality has cultural endorsement.

In later years Woolf achieved ironic perspective on the connection between homosexuality and the male university experience. In *A Room of One's Own* she sketches a portrait of Oscar Browning, a notable—although perhaps atypical— Cambridge don of the turn of the century.[7] Browning, she tells us, would conduct examinations of the girls from Girton and Newnham, proclaim them dunces, opine that the most intelligent woman was inferior to the least endowed man, and then return to his rooms and the arms of a filthy, black-toothed stableboy, who he explained was "a dear boy really and most high-minded."[8] How refreshing, after such condescension, to encounter homosexuals of another sort. "These Sapphists *love* women," Woolf wrote at the beginning of her friendship with Vita Sackville-West.[9] "Sapphism," and not heterosexuality, was perhaps the only equivalent response to homosexuality like Strachey's, and it may be more than coincidence that Virginia's friendship with Lytton crested in 1925, about the time her friendship with Vita became intense.[10]

Although she would come to see Strachey's homosexuality as her father's patriarchal attitude in Edwardian dress, in 1909, at the time of Strachey's proposal and retraction, this consoling perspective had not yet crystallized, and in any case the "homosexual conspiracy" represented a real obstacle to consolidating her self-esteem. However gracefully the two of them had managed it, the fact was that she had been rejected by him, and rejected simply because she was of the wrong sex. In a way she had the worst of two cultural worlds: raised in a Victorian milieu which taught women to be pure and sexless, undervaluing their sexuality, she later moved into a world of men who were self-consciously avant-garde about their sexual behavior and who distinguished themselves from their fathers by not having to do, sexually, with women. She can hardly have been helped in her sexual adjustment by Bloomsbuggery. Not that her reaction was inevitable—her sister was rather aggressively libertine—but it is perhaps understandable.

Oddly, she seems to have simultaneously registered the rejection and yet not, in some way, finally accepted it. Even after the fiasco of the retracted proposal both Virginia and her sister continued to think of Lytton as an option. In March 1912 Virginia wrote a letter to Molly MacCarthy in which she presented marriage to Lytton as a possibility, though one to be resisted: "No, I shan't drift into a bloodless alliance with Lytton—though he is in some ways perfect as a friend, only he's a female friend."[11] Two months later she agreed to marry Leonard Woolf. The engagement announcement she sent to Strachey was brief but pointed:

> Ha! Ha!
> Virginia Stephen
> Leonard Woolf

She had managed it so that it was no longer a question of Strachey rejecting her, but of her rejecting Strachey.

Bloomsbury was nothing if not inventive about domestic arrangements and rather prided itself on the many variations it played on the theme of sex, "with such happy results," Woolf writes in her memoirs, "that my father himself might have hesitated before he thundered out the one word which he thought fit to apply to a bugger or an adulterer; which was Blackguard!"[12] The fidelity of their parents was not, they realized with what seemed to them revolutionary insight, the only or perhaps even the highest form of married life.

*Lytton Strachey in 1917.*

One of the oddest arrangements was Strachey's, and we may imagine the kind of "bloodless alliance" there might have been between him and Virginia because Strachey did in fact manage to land himself in such a situation, a sexless but enduring relationship with a woman. The woman was Dora Carrington, who met and fell desperately in love with Strachey when she was an art student. She could not have him; she could not give him up. What evolved was a *ménage à trois*, with Strachey, Carrington, and Ralph Partridge living together, Strachey in love (on and off) with Partridge, Partridge with Carrington, and Carrington with Strachey. Partridge slept with both. Carrington kept house and painted a little. At some point Partidge forced Carrington to marry him but this made no difference in their arrangement. It is, some will find, a rather seamy story, yet Leonard Woolf, with some psychological insight, points out its inner logic: Carrington was the kind of person who is only happy in pursuit. Loving a homosexual, who was perpetually unavailable, she could remain perpetually in love. Never attained, he remained an object of desire. This made for a kind of stability, and the relationship lasted fifteen years.[13] Shortly after Strachey died, Carrington committed suicide.

Carrington's life presents an example of the psychic pitfalls Woolf avoided by not pursuing that particular alliance. She was rejecting whatever perverse attraction there may be in living with a man in perpetual flight from you; and in addition, quite apart from his sexual predilictions, Strachey was a demanding and difficult man. Carrington more or less sacrificed her art to keep his household functioning. Virginia Woolf, so careful a guardian of her talent, so aware after life with Leslie Stephen of the sacrifices men can extract from talented women, was unlikely to do the same. But perhaps the fact that marrying Strachey would have been a re-enactment of her life with father explains some of its attraction. The model, however masochistic, was there, and it was a potent one.

Why such an independent person wanted to marry at all may seem something of a mystery, but as a young woman Virginia Woolf was not particularly daring. She wanted the usual things women want from marriage—status, companionship, children, sexual experience—and though these might have been obtained in other ways, without marriage, for one of her temperament it was impossible. To spend the rest of her days as merely "a virgin, an aunt, an authoress" seemed a shriveled fate, an endless prolonging of Hyde Park Gate life. She longed for the normal experiences of women, and marriage promised her that. Also, her vanity was at stake. "Am I to have no proposal then? If I had had the chance, and determined against it, I could settle to virginity with greater composure than I can, when my womanhood is at question."[14] Vanessa, married, a mother, happy, sane, and productive, was a constant reproach to her sister. "To be 29 and unmarried—to be a failure—childless—insane too, no writer"—these were her worst fears.[15]

But if she didn't want to stay single, she did in fact have many doubts about marrying. "I'm thinking a good deal . . . about marriage," she wrote Vanessa in 1911. "My quarrel with it is that the pace is so slow."[16] She seems to have felt that a writer needs to live more intensely than is possible in the daily, numbing contact of marriage. More concretely her insanity was a problem, her desire for independence scarcely less so, and of course her aversion to sex. Vanessa, who knew her best, came to conclude only gradually, "impressed by the pathos of her situation," a loneliness made even more difficult by the necessity of living with Adrian, who did not appreciate her, that "in spite of all drawbacks she had better marry."[17] Still, Vanessa could not imagine what her sister would do with children.

In Chapter 18 of *The Voyage Out* Hewet, who as I have suggested is Rachel's alter ago, her affirmative, more outgoing complement, contemplates the range of married life as a series of pictures, most of which he finds unattractive. "He tried all sorts of pictures, taking them from the lives of friends of his, for he knew many different married couples; but he saw them always, walled up in a warm firelit room." Two people "walled up" together—a particularly charged and horrid image to Virginia Woolf. Unmarried people, on the other hand, seem to Hewet "active in an unlimited world," and "all the most individual and humane of his friends were bachelors and spinsters" (295). Terence's meditations articulate an intellectualized, rational concern with marriage which is dramatized less obviously throughout the book, for although we examined *The Voyage Out* largely in terms of Rachel's relations with the two men who most directly effect her, the cast of characters is in fact quite extensive, and much of the novel consists of social scenes, picnics, teas, after-dinner meetings, in which the English guests at Santa Marina are vividly and often comically presented, as in an Austen or a Forster novel. "I want to bring out a stir of live men and women against a background," the author explained to Clive Bell,[18] but a more specific purpose reveals itself, for the guest register at the hotel reads like a discouraging catalogue of women's responses to matrimony.

Susan Warrington, for one, greets marriage enthusiastically. A rather ordinary, good-hearted soul, she latches onto the first man who seems willing, and they get engaged. She is very happy, but Terence scorns her: "she had no self" (156). Evelyn Murgatroyd, Susan's opposite number and the very embodiment of "self," is a congenital flirt with a real emotional disability that makes it unlikely she will ever commit herself to anyone. Rachel, the third of the young unmarried women, remains poised between the possibilities represented by the other two, commitment without selfhood and selfhood without commitment, as though Woolf is asking which nature is really hers, which the truer impulse.

The older women supply few enticing images of marriage. Miss Allan had avoided the whole problem by dedicating herself to her work and the support of her brother. Tough and self-reliant, she is sympathetically presented, fore-shadowing Lily Briscoe and Miss La Trobe of the later novels; yet her lot seems rather barren. Mrs. Thornbury and Mrs. Elliott suggest the liabilities of family life for a woman: the former sentimental, wholly immersed in the lives of her children, and the latter with no children, querulous, edgy, fussing over her husband. Neither has developed—marriage has extinguished their characters, and Terence's comment is harsh: "There can be no doubt it would have been better for the world if these couples had separated." He is skeptical even of the Ambroses, for, with all the love between them, "was not their marriage too a compromise?" "She gave way to him; she spoilt him; she arranged things for him; she who was all truth to others was not true to her husband, was not true to her friends if they came in conflict with her husband." What Terence describes would sound to a man, I venture to guess, like a splendid marriage; that he finds Helen's acts of compromise a degrading betrayal of her integrity reveals again his essentially feminine outlook.

One guest is conspicuously absent from Terence's considerations of the mingled blessings of matrimony—Mrs. Flushing, the eccentric aristocrat, cared for by a husband who enjoys her flamboyance and whom she clearly dominates. It would have been easy for Woolf to have Terence present this marriage as another failure, but she does not, perhaps because she secretly feels it is a success but cannot consciously endorse the model of a marriage in which the wife is dominant. Yet if any of the marriages sketched in *The Voyage Out* foreshadows the Woolfs' it is that of the Flushings.

Terence's melancholy meditation on marriage concludes with an optimism we expect if we see him as Woolf's positive and willed response to her innate timidity, and he decides that however other people have failed in marriage, becoming smug, unadventurous, compromised, he and Rachel will be "free together" (298). In the whole of his meditation, marriage presents itself only as a challenge to selfhood with little

hint of the positive potentials of intimacy beyond a perfunc-
tory "we'd share everything together." The most successful
marriage would be a species of peaceful coexistence in which
neither partner intruded on the other's psychic space, two
people with rooms of their own inhabiting the same house.
Perhaps only a woman who is enormously concerned about
fostering her own talent could find this ideal of marriage appealing.

If the alternating currents of Terence's thought reflect
Virginia Woolf's ambivalence about intimacy in the years
before she committed herself to Leonard Woolf, a concern
with sex is conspicuously absent. That she wanted to marry
for reasons of companionship and to satisfy an image of her
own sexuality, rather than to satisfy a real sexual need, we
may gather from her willingness to accept Strachey, whom,
homosexuality aside, she found physically repulsive. For
Leonard Woolf, too, she felt no physical attraction. "There
are moments," she wrote him with shocking candor during
their courtship, "when you kissed me the other day was
one—when I feel no more than a rock."[19] As it turned out,
she was frigid. Upon returning from their honeymoon, the
Woolfs consulted Vanessa about Virginia's "coldness." Having experienced sex, she couldn't understand what all the
fuss was about. There is no evidence to suggest that she ever
found out, and there is some evidence that shortly after the
honeymoon the Woolfs ceased entirely to have sexual relations.[20]

Yet she had insisted, in the letter in which she scorned a
bloodless alliance with Strachey, that she would marry only
if she could find someone who would make her vehement.

> I began life with a tremendous, absurd ideal of mar-
> riage; then my bird's eye view of many marriages
> disgusted me, and I thought I must be asking what was
> not to be had. But that has passed too. Now I only ask
> for someone to make me vehement, and then I'll marry
> them!

What, we must ask, does "vehemence" mean in this context and what "bloodlessness?" I would suggest that a vehement relationship would be one which ratified and intensified her sense of herself and not, as we might expect, one which elicited passionate feelings about her companion. The letters which Leonard and Virginia exchanged after he had proposed and while she was making up her mind whether or not to marry him are remarkable not only for their candor but for the fact that his deal with his feelings about her, whereas hers are concerned with her feelings about herself:

> I sometimes feel that no one ever has or ever can share something—Its the thing that makes you call me like a hill, or a rock. Again, I want everything—love, children, adventure, intimacy, work. . . . So I go from being half in love with you, and wanting you to be with me always, and know everything about me, to the extreme of wildness and aloofness. I sometimes think that if I married you, I could have everything—and then—is it the sexual side of it that comes between us? As I told you brutally the other day, I feel no physical attraction in you. . . . And yet your caring for me as you do almost overwhelms me. It is so real, and so strange. Why should you? What am I really except a pleasant attractive creature?[21]

I doubt that she intended it as a test, but this letter in itself must have been a trial of Leonard's devotion. His conviction that she was so much more than "a pleasant attractive creature," his ability to convince her of this, too, seem important factors in the success of their marriage. Virginia Woolf, who had so strong a faculty of "seeing" other people, who created fantasy images of other people which she expected them to live up to, had little ability to "see" herself. She suspected she was vapor; Leonard convinced her she was real.

The extraordinary fact is their marriage *was* a success. What pleasure Leonard got from this sexless union (and he was known in Bloomsbury as a passionate man) we can only imagine: she was charming, constantly interesting, and it is clear that he adored her and considered her a genius. In some way his protective, maternal role must have satisfied him. People described them as a Biblical couple, Joseph and Mary. As for Virginia, after more than ten years of living with Leonard she declared to Vita Sackville-West that the two of them seemed to be the only women in London who enjoyed being married. In a constant debate with her sister over the relative merits of maternity and marriage, Virginia always defended matrimony which, as an institution, Vanessa increasingly detested.

No doubt the success of Virginia's marriage—as with Vita's—had something to do with her minimal investment of sexual passion in it. It could be a wholly reasonable relationship, a comfortable living arrangement which allowed her to work well, supported and loved by an intelligent man who valued her not only as an artist and a genius but also as a woman. To many people such a marriage might itself seem bloodless, if not even—less kindly—"sick," but it could not have seemed so from Virginia's point of view. Whether or not she responded to Leonard's passion, it was there. On her part, at any rate, their union involved no self-hatred, no courting of rejection, as a permanent alliance with Strachey would have. For a woman whose writing was more important to her than anything, such a marriage seems not just a wise decision, but a miracle. Erik Erikson distinguishes between the crises of identity and of intimacy, but the crisis of Woolf's late twenties, reflected in *The Voyage Out*, lies somewhere between the two, in the area where intimacy impinges on identity. It may be that for a man it is possible to "establish an identity" and then test his capacity for intimacy, but for a woman, any identity, any commitment to self, has been likely (with few exceptions until relatively recent times) to be tentative, until she has seen whom life put in her way to live with.

In Virginia Woolf's case, "life," and her own resolute

ability to say no to inappropriate offers (there were others besides Strachey), put in her way a man uncannily constituted to nurture her work as a writer. "Leonard wants me to say that if I cease to write when married, I shall be divorced," she wrote Violet Dickinson.[22] "L. thinks my writing the best part of me. We're going to work very hard."[23] If the Woolfs' marriage had not been so happy and if they had not both been remarkably productive people, one might find it pitiful, a marriage of chums who share a dining room and a play room in the basement (the Hogarth Press) but not a bedroom and not a study, a marriage in which the man becomes periodically his wife's nurse, mothering her through periods of insanity. But Leonard never objected, his reverence for his wife glows through the lucid prose of his autobiography, and the last words Virginia wrote were to him: "I don't think two people could have been happier than we have been."[24]

No one was more aware of her selfishness than Woolf herself or blamed her more for it—her letters are full of self-condemnation, passages in which she attacks her own vanity and egotism and wonders how anyone could love her. But artists have to run the risk of selfishness; it is an occupational disease. In the final analysis, the care and solicitude she enjoyed from her husband was not much more than her father had expected as his right, and she exacted it with a good deal less sacrifice from Leonard than her father had from his women—he continued to write his own books, to engage in politics, to run the Hogarth Press. Perhaps using her illness as other artists, notably Proust, have used illness, for self-protection, she managed in her marriage to turn the tables on Victorian patriarchy. And if Leonard played Carrington to Virginia's Strachey, remember it was Leonard who pointed out the satisfactions of Carrington's role.

In 1912, however, when she accepted Leonard, the form her marriage would evolve was not clear: she did not know she was frigid, and she expected that in the normal course of things she would have children.[25] To accept Leonard, then, represented a willed commitment, if not a felt impulse, toward normal intimacy and sexuality. If the flame of sexuality burned low in Virginia Woolf, its prestige, due no doubt to the powerful influence of her sister, remained high. Marriage to Leonard allowed her to join what she saw as the mainstream of life, and to assert that she was a woman, not a defective boy. In terms of sexual style as well as intellectual style, the rejection of Strachean Bloomsbury suggests a movement from self-denigration to self-affirmation, from exclusiveness to an attempt to live the common lot of humanity.

In marrying Leonard Woolf, Virginia married Cambridge, but Cambridge with a difference. Intellectually Woolf was part of the inner circle; like Strachey, he was an Apostle. Socially, however (in what George Duckworth would have considered "society"), he was an outsider, a "penniless Jew" (Virginia's words) from Putney. And returning to London in 1911 after seven years in Ceylon as a civil servant, he was very different indeed from his college friends. He had had the experience "of being a sahib amongst natives, utterly removed from all those friends with whom one could be entirely open, the jokes, the high seriousness, the intellectual communion of Cambridge."

> He learnt to travel and to live alone, to undertake the duties of a policeman and to exert the authority of a magistrate, to send men to their deaths and to watch them hang, to perform the endless and endlessly boring tasks of empire. Hardest of all, he had to deal and come to terms with compatriots who, in a moment of impatient despair, he described as a "stupid degraded circle of degenerates and imbeciles."[26]

He was forced to develop considerable flexibility and tolerance. While holding onto the best of Cambridge, his experiences forced him to develop a wider sympathy.

Virginia Woolf was never one to appreciate the principle of opposites attracting. As she put it in *The Voyage Out*, age is one barrier, learning another, and sex another. The fact that Woolf was Jewish made him seem "foreign" to her, and the exoticism did not add to his attraction. But temperamentally the two had much in common by the time of their marriage. They were both intellectual, verbal, disciplined, hard-working, and reserved. They developed a certain chastity of both intellectual and personal style which was unshared by Vanessa and her more free-wheeling friends. Perhaps most importantly, they each possessed democratic sympathies and a political consciousness, expressed in rather different forms, but created by analogous experiences of exclusion. Leonard returned from Ceylon anti-imperialist, and he soon became a socialist; he worked on behalf of the Labour Party and the Fabians, and Virginia, in her way, worked too.

She taught at Morley College, an evening institute for working men and women, faithfully from 1905 to 1907, before Leonard was on the scene. Others of her family began teaching there, too, but she was the only one who stuck with it, planning her lessons dutifully and at great length in advance. Later, for some years, she presided over the monthly meeting, held at her house, of the Richmond Branch of the Women's Co-operative Guild. Responsive to the plight of women undereducated through no fault of their own, she was pleased that the Guild did "somehow stand for something real to these women" and sympathized with their "deeply hidden and inarticulate desire for something beyond the daily life."[27] Can one imagine Lytton Strachey lecturing to a group of working people on literature, or presiding over a discussion of conscription with Richmond ladies? Only, perhaps, in the spirit of *épatisme* with which Wilde toured the mining camps of America. Picture, if you will, two incidents. First, Lytton Strachey, applying for conscientious objector status during World War I, is summoned before a tribunal to present his case. He sends his brother James before him, like a page, bearing a large pillow. Second, Leonard and Virginia Woolf are returning from a costume party dressed as, respectively, Lewis Carroll's Carpenter and the March Hare. In a lonely part of London, they come upon a prostitute being taunted by some passersby and harassed by the police, and, forgetting how absurd they look in their costumes, Leonard intervenes on her behalf. The Woolfs, totally oblivious of appearances—Strachey manipulating them like a master. Strachey's impulse is stylishly to thumb his nose, to outrage; the Woolfs' impulse is toward sympathy.

Virginia Woolf's commitment to the ladies of Richmond and the part of the population they represent, disadvantaged, earnestly seeking enlightenment, carries through, I would argue, into her criticism and even, in a personal way, into her fiction. It appears as a kind of large-mindedness, a dedication to nothing less than the most important concerns, "life, death, etc."[28] Continually she poses to herself the ultimate questions for a writer and critic: why write books at all? why read books? why write about books? The answer is, to live more intensely and to help other people to live more intensely. The initial impulse is Paterian, "to burn always with a hard, gemlike flame," but Woolf is aware of a contract with the reader, the writer's obligation to make his or her reader see that hard gemlike flame as well. That is why charges of Bloomsbury snobbism so infuriated her. Given the limits of her experience, she tried fervently not to be cut off. Of course, she writes in an unsent, enraged reply to a *New Statesman* attack, of course she is a highbrow; she is proud to be a highbrow because lowbrows, who form the great part of the population, need them so. "Since they are lowbrows, engaged magnificently and adventurously in riding full tilt from one end of life to the other, they cannot see themselves doing it. Yet nothing interests them more. It is one of the prime necessities of life to them—to be shown what life looks like. And the highbrows, of course, are the only people who can show them."[29] Inhabiting a tower, the high-born maiden can at least use her position to some advantage: she becomes in her own eyes a kind of existential lookout.

Once more I will contrast Strachey's spirit with Woolf's, in order to portray her distinctive place within Bloomsbury.[30] Strachey's considerable talent, best represented by *Eminent Victorians* and *Queen Victoria,* is mobilized by rejection, whereas hers is energized by an effort to understand and sympathize. Even her prose style is more democratic than his: fluid, explorative, tentative, trying to mold itself sinuously to the shifting currents of emotion, it demands a reader's participation to fill in the gaps, to follow poetic leaps. Strachey's elegant periods, modeled on the classical eighteenth-century prose he admired, allow for nothing but acceptance and structure response in so totalitarian a fashion that, as we would against any tyranny, we rebel. To an admirer of Sterne's delicate prose, such as Woolf, Strachey's must have seemed like "the arid scimitar of the male,"[31] smiting and smiting. No wonder, rivalry aside, they did not much care for each other's work.

To read *Eminent Victorians* is to be aware of a first-rate mind in the service of trivial, perhaps atrophied emotions. With an adolescent's intolerance, Strachey puts stupid, pretentious people in their place. He would have liked to be seen as the spirit of reason, proceeding through the dusty house of history with the torch of enlightenment in hand, clearing out cobwebs, but I, for one, persist in seeing him as a little boy dropping water bombs out of a second-story window onto the grown-ups below. He remains, to some extent, forever the clever undergraduate, whereas Woolf, perhaps because she hadn't the chance to be a clever undergraduate, was forced to become something larger.

# 5

# Transitions
# and Experiments

In 1915 Virginia Woolf was the author of an occasionally brilliant first novel. In 1922 she began
*Mrs. Dalloway,* the first of her novels in which personal style and personal subject mesh consistently
to produce a work unquestionably of the first rank.
By that time she had won a small following in both
England and America and a reputation, supported
partly by her fiction and partly by her critical writings, for innovation and experiment. In the stories
of *Monday or Tuesday* (1921), especially in "The
Mark on the Wall" and "Kew Gardens," which had
been issued earlier by the Hogarth Press,[1] she

worked out the lyrical, oblique approach in which her best later works would be written. The years between 1915 and 1922 therefore represent a crucial moment in her artistic development. Of *Jacob's Room* (1922), the culminating work of this period, she said, "There's no doubt in my mind that I have found out how to begin (at 40) to say something in my own voice."[2]

But why did finding her own voice take so long? She had been writing for close to twenty years. Had the seven-year apprenticeship of writing *The Voyage Out* counted for nothing? Her second novel, *Night and Day* (1919), seems—in terms of fictional technique—something of a step backward. Why? In these pivotal years I see a fascinating inner drama being played out, in which the inevitable struggle between tradition and the individual talent is complicated by the fact that the tradition of fictional form was, or was perceived by Woolf to be, masculine, whereas her talent was feminine. In order to develop a distinctively personal way of writing, she had to rebel against traditional expectations of what the novel should be and a traditional form whose authority and prestige she could not easily deny because they were, in a sense, paternal. *Night and Day* and *Jacob's Room* are most interesting when read in conjunction with her contemporary criticism and seen as stages in a process of self-realization. She found her own voice, as she says, her style, in *Jacob's Room;* the next stage was to locate her sympathies.

Katharine Hilbery, the heroine of *Night and Day,* comes from a family with a tradition of intellectual achievement. Her father edits a prestigious journal, and her mother, a vague but warm-hearted woman, has been trying for years to write the official biography of her father, Richard Allardyce, a famous poet of the nineteenth century. Their house in Chelsea is a center of contemporary intellectual life. The clever young men who write for Mr. Hilbery drop in frequently for tea. The house also serves as something of a museum to the glory of past Allardyces, and Katharine, who helps her mother with her haphazard efforts to write the great poet's life, invariably shows visitors the relics—paintings, the writing desk, the letter from Shelley. *Night and Day* presents superbly an atmosphere and a problem from which few of us suffer, although it must be endemic among Huxleys, Stracheys, and Darwins, and in this country, in a different form, among Roosevelts and Kennedys—I speak of the burden of the past in family dress. The Stephen children, we might expect, suffered from it, too, but when Vanessa Bell praised *Night and Day* for its illumination of their life at Hyde Park Gate, Virginia replied that she hadn't thought she was describing their own form of hell.[3]

Despite Virginia's disclaimer, it is hard not to read this novel as autobiographical—not so much in its details, perhaps, as in its spirit. Katharine Hilbery is no rebel, and in a spirit of acquiescence to her family's expectations and society's demands, she engages herself to marry William Rodney, a rather effete gentleman and dabbler in the arts for whom she feels no strong emotion. She does not believe in love or passion; one has to marry, so one might as well marry Rodney. But strangely, she begins to find herself attracted to one of her father's clever young men, Ralph Denham, who is in law and who is distinctly inferior in social position to herself and Rodney. She observes that Mary Datchet, a feminist friend, is very much in love with Ralph. She wonders if there might not be another dimension to life, an intense and passionate dimension, about which she knows nothing.

Katharine's bewildered and wistful hypothesis of the existence of passion is extremely poignant, and the poignancy increases when one bears in mind Virginia Woolf's emotional temperature. A book about love from the point of view of someone who fears she has missed out on it, *Night and Day* has some of the autumnal quality of *Persuasion*.[4] Life is moving on, chances are being missed, there is little time left for getting down to the business of living. It is characteristically a mood of beyond thirty, the mood in which one considers the discipline and hard work of one's young adulthood wasted and misguided, in which one thinks nostalgically of the passionate attachments of adolescence.

If one is a writer, this unrest may be channeled into a book, but what a restrained and quiet book this one is! Rodney, Denham, and Katharine sort out their passions and plan their future over tea, in taxis, by the fire, in walks along the Embankment, and overthrow the accepted social order (that engagements are not broken, that the abandoned woman does not help her ex-fiancé to find a new bride, that great poets' granddaughters do not marry law clerks) so discreetly and placidly that one hardly knows anything of moment has happened. *Night and Day* is a pleasant book to read, but nothing in it makes one breathe more quickly or disturbs one's mind when the book is put away. It shows what sheer intelligence and determination can produce in the way of a novel, and also their limitations.

Critics have reached remarkable unanimity about the place *Night and Day* occupies in Virginia Woolf's career—it is her attempt to prove herself the master of the classical tradition of the English novel, to create solid characters and place them in realized settings, to have them speak to one another in credible dialogue and to advance the plot through dramatic scenes.[5] It is as though an abstract expressionist painter felt he must prove himself the master of classical figure-drawing before he discarded the representational, and so Woolf presented the novel in later years: "How beneficent of you and Philip," she wrote to Ottoline Morrell, "to take down my old books again! I can't believe that any human being can get through *Night and Day* which I wrote chiefly in bed. . . . But it taught me a great deal, or so I hoped, like a minute Academy drawing: what to leave out by putting it all in."[6]

Keats set himself to write *Endymion* as a "test of invention." By downplaying the importance of the work—it was only a prelude to future works—he could write quickly and copiously, and in the process he learned a great deal about poetry. Woolf's gains from *Night and Day*, I suspect, were largely psychological. She proved she could write novels, not just one novel, and from her comment to Vanessa disclaiming autobiographical content, one gathers she proved also (at least to her own satisfaction) that she could create characters who were not herself. Most important, for a writer who would come to value her own work for "some queer individuality"[7] it possessed, whose strength came so much from innovation and the development of an intensely personal style, whose greatest fear was that her novels were so much herself that no one else could possibly see anything in them, to clear the decks, as it were, by writing a novel in which there was nothing personal at all, which was as traditional as she could make it, seems right—the act of piety before the act of rebellion. Perhaps in some way she wanted *Night and Day* to be sterile, so as to force herself into the far more perilous task of finding a fictional form that would uniquely express what she was, and E. M. Forster may have given her exactly the criticism she wanted when he said he liked the book less than *The Voyage Out*.[8]

"Modern Fiction," published in the *Times Literary Supplement* in 1919, illuminates the inner drama involved in the writing of *Night and Day*. Her first attack on Bennett, Wells, and Galsworthy and on the "materialism" of the traditional form of the novel—plot, setting, and all those formal features which ratify the importance of the external life as opposed to the life of the mind—it should be read as a self-justifying statement about her own work as well as an objective discussion of the contemporary literary scene.

Her view of progress in the arts is Carlylean: the new spirit of the twentieth century cannot be contained in the "vestments" of another era.

Whether we call it life or spirit, truth or reality, this, the essential thing, has moved off, or on, and refuses to be contained any longer in such ill-fitting vestments as we provide. Nevertheless, we go on perseveringly, conscientiously, constructing our two and thirty chapters after a design which more and more ceases to resemble the vision in our minds. So much of the enormous labour of proving the solidity, the likeness to life, of the story is not merely labour thrown away but labour misplaced to the extent of obscuring and blotting out the light of the conception. The writer seems constrained, not by his own free will but by some powerful and unscrupulous tyrant who has him in thrall, to provide a plot, to provide comedy, tragedy, love interest, and an air of probability embalming the whole so impeccable that if all his figures were to come to life they would find themselves dressed down to the last button of their coats in the fashion of the hour. The tyrant is obeyed; the novel is done to a turn. But sometimes, more and more often as time goes by, we suspect a momentary doubt, a spasm of rebellion, as the pages fill themselves in the customary way. Is life like this? Must novels be like this? [9]

This familiar passage, read as personal statement, dramatizes an inner conflict between authority and inspiration. "We go on" dutifully turning out the two-and-thirty chapters (*Night and Day*, published in the same year as this essay, has thirty-four), despite the fact that they betray our vision of life. The struggle she describes between conception and realization is clearly not that of Galsworthy, whose vision, whatever we may think of it, is rather comfortably embodied in *The Forsyte Saga*. (Bennett, Wells, and Galsworthy, whom she would attack again in 1924 in "Mr. Bennett and Mrs. Brown," were straw men, as Woolf later and privately admitted. The real battle was not with those relatively mediocre realists, but with Tolstoy, the greatest realist of all.) What, then, prompted this "labour thrown away?" What was the lure of traditional form? It does not sound like inertia, or even lack of imagination, but a kind of compulsion. The "powerful and unscrupulous tyrant" who keeps the writer "in thrall" and forces her against her will to provide plot and probability is, of course, an internalized tyrant.

In another context, Woolf would describe a similar struggle between her artistic integrity, her sense of what she wants to write, and a kind of tyrant who tells her what she ought to write. "Professions for Women" describes how, in her early years of reviewing, a "phantom" whispered in her ear: be gentle, flatter, sympathize—you are a woman writing about a man's book. This phantom, dubbed "the angel in the house," represented Woolf's vestigial belief in the Victorian conception of woman as self-sacrificing servant to man's emotional needs. The powerful formalist tyrant who made her write *Night and Day* is the male equivalent to the angel in the house, like her an internalization of cultural expectations—in this case, expectations about what fiction should be.

"Modern Fiction," read as personal statement, seems designed to encourage the writer to be herself and not to try to fit herself into a pre-existing (masculine) model of the novelist. Although the essay purports to speak for a movement and mentions Joyce, it is really a self-exhortation to rebellion.

> Examine for a moment an ordinary mind on an ordinary day. The mind receives a myriad impressions—trivial, fantastic, evanescent or engraved with the sharpness of steel. From all sides they come, an incessant shower of innumerable atoms; and as they fall, as they shape themselves into the life of Monday or Tuesday, the accent falls differently from of old; the moment of importance came not here but there; so that, if a writer were a free man and not a slave, if he could write what he chose not what he must, if he could base his work on his own feelings and not upon convention, there would be no plot, no comedy, no tragedy, no love interest or catastrophe in the accepted style, and perhaps not a single button sewn on as the Bond Street tailors would have it. Life is not a series of gig lamps symmetrically arranged; life is a lu-

minous halo, a semi-transparent envelope surrounding us from the beginning of consciousness to the end. Is it not the task of the novelist to convey this varying, this unknown and uncircumscribed spirit, whatever abberation or complexity it may display, with as little mixture of the alien and external as possible? [10]

On the one hand freedom, writing as one chooses, true feeling (the individual talent) and on the other, slavery, writing as one must, convention, plot, tragedy, love interest *and* buttons sewed on as Bond Street tailors would have them (tradition). The Bond Street tailors are an anomalous detail interjecting into a discussion of the well-made novel a spectral image of the world of well-made men's clothing.[11] Accustomed to domestic tyranny, having chafed against conventional sentiment from at least as far back as the time of her mother's death, having wished to be able to speak what she felt and not what she ought to say, and having been thwarted, in various ways, by her father and half-brother, Woolf carried over some of the passionate resentment built up in the Kensington years against male domination into this ostensibly literary manifesto.

The novel of certainties, firm characters in a firm setting, a plot solidly in the hands of an omniscient narrator, the novel which relied for its impact on moral certainties as well (for example, that all readers would react with horror to Anna Karenina's adultery)—this kind of novel was masculine. Certainty and stability played little part in Woolf's sense of herself, and it was on her sense of herself that she predicated the new form of the novel: shifting, subjective, unassertive in its moral stance, it would impose no rigid thirty-two chapters on experience, but would let the emphasis fall where it might. Authority, the rigid imposition of form upon matter, whether the matter be subject peoples or the fictive stuff of life, is associated for Woolf with masculinity, and the critical arguments she makes in 1919 and 1924 on behalf of innovation in fiction prefigure her feminist arguments of 1929 and 1938.

The psychologist David McClelland, feeling the need for a distinction between masculine and feminine personality traits that would not be prejudicial to the feminine (as, for example, the oppositions active-passive, independent-dependent are prejudicial), devised an experiment employing two sets of geometrical forms, in one of which the figures were closed and in the other open, with their parts unconnected.[12] McClelland found that by and large men preferred the closed forms and women the open ones, and from this geometrical preference he developed a formulation of style: a preference for assertion, for the clearcut and unambiguous, a tendency to impose definite structure and definite limits, characterizes the male personality, while the female concerns itself more with context, prefers to draw no rigid boundaries between inner and outer, abhors the definite as a limitation.

McClelland's formulation of masculine and feminine traits is certainly not offered here as truth but because it echoes strangely and suggestively formal descriptions of the modern novel as opposed to the classic novel of the nineteenth century. Alan Friedman, for example, talks about the "open" form of the twentieth-century novel as opposed to the "closed" form of the nineteenth century; Frank Kermode points out the loss of the "sense of an ending" and its implications.[13] Modern literature distrusts strong authority. Even writers as didactic as Lawrence, as aggressively masculine as Hemingway concentrate on ambiguities of character, wavering points of the ego, instabilities and doubts rather than certitude. The ending of *Women in Love* is a case in point: all is unresolved; assertion is met by counter-assertion; nothing is concluded, the novel merely stops. It suggests that experience is a continuum without pattern, of which the novel can record only an arbitrary segment. Invoking McClelland's useful formulation, one could therefore characterize the innovations in early twentieth-century novels as a feminization of fiction, and, viewing them in this light, one can perhaps more readily understand how the form of the novel presented itself to Virginia Woolf as a sexual issue.

Because it encapsulates Woolf's impulse to rebellion against and mockery of patriarchal pomp and authority, which is a recurrent feature in her life and work, I bring up here an incident from her life—the *Dreadnought* hoax. I believe I am not the first to connect her statement in "Mr. Bennett and Mrs. Brown" that in or about December 1910 human character changed with the fact that the great event of her life in 1910 was that massive practical joke. In February of that year, Virginia, disguised in blackface, beard, caftan, and turban as an Ethiopian prince, along with her brother Adrian, Duncan Grant, and a few other intrepid jokesters, boarded the H.M.S. *Dreadnought*, the pride of the British Home Fleet, and received the royal welcome the Navy owed so splendid a prince and his entourage. A photograph of the emperor of Abyssinia and his suite provides hilarious documentation: [14] looking at these unmistakably English faces, you realize how rigid and unquestioning, how foolish or merely self-absorbed, how blind the officers of the *Dreadnought* had to be not to suspect the imposture. And that, of course, was the point of the hoax: to make fun of that great institution, the Navy, and perhaps, incidentally, the authority of princes. Virginia must have enjoyed the chance to dress up as a man, and for her the symbolic essence of this escapade was the chance to defy and ridicule an authority specifically masculine. The resplendent, uniformed obtusity of the British naval officers became the very image of masculine folly and the *Dreadnought* hoax itself a primal event, the acting out of her own rebellion against paternal authority. She told the story for years after, enormously proud of the part she had played, hugely and continually amused by it; Vanessa had thought her sister should have nothing to do with it. Substitute Bennett, Wells, and Galsworthy for the

*Participants in the Dreadnought Hoax (1910). Virginia is seated on the sofa.*

gold-encrusted officers, or imagine Woolf as a critical David. taking on Goliaths, flinging the protean, elusive nature of life at their cumbersome fictional machines, and we see how the *Dreadnought* hoax is emblematic of much of her career.

Although stylistically, formally, they are exciting, Woolf's transitional works are ultimately unsatisfying. "The Mark on the Wall" and "Kew Gardens" represent daring innovations in technique, but she had not yet found a subject which would allow her to express her humane experience of life. "The Mark on the Wall" is a reverie, taking off from the contemplation of a spot which may have been made by a nail, may be a snail. "I" (which Woolf will call, in *A Room of One's Own*, a convenient term for someone who has no real being) contemplates the insubstantiality of life and the unreality of "the masculine point of view which governs our lives, which sets the standard, . . . which soon, one may hope, will be laughed into the dustbin where phantoms go, the mahogany sideboards and the Landseer prints, Gods and Devils, Hell and so forth, leaving us all with an intoxicating sense of illegitimate freedom—if freedom exists."[15] The mark is an excuse for such meanderings. In "Kew Gardens," a lovelier piece of writing, she tries to describe the fragmentary, transient nature of what *is* real, people passing, wisps of conversation, nature in motion, the wafting of life through the gardens, from the point of view of—of all things—a snail. A unique but ultimately disappointing vantage point from which to observe the flow of life. Woolf has not yet found a fictional body to inhabit. She captures wonderfully the movement of life in a great city, but it will be much more interesting when the center of consciousness is Mrs. Dalloway and not a snail in a flower bed.

Of the stories in *Monday or Tuesday* the most interesting to me is "A Society." It cannot match for sheer beauty of prose either "Kew Gardens" or "Mark on the Wall," but it has bite. A group of women set out to investigate how well men are doing, ruling England. One, disguised as an Ethiopian prince, goes to visit His Majesty's Navy. One goes to the Law Courts, another to Oxbridge, another to the Royal Society. They want to know if it is worthwhile to sacrifice their youth to raise the future leaders of the country. Everywhere they encounter pomposity and futile activity. They discover that as boys men are charming—they enjoy life and help other people to enjoy it. But once taught to cultivate their intellects, they become (alas) barristers, generals, authors, professors. They keep themselves busy—ultimately, by making war. "For Heaven's sake let us devise a method by which men may bear children! It is our only chance. For unless we provide them with some innocent occupation we shall . . . perish beneath the fruits of their unbridled activity."[16] This light satire of men's use and misuse of power, an imagined extension of the *Dreadnought* hoax, reveals the gap at this point in Woolf's career between her social concerns and her development of technique. She cannot seem to combine in one story the sophisticated style of "Kew Gardens" and "Mark on the Wall" and the content of a story like "A Society."

In *Jacob's Room* Woolf sets out to prove the point of "Modern Fiction." She presents Jacob Flanders' life so that the accent falls not here, where we expect it, but there, where we do not. The book is a collection of fragments—Jacob playing on the beach as a boy, Jacob at Cambridge, Jacob at dinner, at luncheon, with women, in the reading room of the British Museum, trying to respond to the beauty of Greece. Major facts—such as his death in World War I—are not mentioned, but must be deduced from their incidental effects: his friend, Bonamy, and his mother clear out his room and wonder what to do with his shoes. There is no comedy, no tragedy, no plot, and little love interest. About all we know of Jacob is that he is "distinguished-looking." Reading this novel has the same fascination as flipping through a stranger's snapshot album. You know he had a life; you know he was real to various other people who turn up in the album's pages; you know some of them loved him deeply, but you wonder why and what he was really like. One would be tempted to say that Woolf had failed to create a central character, if that were not so patently the purpose of the book—to present its central character as unknowable. Jacob is one of a series of figures in Woolf's work at this time who represent Human Nature in a rather abstract form—"Mrs. Brown," sitting across from you in a railway car, or "Minnie Marsh" (in "An Unwritten Novel"). How can a novelist do them justice? Woolf wonders. Bennett would tell you how much rent they pay or describe for you the view from their flats. But Jacob's rent, even Jacob's room, is beside the point. We must be content with whispers and hints, fragments and shadows.[17]

. . . Life is but a procession of shadows, and God knows why it is that we embrace them so eagerly, and see them depart with such anguish, being shadows. And why, if this and much more than this is true, why are we yet surprised in the window corner by a sudden vision that the young man in the chair is of all things in the world the most real, the most solid, the best known to us—why indeed? For the moment after we know nothing of him.

Such is the manner of our seeing. Such the conditions of our love.[18]

It is quite likely that in writing about Jacob, Woolf had in mind her brother Thoby, one of those shadows she embraced so eagerly and saw depart with such anguish. The bare bones of Jacob's life are those of Thoby's: childhood at the seashore, Cambridge, London, a trip to Greece, early death. Thoby Stephen appealed to people as Jacob does, not for anything you could put your finger on, except his beauty, but for some indefinable quality of distinction emanating from him. The most moving parts of *Jacob's Room* capture the emotion of yearning for someone you cannot have and whom, in any case, you do not really know.

In another view, however, neither Jacob nor Thoby is the subject of *Jacob's Room*, except insofar as each of them enjoyed the usual advantages awarded to upper-class English men, for the novel may be seen as concerned with the fate of British civilization, masculine, needless to say, nurtured on public-school Hellenism, reinforced by Cambridge, kept up by reading Marlowe and Shakespeare at the British Museum, killed off in World War I. The book is permeated by the envy—and irony—that generally colors Woolf's treatments of Oxbridge and its products. We get an outsider's view, for example, of the King's College chapel, where Jacob and Timothy Durrant sit, wondering why they let women inside. At the Parthenon, too, Jacob will object to the presence of women—they disturb the aesthetic arrangement. The lines between Greece and England cross and recross: the Elgin

Marbles are in London, a statue of Achilles in Hyde Park; Jacob and his friends read the classics at Cambridge, where the *genius loci* is the head of a beautiful Greek boy; when Jacob goes to Greece he sends letters back to Bonamy about the roots of civilization. From the Greeks to Shakespeare to the young men of Cambridge, the line of inheritance is clear, and the reminder that culture is a masculine preserve functions as a leitmotif of the book. Julia Hedge, the feminist, sits in the reading room of the British Museum contemplating the gilt names curving around the dome and wishing room had been left for a Brontë or an Eliot.

And where does this civilization lead? The answer is underlined by Jacob's fate. Thoby Stephen's life and Rupert Brooke's death could have served as personal markers for Woolf of the care that is lavished on men's intellects and of how, fighting to save the civilization they have been taught to revere, they throw themselves away. Woolf had already hinted in "A Society" at her notion that leaving the business of civilization entirely to men produces wars, although she would not articulate it fully—some would say stridently— until *Three Guineas*, written on the verge of World War II. If not the major theme of *Jacob's Room*, this ironic view of Western civilization provides an important subtext.

In writing *Jacob's Room*, however, Woolf was excited mainly by the technical experiment it represented. "Conceive *Mark on the Wall*, *K[ew] G[ardens]* and *Unwritten Novel* taking hands and dancing in unity."[19] Compare this conception to the inspiration of *To the Lighthouse*, a vision of her father in a sailboat,[20] and you see how the earlier book is energized by formal concerns, the later one by content. When Woolf despaired about *Mrs. Dalloway*, it was from worry that her central character was too shallow. When she despaired about *Jacob's Room*, it was from worrying whether Joyce hadn't done the same thing better.[21] Without drawing a naive distinction between form and content—for certainly much of the content of *Jacob's Room* is generated by its form—I think one can still say that a great deal of the richness of Woolf's mind is not finding its way into her work of this period. The subtext of *Jacob's Room* suggests that the gap between formal concerns and social concerns which characterizes Woolf's post-war work extends to this novel as well. At times the narrator contemplates Jacob, very much as she contemplates the mark on the wall, as an incidental starting point for beautiful reveries. At times we see life from Jacob's point of view, but Jacob's point of view is scarcely more energetic than that of the snail in "Kew Gardens." As in "Kew Gardens," there are exquisite descriptive passages capturing the rustle of life in city streets, which make me think of Woolf's next book and again make me long for Mrs. Dalloway as a central consciousness. Something is missing in *Jacob's Room,* and I would suggest that that something is not Jacob, but women. Jacob lingers in the imagination more as a beautiful statue than as an enigma. "Oh women are my line and not these inanimate creatures!"

# 6

# The Love of Women

The character who will most occupy Woolf's mind
for the next few years is a society woman, a Westminster hostess—Mrs. Dalloway. There is considerable evidence that in creating Mrs. Dalloway Woolf
had a particular model in mind, Kitty Maxse, the
fashionable lady who had graced the Stephen tea
table while she was still Miss Lushington and whose
marriage to Leo Maxse had been helped by Julia
Stephen's matchmaking activities. Those who knew
Mrs. Maxse say that Mrs. Dalloway does not much
resemble her, and Quentin Bell explains this by saying that Virginia Woolf did her best portraits when

she was in love with her model and that she was not in love with Kitty Maxse.[1] But Kitty Maxse was not the only society woman in Woolf's life, and some of them she was in love with. *Mrs. Dalloway*, I would suggest, is her tribute to a kind of woman that most of her friends disliked. They assumed Virginia Woolf shared their dislike, and they were wrong. As a result Lytton Strachey, for example, misread *Mrs. Dalloway*, convinced it had to be a satire of a shallow woman. He found Clarissa disagreeable and limited, and wondered why Virginia alternately laughed at her and then "covered her" with herself.[2] Why Virginia Woolf found these women of title and fashion so alluring is a question that bears going into, and to find the answer we must explore more closely her relationship with her mother and, more particularly, the impact of Mrs. Stephen's death.

Recalling in later years her mother's death in 1895, Woolf remembered chiefly her own absence of grief. The event seemed to her then like a melodrama which the adults acted out with stricken seriousness, but which the young people found rather comic. "Remember turning aside at mother's bed, when she had died, and Stella took us in, to laugh, secretly, at the nurse crying. She's pretending, I said, aged 13, and was afraid I was not feeling enough."[3] In the fictionalized version of this scene in *The Years*, when Mrs. Pargiter dies, her daughter Delia looks on distantly, wondering if she should kneel. She thinks her father plays his role very well, running down the hall with his fists clenched, screaming her mother's name.

Freud tells us that when we lose a beloved person we must go through a painful and protracted process of detaching ourselves emotionally from the one who has died and of coming to accept the loss before we can love someone else. This is the function of mourning, and, unpleasant as it is, the expression of sorrow can be healthy and useful; the unhealthy alternative would be to deny that the loss has occurred. After Julia Stephen's death, Leslie Stephen entered wholeheartedly into the business of mourning, plunging the household at Hyde Park Gate into black-crepe gloom, giving up their house at St. Ives which he associated inevitably with Julia, weeping, demanding sympathy from everyone around him, talking and of course writing obsessively about Julia and berating himself for how badly he had treated her, while at the same time trying to convince himself he had treated her well.

His children did not enter into his grief and were, in fact, offended by the whole process of mourning. They wanted life to continue as before and felt their joys were being unfairly blighted, their father self-indulgent and self-pitying. Psychoanalysts explain children's cruelty by telling us that adolescence itself is a kind of extended mourning, a gradual detachment from the parents who have been until then major objects of love, and that until children have been through adolescence, have been initiated into loss, it is impossible for them to do the work of mourning which Freud describes.[4] Typically adolescents who lose a parent curtail their grief, weep little, try to immerse themselves in the everyday activities of life and to deny the finality of their loss, just as the Stephen children did. Sensitive ones, like Virginia, are afraid of their own emotional emptiness and fear they ought to be feeling more.

Because they are in a stage of rebellion and hostility, adolescents are likely to suffer terribly from guilt when a parent dies, yet not every adolescent who loses a parent is maimed. Put baldly, the more hostility, the stronger the fleeting, unexpressed wish for the parent's death, the more difficult it becomes to admit the reality of the death. In this context it is useful to contrast Vanessa, who emerged from adolescence with a healthy appetite for love and sex, with Virginia.

Goddess, madonna, saint, Julia Stephen was a hard act for her daughters to follow, a fearsome opponent in that rivalry that always exists between women and their female offspring. In contrast to Stella Duckworth, who tried to be exactly like their mother, both Virginia and Vanessa chose to distinguish themselves from her by rejecting her exclusive devotion to home and family, Vanessa determining to paint and Virginia to write. But Virginia cut herself off from their mother even more aggressively than Vanessa. Vanessa told this story of Virginia at the age of six or so:

> I remember one evening as we were jumping about naked, she and I, in the bathroom. She suddenly asked me which I liked best, my father or mother. Such a question seemed to me rather terrible—surely one ought not to ask it. . . . However, being asked, one had to reply and I found I had little doubt as to my answer. "Mother," I said, and she went on to explain why she, on the whole, preferred father. I don't think, however, her preference was quite as sure and simple as mine. She had considered both critically and had more or less analyzed her feelings for them which I, at any rate consciously, had never attempted.[5]

The unmistakably sexual setting of this episode highlights the style of Virginia's declaration. In contrast to Vanessa's simple and spontaneous confession of her preference, Virginia had "analyzed her feelings," and the intellectual, analytic spirit is in itself strong proof of her identification with her father. (Later she was to feel guilty over her obligation, as a writer, to analyze her emotions, and to fear that it prevented her from feeling.) By the age of nine, when she began producing the *Hyde Park Gate News* and sent off her first story to *Tit-Bits*, this identification (she would, like her father, be a writer) had shaped itself into a calling.

There was a crucial difference too between Vanessa's experience and Virginia's in the long period following their mother's death. When Stella Duckworth died, two years after Julia, Vanessa was called upon in turn, as the eldest daughter, to replace her mother in running the household, to be her father's adjutant and to deal with him in all matters of finance. This was a most unpleasant business, for Leslie, with an irrational fear of ending his days in the poorhouse, screamed and raved at whoever presented the account books to him. Every week, to get him to sign the checks to pay the bills, Vanessa had to endure a scene. It was odious and painful, yet in some ways a bracing encounter with reality. Taking care of father could be no fantasy goal when it was so clearly an awful business; one had best get out of it as soon as possible. Quite reasonably Vanessa could express a great deal of anger towards her father, and so (though not to his face) she did. She looked forward frankly and rather indecently, Virginia thought, to his death. For Virginia herself, who did not have to deal with him, Leslie was more remote than ever, sunk in his misery. And it is not fanciful to imagine her receiving the message from her father that she was no help, for he said as much, by what he left unsaid, in a passage of the memoir he wrote in 1895 just after Julia's death, which the children named "The Mausoleum Book":

> You, my darling Stella, have helped me more than any one. My George and Gerald have helped me too; but in grief like mine a woman can do more, and a woman who reminds me at every turn of her darling mother can give me all the comfort of which I am susceptible.[6]

In the family myth which grew up around Julia Stephen, Stella was like her mother, Vanessa was like her, but less so, and Virginia not at all. With neither the favored place of Vanessa and Stella nor an object for her anger, what anger she had may well have been turned inward and directed at herself.

This partial explanation of why Julia's death affected Virginia so much more than Vanessa is frankly conjectural, but that it did affect her distressingly is certain. It was shortly after her mother's death that she suffered her first major mental breakdown, and thereafter, whenever she was mad, one symptom reappeared which Leonard Woolf noted and was puzzled by, and which is almost surely connected with continued guilt about her mother's death.

> It was extraordinarily difficult ever to get her to eat enough to keep her strong and well. Superficially I suppose it might have been said that she had a (quite unnecessary) fear of becoming fat; but there was something deeper than that, at the back of her mind or in the pit of her stomach a taboo against eating. Pervading her insanity generally there was always a sense of some guilt, the origin and exact nature of which I could never discover; but it was attached in some peculiar way to food and eating. In the early acute, suicidal stage of the depression, she would sit for hours overwhelmed with hopeless melancholia, silent, making no response to anything said to her. When the time for a meal came, she would pay no attention whatsoever to the plate of food put before her and, if the nurses tried to get her to eat something, she became enraged. I could usually induce her to eat a certain amount, but it was a terrible process. Every meal took an hour or two; I had to sit by her side, put a spoon or fork in her hand, and every now and again ask her very quietly to eat and at the same time touch her arm or hand. Every five minutes or so she might automatically eat a spoonful.[7]

No accident that one remembers Mrs. Ramsay presiding over the distribution of her *bœuf en daube*, for this expresses the connection between food and maternal love which is universal from infancy. Oliver Twist, holding out his porridge bowl and asking, in that famous scene, for "more," wants not just more porridge but more of the affection an orphan is starved for. But Virginia Woolf wanted less, felt she had already taken too much. When she was ill, "she would maintain that she was not ill, that her mental condition was due to her own fault—laziness, inanition, and gluttony," and even when well, she was convinced that "she ate too much and lived a life too lethargic and quiet."[8] She had taken too much from her mother, done too little, given too little love in return, and her mother had died. Unworthy of sustenance, she punished herself by refusing to eat.[9]

At the same time she was always hungry for affection. The natural adolescent process of detachment from her mother ended catastrophically with her mother's death, and instead of the real woman who inspired in her growing daughter a mixture of hatred and love, an idealized phantom mother haunted her mind. In this idealization "The Mausoleum Book" must have assisted. It was intended as a letter from Leslie Stephen to his children and stepchildren, to "fix" for them all some memories of Julia. In this domestic portrait, no flaw is admitted. Julia's goodness is "unspeakable." "The very substance of her life was woven out of her affections." She loved to love, and her love was "holy and tender." " 'Reverence' is the word which comes naturally in speaking of that perfect type of noble womanhood." It is a Victorian saint's life he writes, and cloying and sentimental as we find it, "The Mausoleum Book" embodies a religious ideal in which love of God has been replaced by love for other people, particularly the members of one's own family. As for himself, the best achievement of his life was not his work but his marriage with Julia, to have allowed that noble nature to pour out, "making one little fragment of the race happier and better and aware of a noble ideal."

After writing *To the Lighthouse* Virginia Woolf confessed that she could not really remember her mother—she had been too young at the time of her death. To create Mrs. Ramsay she relied partly on her observation of Vanessa and partly on the idealized image of Julia fixed in their memories by "The Mausoleum Book," an idealization against which, at last, in *To the Lighthouse*, she was to rebel. Before *To the Lighthouse*, however, Julia Stephen remained for her daughter the perfect, idealized mother of early childhood, never known to the point of disillusionment. Virginia sought this ideal for much of her life and found it in a series of quasi-maternal figures, beginning with her sister and including Violet Dickinson, Vita Sackville-West, and even her husband. What she wanted from these people was the solace and affection, the unearned, unconditional love one expects from a mother.

Woolf's correspondence with Violet Dickinson provides graphic evidence of this, for its keynote is a pathetic need for affection. "Write to me, and tell me that you love me dearest. I wish no more. My food is affection." When Violet takes a trip, Virginia warns that "letters must come hot from the Equator with praise, or I shall give up literature and take to marriage."[10] The friendship and correspondence were at their most intense from 1902 and 1907, when Virginia was in her early twenties. She wrote to Violet about three times a week, letters full of news about her efforts to establish herself as a journalist, but most interesting for the nature of her endearments and her fantasy image of herself and Violet. "I wish you were a Kangaroo and had a pouch for small Kangaroos to creep to."[11] Violet, a tall woman, substantial both physically and emotionally, becomes in Virginia's imagination a protective mother kangaroo and herself a little wallaby (an animal resembling a kangaroo but smaller). In times of crisis, for example in 1906 when Thoby Stephen died of typhoid and Violet herself was sick, Virginia indulged more heavily than ever in the kangaroo baby-talk: "Wall [Wallaby, i.e. Virginia] rubs his soft nose in the quilt. He is a dear little beast, and loves his mother." "Is mother wallaby soft and tender to her little one? He will come and lick her poor lean mangy face."[12] When, at the zoo, she saw a kangaroo with a baby in its pouch, licking its nose, she cried, "That is Violet." There is a photograph of Violet and Virginia taken in 1902 which explains as well as words the older woman's appeal to the younger: Violet sturdy, solidly rooted, enormously tall, Virginia fragile and clinging, her

*Violet Dickinson.*

head reaching only to Violet's shoulder, on which it rests. Violet was thirty-seven at the time, Virginia was twenty; they might have been mother and daughter, and in many practical matters Violet acted the maternal role. When Virginia went to Italy and forgot her fur slippers, Violet sent a new pair after her. When she needed a new dress, Violet went out to buy the material. When she got married, Violet sent her a cradle.

More than once, Virginia presents the kind of love she

wants from Violet as the loving care a sick person gets from a nurse. In 1903 she recalls having told Violet that she should like to be nursed by her when she is ill and finds this "typical of so much in our lives." In turn, what she wants from Violet typifies what she wanted from women in general:

> I wish I could be an invalid and have ladies. I am so susceptible to female charms, in fact I offered my blistered heart to one in Paris, if not to two. But first by a long way is that divine Venus [the Louvre statue] who is Katie and you and Nessa and all good and beautiful . . . women—whom I adore. I weep tears of tenderness to think of that great heart of pity for Sparroy [another pet name for herself] locked up in stone—never to throw her arms around me—as she would, if only she could—I know it and feel it. Honestly there was a look of Katie in her stupid beautiful head, and Katie in a bath towel would have what you call a bust just like hers, only Katie won't ever open her arms (which aren't of stone—the Venus hasn't got any by the way) for this poor Sparroy to enter.[13]

This effusion is distinctively, and poignantly, Woolf: I can't imagine many people who would look at the Venus de Milo and see a maternal figure whose "great heart of pity" was "locked up in stone," who would throw her arms around them and comfort them if only she could. The missing arms become, not an accidental defect, but an important part of the statue's image and its emotional impact. Leslie Stephen had said of his wife's beauty, "It was just the perfect balance, the harmony of mind and body which made me feel when I looked at her the kind of pleasure which I suppose a keen artistic sense to derive from a masterpiece of Greek sculpture."[14] Looking at one masterpiece of Greek sculpture, his daughter sees a symbol of unavailable maternal love. But as for "the harmony of mind and body," Virginia demurs—the Venus' head is "beautiful" but "stupid."

The Katie she talks of is Katherine Thynne, daughter of

the Marchioness of Bath and later Lady Cromer, one of the circle of aristocratic young women to which the well-connected Violet, a relative of the Edens, introduced Virginia. Virginia adored them: Katie, her sister Beatrice, their friend Lady Robert Cecil (Nelly). They "dressed very badly" but held themselves superbly; they "left beautiful spaces behind them."[15] Like Matthew Arnold's before her, Woolf's affection for the aristocracy is part aesthetic, part moral; they worship Pan and Bacchus rather than Mammon and Respectability, the gods of the Philistines. "We spent the whole afternoon under a tree in the garden," she writes in 1903 of "An Afternoon with the Pagans." "Katie lay stretched on a long couch, in the carelessness of perfect grace. She doesn't think how she looks. She just flings out her superb limbs, like a child resting after its play." [16] They seemed like "beings moving in a higher world, with voices like the ripple of Arcadian streams."[17] She admired their insouciant grace, the way their very awkwardnesses became signs of a magnanimity of spirit. She would respond to a similar largeness and openness in Vita Sackville-West, "so dashing in her long white legs with a crimson bow; but rather awkward, forced indeed to take down her stockings and rub her legs with ointment at dinner, owing to midges. I like this in the aristocracy. I like the legs; I like the bites; I like the complete arrogance and unreality of their mind."[18]

Stephen Spender, in trying to explain the attraction of sailors, stableboys, and gondoliers for well-educated British male homosexuals, suggests that the difference in class provides the sense of "otherness" usually supplied in sexual relationships by a difference in sex.[19] His suggestion applies interestingly to Woolf's feelings about women. Making a distinction which it would no doubt be unnecessary to mention on the other side of the Atlantic, I would emphasize that Virginia Woolf was not of the same social class as the young ladies with whom she was so happy. Her connections were mostly upper middle class. The women who excited her imagination had titles, or their parents did. Not only were they rich and privileged, they had been rich and privileged for so long they could afford to be frivolous and eccentric.

In a Memoir Club contribution of the thirties Woolf asks a question many have asked about her: "Am I a Snob?" Her answer is "Yes." However, the memoir explores not her cultural elitism but her attraction to the aristocracy. "Am I a snob?" leads to another question, somewhat facetious, which might be paraphrased: Why is it that invariably, in the pile of letters on her table, the one with the coronet floats to the top? To answer this she recalls a lunch, when she was younger, with Lady Bath and her daughters. She sat "shivering with ecstasy," a snobbish ecstasy perhaps, but made up of "pleasure, terror, laughter and amazement." Lady Bath sat at the head of the table with two Waterbury watches on cushions before her, and yet what cared she for time? She seemed to have enormous leisure. She nodded off to sleep. She flung occasional questions at the butler which he dutifully answered: "What's marl, Middleton?" "Who just rode by?" Katie gave the dog a bloody bone directly from her plate.

> As I sat there, I felt these people don't care a snap what anyone thinks. Here is human nature in its uncropped, unpruned natural state. They have a quality which we in Kensington lack. Perhaps I am only finding excuses for myself, but that seems the origin of the snobbery which now leads me to put this letter on the top of the pack— the aristocrat is freer, more natural, more eccentric than we are.[20]

There are two distinctions made at two points in Woolf's life embedded in this passage. The first is between the aristocracy and the upper middle class: "they have a quality which we in Kensington lack" was a thought she had while sitting at lunch with Lady Bath, as a young woman oppressed by her respectable philistine relatives. The other distinction is between the aristocracy and her Memoir Club audience of Bloomsbury intellectuals and artists: "the aristocrat is freer, more natural, more eccentric than we are."

"Am I a Snob?" seems a calculated dig at the snobbery of artists, writers, and intellectuals, which created a world too insular for Virginia Woolf. In women of fashion like Lady Bath, Margot Oxford, Ottoline Morrell, and Sybil Colefax, she sought escape. If someone asked her whether she would rather meet Einstein or the Prince of Wales, she would plump—she vaunts—unhesitatingly for the prince. In fact, she began to get tired of going to Sybil Colefax's parties, because she was invariably asked to meet other writers. For that, she did not need Sybil. Her response was to invite Sybil to see her at her own house, where she could receive her in her messy study, her fingers covered with ink, and could in privacy confront her anti-self. "She would exclaim, 'Oh how I long to be a writer!' And I would reply, 'Oh Sybil, if only I could be a great hostess like you!' "[21]

There is more, however, to Virginia Woolf's feeling for the aristocracy than Arnoldian moral-aesthetic approval. Its keynote is a mixture of fascination and condescension. This is clear in her attitude to Vita, whom she valued not for her writing but for the way she scratched her legs, and in her thoughts about Katherine Thynne, who, like the Venus de Milo, impressed her as beautiful but stupid. As was the case with that other woman who reminded people of Greek goddesses, Virginia did not look to the aristocratic young ladies for intellectual eminence, and I suspect that had she been awed by the brains and talent which some of them, notably Nelly Cecil, did in fact possess, she would have abandoned them as altogether too frightening.[22] Instead she welcomed their spontaneity about emotions: "Beatrice took us driving today; she brings tears to my eyes sometimes. 'I like being stroked. No one strokes me,' she says simply as a child."[23] Not unreasonably, she turned to them for love and emotional support—Venuses who, unlike the armless Venus, might conceivably open their arms to take her in. Collectively, I would suggest, the Nellies and Katies represented a romantic and glamorous but also distinctly maternal world to Virginia, with now one woman, now another, surfacing as the chief focus of affection.

Mrs. Dalloway is no more a portrait of Kitty Maxse than she is a portrait of the flamboyant Ottoline Morrell, yet at one point Woolf referred to *Mrs. Dalloway* as her "Garsington novel."[24] (Garsington was Ottoline's country house.) Mrs. Dalloway is a representative of a class of women which stimulated Woolf's imagination, and the novel is largely a celebration of a self-made image, "that divine Venus who is Katie and [Violet] and Nessa and all good and beautiful women whom I adore." Clarissa Dalloway (unlike Mrs. Ramsay) is not a strikingly maternal figure, and she was certainly not intended to represent Julia Stephen, but in *The Voyage Out* she belongs to the social sphere in which Virginia frequently sought the maternal element: she is the daughter of a peer. In *Mrs. Dalloway,* although she is demoted, the daughter merely of Mr. Justin Parry, country gentleman, she is still very much a society woman, and indeed how you respond to *Mrs. Dalloway* depends to some extent on how you feel about society women. If you assume, beyond convincing to the contrary, that a woman who spends her days at luncheons and teas and her evenings making polite conversation must be idle and trivial, you will read the book totally as satire—as Lytton Strachey did—and wonder why the satire isn't sharper. But Woolf herself, for reasons I have suggested, romanticized the world of fashion, and *Mrs. Dalloway,* in which she sympathetically identifies with a Westminster matron, her anti-self, and imaginatively inhabits her body, is something of a declaration of independence from Bloomsbury attitudes and represents a discovery of uniquely personal subject matter. The sexual energy which was lacking in *Jacob's Room* is present in the writing of *Mrs. Dalloway,* and for the first time the full richness of Woolf's imagination is released in a novel. In terms of subject matter and point of view, the difference between *Jacob's Room* and *Mrs. Dalloway* is analogous to the difference between masculine early Bloomsbury, where Virginia felt confined and oppressed by the sterility of intellect, and the more feminine world she later contrived for herself, which could include the champagne intoxication of Ottoline's house in Bedford Square. *Mrs. Dalloway* is the first novel in which she taps unabashedly the great reservoir of feminine experience.

# 7

# Mrs. Dalloway

I read *Mrs. Dalloway* as celebration, not as satire—a celebration of the ecstasy of living and an elegy for the swift passage of that ecstasy. It alternates between visions of beauty and despair, between exhilaration and melancholy; it communicates the perilousness of living and the precarious position of the sensitive mind assaulted by the material world. It is perhaps the most schizophrenic of English novels, and, along with De Quincey's *Confessions of an English Opium Eater,* the one most likely to appeal to any remnants of that culture which looked to drugs for an alternative, transcendental reality. In writing about the mad delusions of Septimus Warren Smith, Virginia Woolf described her own insanity and feared people might not be interested in so alien an experience; in fact, she provides the best description of a kind of visionary state many people in the twentieth century have experienced in other ways, not all drug-induced.

Creativity and madness are the central subjects of this book: the impulse towards life and the impulse towards death, the sane and the insane, representing two impulses or currents within Virginia Woolf. This is the first of her novels to be structured, as her greatest ones are, by alternating rhythms of feeling. *Mrs. Dalloway* represents Woolf's fullest self-portrait as an artist; it contemplates the relationship between her own madness and her creativity. In presenting a society woman as at least partially analogous to an artist, she also suggests a critical view of various kinds of masculine creativity—law-making, soul-curing, empire-building. The richness of the novel emerges from two dynamic juxtapositions: that of Mrs. Dalloway and the Prime Minister, and that of Mrs. Dalloway and Septimus Warren Smith, the former contrasting characteristic masculine power with one version of female power, the latter suggesting the much less clear-cut contrast between a kind of divine intoxication which is the basis of all creativity and insanity pure and simple.

On June 23, 1922, Woolf mentions for the first time the short story "Mrs. Dalloway in Bond Street" as something she will write in the future, and on August 16 she seems well into it. On August 28 she predicts that the story will be finished on September 2 and wonders what to do next. The chapter on Chaucer for *The Common Reader?* Or, "shall I write the next chapter of *Mrs. D.*—if she is to have a next chapter; and shall it be *The Prime Minister?*"[1] By October 6 she had finished "Mrs. Dalloway in Bond Street" and sketched out the rest of a novel, "a short book consisting of six or seven chapters each complete separately," of which the second was to be "The Prime Minister." "And all must converge upon the party at the end."[2]

"Mrs. Dalloway in Bond Street," published as a short story in *The Dial* in 1923, is roughly analogous to the first sixteen pages of *Mrs. Dalloway*, in which Clarissa, responding intensely to the vitality of the city street, walks to the florist to buy flowers for the party she will give that evening. In the short story she is buying gloves, the French kind with pearl buttons which one could get so easily before the war, but which are now hard to find. The story insists more than the novel on its setting in the aftermath of World War I and concentrates thematically on what endures and what has been lost after a period of great upheaval.

In a larger sense, too, the story is concerned with change and permanence. As she walks down the street, feeling a tie between herself and members of the Parry family who walked down Bond Street in decades long past, Clarissa is haunted by scraps of poetry: "From the contagion of the world's slow stain . . . Fear no more the heat o' the sun . . . And now can never mourn, can never mourn." In the novel the scraps of *Adonais* which sound the note of death in the story vanish, but "Fear no more the heat o' the sun," the tag from *Cymbeline*, continues to be the leitmotif of Clarissa's underlying despair, of her wish for easeful death, and recalls too, more indirectly, the miraculous world of Shakespeare's romances in which what is lost may yet be found again. "Mrs. Dalloway in Bond Street" ends with Clarissa's reunion in the glove shop with a woman who was once important to her, now an old brittle person complaining about the quality of gloves, who fulfills in the story the function of Sally Seton in the novel. She returns from the past only to prove that people's imaginative visions of her are more enduring than the woman herself.

Shelley's lines may be gone in the novel, but his spirit persists in the book's sense of life as a gradual process of loss and compromise, death as a kind of purity. Clarissa, over fifty, weakened by illness, feels painfully the passage of time and, fighting her impulse to withdraw, forces herself to grasp as much as she can of life, of sensation, of intensity. What distinguishes her is the intensity of her imaginative participation in life; in her own way, she is enacting for us the process of sympathetic imagination, of projecting oneself into the flow of life, into other people, other objects, which is in this novel the essence of art.

There is no way fully to explain or analyze the lift of the spirit that occurs when one reads certain parts of *Mrs. Dalloway*.[3] It is one of the most buoyant books ever written, for Woolf has transfused her own spirit of ecstatic response into her heroine:

> Such fools we are, she thought, crossing Victoria Street. For Heaven only knows why one loves it so, how one sees it so, making it up, building it round one, tumbling it, creating it every moment afresh; but the veriest frumps, the most dejected of miseries sitting on doorsteps (drink their downfall) do the same; can't be dealt with, she felt positive, by Acts of Parliament for that very reason: they love life. In people's eyes, in the swing, tramp, and trudge; in the bellow and the uproar; the carriages, motor cars, omnibuses, vans, sandwich men shuffling and swinging; brass bands; barrel organs; in the triumph and the jingle and the strange high singing of some airplane overhead was what she loved; life; London; this moment of June.[4]

Loving life is equivalent to making it up, building it round one, creating it every moment afresh, and the answer which *Mrs. Dalloway* offers to the decay of the spirit, the deaths it variously records, is intense response to the moment.

Virginia Woolf had turned forty when she began this novel, and her diary reveals an increasing awareness of the passage of the time as well as a keen desire not to waste the time that was left her. This passage is typical:

I went to Golders Green and sat with Mary Sheepshanks in her garden and beat up the waters of talk, as I do courageously, so that life mayn't be wasted. The fresh breeze went brushing all the thick hedges which divide the gardens. Somehow, extraordinary emotions possessed me. I forget now what. Often now I have to control my excitement—as if I were pushing through a screen; or as if something beat fiercely close to me. What this portends I don't know. It is a general sense of the poetry of existence that overcomes me. . . . The sight of two coffins in the Underground luggage office I daresay constricts all my feelings. I have the sense of the flight of time; and this shores up my emotions.[5]

Had she been writing decades later we might say her attitude was existential: the imminence of death conditions and enhances her response to life. As it is, pointing to her knowledge of the romantic poets, to her age and her frail constitution, perhaps suggests more accurately the sources of the urgency which permeates *Mrs. Dalloway*.

Suffused as it is with the spirit of romantic poetry, the first section of *Mrs. Dalloway* may be illuminated by Keats's proposition that "every mental pursuit takes its reality and worth from the ardour of the pursuer." Keats distinguishes things "real," like the sun and stars, from things "semi-real," like love and the clouds, which require, in his lovely phrase, "a greeting of the spirit" to make them come fully to life, and these in turn from "nothings," which are wholly dignified "by ardent pursuit." Clarissa Dalloway, living her day, preparing for her party, has to do mostly with things that require a greeting of the spirit or with nothings dignified by the ardour of the pursuit: "now it was a bed of tulips, now a child in a perambulator, now some absurd little drama she made up on the spur of the moment" (87). In a context which elevates enjoyment to a touchstone of goodness, Clarissa's sheer enjoyment of life is emphasized ("And of course she enjoyed life immensely. It was her nature to enjoy. . . . She enjoyed practically everything" [87]), and in her enjoyment there is nothing passive: we receive but what we give.

The products of her creativity may seem comically slender: "that network of visiting, leaving cards, being kind to people; running about with bunches of flowers, little presents; So-and-so was going to France—must have an air-cushion" (86). But the comedy is loving. This is the creativity of everyday feminine life. Its goal is connection, establishing relationships rather than making monuments, so that one is struck repeatedly by images of threads and webs in *Mrs. Dalloway*, the invisible ties between people woven by Clarissa. Frost's sonnet "She is as in a field a silken tent" commemorates the same kind of creativity.[6]

What dignifies it is not only the ardor of the pursuit but also the forces against which this campaign of genteel creativity is waged, the forces of chaos and death. Stephen Spender, discussing the nature of Woolf's political insight, notes acutely that her imaginative power, "although it is concentrated often on small things—the light on the branches of a tree, a mark upon a whitewashed wall—nevertheless held at bay vast waters, madness, wars, destructive power."[7] Like other great works of the postwar period (*The Good Soldier, The Waste Land, Ulysses* come to mind), *Mrs. Dalloway* pits civilization against destruction, culture against chaos; the frailty of culture—as well as its potential for triviality—is all the more striking because it is embodied in a fragile birdlike woman who gives parties.

Lady Bexborough, that noble figure who expresses the heroism of society, its willed determination to maintain civilized values in the face of death and suffering, appears in "Mrs. Dalloway in Bond Street" sitting upright and alone in her carriage, "borne past like a queen at a tounament, though she had nothing to live for and the old man is failing and they say she is sick of it all."[8] In the novel, too, Lady Bexborough is Clarissa's ideal, projecting stoic endurance in a meaningless world. Lady Bexborough holds herself upright; Lady Bexborough opens a bazaar holding in her hand, they say, the telegram informing her that John, her favorite, has been killed in the war. The situation is more or less repeated when Mrs. Dalloway goes on with her party after hearing of Septimus' suicide, not out of callousness, but as a reaffirmation of life and creativity against the power of death and disintegration.

The experience of World War I drove Freud to postulate the existence of a death instinct, a compelling urge in mankind not to be, to return to primordial unconsciousness. He first suggested the conflict between Eros and Thanatos in *Beyond the Pleasure Principle*, published in English in 1921. I am not suggesting that Woolf read Freud's work at this time (there is no evidence that she did), but that such ideas were part of the postwar cultural climate.

The postwar theme of culture battling anarchy, of public grace masking private sorrow is suggestive, yet the attitude towards society *Mrs. Dalloway* rests on does not represent solely Woolf's response to World War I. At twenty-one she had formulated it in her diary essay "Social Success" in words we may recall:

> Mrs. Thingamagig is more amusing than ever tonight— didn't she lose an only son in the war? . . . You may call her heartless but surely she does more good by making the world laugh than by sitting at home and weeping over her own sorrows. The truth is, to be successful socially one wants the courage of a hero.[9]

By 1922, the years of Woolf's initiation into society, the years in which the socialite Kitty Maxse was a presence in her life, the years of her intense friendship with Violet Dickinson, in which Violet was to Virginia the kind of mentor and surrogate mother that Kitty was to Vanessa, were almost two decades in the past. But that year two events served to bring Violet and Kitty back to mind. First, in February, four months before the first mention of "Mrs. Dalloway in Bond

Street," Violet paid a call which sufficiently impressed Virginia for her to devote some space to it in her journal.

> She told me she had no wish to live. "I'm very happy," she said. "Oh yes, very happy—But why should I want to go on living? What is there to live for?" "Your friends?" "My friends are all dead." "Ozzie?" [Her brother.] "Oh, he'd do just as well without me. I should like to tidy things up and disappear." "But you believe in immortality?" "No. I don't know that I do. Dust, ashes, I say."[10]

Then, in October 1922, Woolf heard that Kitty Maxse had died by falling down a flight of stairs. There was some question of suicide.[11] According to the introduction Woolf wrote for the Modern Library edition of *Mrs. Dalloway* in 1928, in the "first version" of the novel, Septimus, "who is later intended to be [Mrs. Dalloway's] double," did not exist, and "Mrs. Dalloway was originally to kill herself, or perhaps merely to die at the end of the party." This "first version" does not appear actually to have been written but seems to refer to an idea Woolf had at some point for developing "Mrs. Dalloway in Bond Street" into a novel.

I would suggest that what coalesced in Woolf's mind after Violet's visit, in which that salty, chipper woman confessed she had no will to live, and after Kitty Maxse's possible suicide, was an energizing view of fashionable society as a fragile skin stretched over chaos, the chaos of madness, death, and destruction. It is, then, Woolf's great theme, or to use her own word, her most gripping "vision," touching as it does on the sudden destruction of her childhood world through her mother's death. When she saw it enacted in the life of her friends she could return to the sketch written as a young woman, suggesting the heroism of society which ignores and dispels pain, and develop it with mature fictional techniques and real compassion.

Mrs. Dalloway, whatever her limitations, is Woolf's answer to the forces—the masculine forces, Woolf would say—which led civilization into the chaos of war.

"The Prime Minister," the second part of *Mrs. Dalloway* to be written, was never published separately as a short story. It is a rough draft of that part of the novel which describes the passage of a gray limousine through the city streets and the reactions to it of various passersby. "Authority," in almost allegorical fashion, makes its stately progress, and the occupant of the limousine (identified in the manuscript as the Prime Minister) is conceived by Woolf as a "generalized" character, as opposed to Clarissa, who is "particular." [12] This means, I assume, that the Prime Minister is no more than his role in society, whereas Clarissa is seen from the inside as an individuated consciousness.

Mrs. Dalloway and the Prime Minister, then, juxtaposed in this way, were in Woolf's mind from the moment she asked herself how to develop the short story; they generated the novel, even though the juxtaposition of Mrs. Dalloway and Septimus comes to dominate it. Appreciating the seminal contrast between the symbol of authority, known by his clothes and his car, whose description reflects the nature of his power, which is over the externals of life, and the example of private consciousness, fluid, unstructured, responding now to this, now to that perfection in the flux of life, whose power is to affect the inner lives of others, helps you see how *Mrs. Dalloway* develops naturally from the concerns of "A Society," "Modern Fiction," and *Jacob's Room*, which all, in varying degrees of outspokenness, mock the rigidity of masculine authority.

The two characters come together at Clarissa's party:

> And now Clarissa escorted her Prime Minister down the room, prancing, sparkling, with the stateliness of her grey hair. She wore ear-rings, and a silver-green mermaid's dress. Lolloping on the waves and braiding her tresses she seemed, having that gift still; to be; to exist; to sum it all up in the moment as she passed; turned, caught her scarf in some other woman's dress, unhitched it, laughed, all with the most perfect ease and air of a creature floating in its element (191).

Clarissa, the mermaid, perches on the waves and presides over the fluidity of life, encouraging motion, liquidity. As for the Prime Minister, "one couldn't laugh at him. He looked so ordinary. You might have stood him behind a counter and bought biscuits—poor chap, all rigged up in gold lace" (189). Labeled a "symbol of what they all stood for, English society" (189), he is made deliberately unreal, just as the power he represents, the power of laws and systems to affect people's lives, seems in this book unreal. Even Clarissa's air-cushions have a greater effect on the inner life, and the fragile society over which she presides, the gathering of people from Bayswater, Kensington, and Mayfair at her party, has greater cohesion (though even that harmony is precarious) than the nation the Prime Minister rules, to preserve which men like Septimus went to fight in France.

The Prime Minister has his minions, who are, in fact, more important in the "action" of the story than he is, most notably the doctors Holmes and Bradshaw, but also the politicians, Lady Bruton, Elizabeth Dalloway's tutor Miss Kilman, and to some extent Peter Walsh, Clarissa's old friend. What these people share is a lack of respect for the privacy of the soul and a determination to squeeze other people's lives into procrustean beds. Members of Parliament who try to frame laws to impose on human nature are merely wasting their time. But doctors who participate in a similar unreality by counseling proportion to disturbed souls are cruelly as well as laughably irrelevant. Fanatics and ideologues like Miss Kilman, however noble-sounding their motives, commit the crime of "forcing" the soul, where forcing has the meanings of forcible entry into a locked house, of rape, and of making a growing thing bloom out of its proper season. In *Mrs. Dalloway*, Woolf turns Victorian idealism on its head, presenting the urge to say what ought to be rather than what is as the source of much of the cruelty that human beings visit upon one another.

In an unusual passage, so conspicuous for its savage indignation that it disrupts the texture of the novel, Woolf personifies this urge to dictate as the spirit of Conversion, "that Goddess whose lust is to override opposition, to stamp indelibly in the sanctuaries of others the image of herself." Sir William Bradshaw is Conversion's right arm. "He swooped; he devoured; he shut people up." Even the clocks of Harley Street are seen as part of the conspiracy: "Shredding and slicing, dividing and subdividing, [they] nibbled at the June day, counselled submission, upheld authority" (113). The clocks may be inanimate, Lady Bruton and Miss Kilman may be women, but they all participate in an essentially masculine effort to impose a mechanical form upon the natural fluidity of life.

Septimus Warren Smith entered Woolf's plans for *Mrs. Dalloway* on October 16, 1922, with these notations in her working notebook: "Suppose it to be connected this way: Sanity and insanity. Mrs. D. seeing the truth. SS seeing the insane truth. The pace to be given by the gradual increase of S's insanity on the one side; by the approach of the party on the other." Three weeks later, she worries about welding it all together in some general style, and again the pairing of Septimus and Clarissa is important to her. "All must bear finally on the party at the end; which expresses life in every variety . . . while S dies."[13] In creating Septimus, she seems to have cast about for models, wondering if she might not put something of Gerald Brenan in him, the young man who has survived the war and gone into some business, who "takes life to heart: seeks truth—revelations—some reason yet of course it is insanity. His insensitivity to other people's feelings—that is to say he must have the masculine feelings, selfishness: Egoism; but has also an extreme insight; and humility."[14] But largely, as she planned, Septimus was based upon herself and her own experience with madness.

Septimus acts out instincts suppressed in Mrs. Dalloway, withdrawing to live in a self-enclosed dream-world which frequently becomes a nightmare, and finally opting for death, while she continues to push herself to connect with people and to respond to the beauty of the world outside her. In Septimus, Clarissa's creative imagination is carried to the point of madness. If in her the soul of an artist is trivialized by its circumstances, in him the soul of an artist, divorced from the pressure to affect circumstance, grows diseased. His drawers are filled with visionary writings and pictures, proof that the trees are alive, proof of universal love. He, too, experiences life as a succession of piercingly beautiful visions, about which it seems parsimonious to say that they have lost contact with reality: sitting in Regent's Park with his wife, in his mind he "remained high on his rock, like a drowned sailor on a rock. I leant over the edge of the boat and fell down, he thought. I went under the sea. I have been dead, and yet now am alive, but let me rest still he begged" (77).

In a mad distortion of Mrs. Dalloway's ecstatic vision he sees beauty everywhere. Some of his visions, moreover, express a truth or psychological reality which could be expressed in no other fashion; for in some way the dead do walk, though they may not sing behind the rhododendron bushes, and Smith's recurring sensation of falling—into the depths of the sea or burning flames—speaks to some potential for bottomlessness in all of us, and reminds us that while Clarissa may be a mermaid, he is a deep-sea diver and has plunged into depths, has explored areas she systematically closes off. One does not have to invoke R. D. Laing to endorse at least partially the validity of Septimus' response to life. Does one wonder if Keats was mad when he said that beauty was truth?

"Pure poetry," if I may use an imprecise term which I think every reader of Woolf will nevertheless understand, represents one pole of Woolf's imagination, expressed most consummately in *The Waves*. The "Time Passes" section of *To the Lighthouse* is another instance of pure poetry. But even people who do not consider *The Waves* Woolf's masterpiece and who find "Time Passes" the least interesting part of *To the Lighthouse*—people, that is, who are essentially novel-lovers and not poetry-lovers (and I am one of them)—will probably agree that bringing elements of lyric poetry into the novel was one of Woolf's greatest adjustments to that form, stylistically her most distinct achievement. In relatively early novels like *The Voyage Out* and *Mrs. Dalloway*, pure poetry is assigned to the delirious (Rachel) and the mad (Septimus). It is the least traditional, most personal part of Woolf's gift, and the part she most distrusted.

The cleaning woman, stumbling upon some of Septimus' writings, laughs at them. When he tells Rezia how he is falling into an abyss of fire, she actually looks for the flames, "it was so vivid. But there was nothing" (155). Woolf dreaded writing the "mad" parts of *Mrs. Dalloway*, for in them she touched on some of the worst moments of her own life and some of her deepest fears about her art, that it represented the ravings of an isolated person, intelligible to no one but herself. Would the charwoman laugh? Would her friends see nothing where she had seen consuming flames or fawning sunlight? To assume that one's impressions hold true for other people was a privilege and comfort Woolf envied in writers like Jane Austen, but which she thought was unavailable to writers like herself. She makes the best case she can for "Modern Fiction" on historical and technical grounds, and I do not mean to imply that her efforts are insincere; but her real doubts are about herself, and what she is justifying, finally, is her hold on reality.

Septimus Warren Smith's chaotic ramblings are by no means an accurate image of Virginia Woolf's art—her work is disciplined, her prose style amongst the most polished in English literature. Yet insofar as her writing after 1919 represents something new and original in English letters, chaos plays its part. "The emphasis is laid upon such unexpected places that at first it seems as if there were no emphasis at all."[15] She is writing of Chekhov, but she might as well be talking of "The Mark on the Wall," "Kew Gardens," or *Jacob's Room*, with their radical questioning of what it is important to notice, what character consists in, what structure, if any, life has, and what structure the novel.

It would be wrong to romanticize Virginia Woolf's insanity by finding it the source of her genius, though her husband seems again and again in his autobiography to approach doing this himself. Frank Barron, a psychologist who has written perceptively on the creative process, points out the enormous difference between a dreary, limiting psychosis, which merely subtracts from life, imprisoning its victim, and the kind of madness which *is* perhaps allied to genius and which represents an enhancement of life, the ability periodically to let go of one's hold on reality as ordinarily perceived in order to achieve a new synthesis, a creative recombination of fact and vision.[16]

Woolf talked openly, often jokingly, about her insanity, and whether or not on some profound and unknowable level she willed it, consciously she resented her illness as an intrusion on her working life. Quite simply, she was happiest when writing, especially fiction: at such times she felt she was mobilizing all of herself, and "free use of the faculties means happiness." She thought herself "better company, more of a human being" when writing.[17] Sick, she couldn't write, was confined to bed. In 1922 she complained to E. M. Forster that she had wasted five whole years in bed and must be thought of, in consequence, as thirty-five, not forty. But a fascinating afterthought follows: "Not that I haven't picked up something from my insanities and all the rest. Indeed, I suspect they've done instead of religion."[18] What she means by this is uncertain, of course, but I would suggest that in madness she experienced some of the awe in the presence of the unknowable, the potent disorientation, which other visionaries have experienced in religion. "At the very heart of the creative process is this ability to shatter the rule of law and regularity in the mind," writes Barron. "Creation is a stone thrown uphill against the downward rush of habit."[19]

Septimus, without Mrs. Dalloway, is as incomplete a portrait of the artist as she is without him. He may be in touch with the depths, he may dive down into the ocean of the unconscious and come up with a pearl, but she can see that the pearl is displayed and handed around. With a writer as sensitive to her audience as Woolf, the element of sheer communication in art should not be minimized. An early draft of "Mr. Bennett and Mrs. Brown" contains an extremely revealing by the bye: "One writes," she says, "to bridge over the abyss between the writer and the reader, or between the hostess and her unknown guest."[20] This was written while she was working on *Mrs. Dalloway,* and it suggests not only the private resonance of the figure of the hostess, but also her extraordinary concern for establishing a direct, personal relationship with her reader, whom she conceives to be her guest. The source of creativity may be subterranean, it may well up in the privacy of the soul, but if it doesn't rise to the surface and become channeled so others can drink, it is a sterile if sacred fount. Creativity is a rhythmic process, an interplay between opposite states, however we define them: unconscious-conscious, relaxation-assertion, chaos-order, diffusion of identity–integration; Woolf, not surprisingly, will use Coleridge's sexual terms for describing this and insist that the truly creative mind must combine masculine and feminine.

Septimus Warren Smith and Mrs. Dalloway suggest such a polarity, the mad fragmented visions of the shell-shocked soldier and the orderly social creations of the Westminster hostess each insufficient as an image of art, the one risking unintelligibility, the other triviality. Of the two, however, Clarissa is the more complete figure, for the novel suggests that her creative engagement with life—specifically, her ability to bring people together—somehow depends upon her core of isolation.[21]

Mrs. Dalloway experiences an occasional folding in upon

the self, a subsiding or lapsing of energy which alternates with her plunging participation in life. There are, as Richard Dalloway puts it, "tides in the body." In wavelike rhythm, Clarissa seems to draw back and collect herself periodically before splashing again on the shore. Such a moment of strategic contraction of the spirit occurs as she sits sewing, just before the entrance of her old lover, Peter Walsh, and Woolf's beautiful description ties the physical action of sewing to the motion of waves, both in turn mirroring a movement of the soul.

> Quiet descended on her, calm, content, as her needle, drawing the silk smoothly to its gentle pause, collected the green folds together and attached them, very lightly, to the belt. So on a summer's day waves collect, overbalance, and fall; collect and fall; and the whole world seems to be saying "that is all" more and more ponderously, until even the heart in the body which lies in the sun on the beach says too, that is all. Fear no more, says the heart. Fear no more, says the heart, committing its burden to some sea, which sighs collectively for all sorrows, and renews, begins, collects, lets fall. And the body alone listens to the passing bee; the wave breaking; the dog barking, far away barking and barking.
>
> "Heavens, the front-door bell!" exclaimed Clarissa, staying her needle (44–45).

The prose rhythms, of which Woolf is a master, help to re-create in the reader Clarissa's almost hypnotized trance, before the intrusion of the outside world, the doorbell. Clarissa's moments of withdrawal are often signaled by the Shakespearean refrain "Fear no more," suggesting surrender of the will to the amorphous consolation of death; it is the opening of the dirge sung in *Cymbeline* over the body of Imogen, who only seems to be dead and will reawake momentarily, so it suggests also the kind of death which precedes resurrection, the momentary abdication which allows a person to proceed afterward with the active business of living.

Clarissa's reverie as she sews may be compared with Septimus' reverie in Regent's Park:

> Long streamers of sunlight fawned at his feet. The trees waved, brandished. We welcome, the world seemed to say; we accept; we create. Beauty, the world seemed to say. . . . To watch a leaf quivering in the rush of air was an exquisite joy. Up in the sky swallows swooping, swerving, flinging themselves in and out, round and round, yet always with perfect control as if elastics held them; and the flies rising and falling; and the sun spotting now this leaf, now that, in mockery, dazzling it with soft gold in pure good temper; and now and again some chime (it might be a motor horn) tinkling divinely on the grass stalks—all of this, calm and reasonable as it was, made out of ordinary things as it was, was the truth now; beauty, that was the truth now. Beauty was everywhere (77–78).

Just as he perceives that beauty is everywhere he is interrupted, as Clarissa was interrupted by the doorbell, by Rezia saying "It is time." Instead of pulling him back to shore, however, this fragment of reality becomes engulfed in his imaginative wave:

> The word "time" split its husk; poured its riches over him; and from his lips fell like shells, like shavings from a plane, without his making them, hard, white, imperishable, words, and flew to attach themselves to their places in an ode to Time; an immortal ode to Time. He sang. Evans answered from behind the tree. The dead were in Thessaly, Evans sang, among the orchids (78).

What in Clarissa is an alternating ebb and flow becomes in him a resistless undercurrent bearing him out to sea. Septimus' visions of beauty as truth and of the terrors of living are only quantitatively and not qualitatively different from

Mrs. Dalloway's reactions, and insofar as the novel is, as Woolf intended it to be, a study of sanity and insanity, it seems to suggest rather startlingly that sanity and insanity are merely two points on the same continuum and not two radically different states. There is, then, poignant accuracy in Leonard Woolf's choice of words in describing his wife's mental illness: four times in her life, he writes, "she passed across the border which divides what we call insanity from sanity."[22]

The issue, as so often in Woolf, is autonomy, the mind's dominion over itself, and when Septimus kills himself to preserve this, Clarissa can intuitively understand, even though her own demands for integrity are less extreme:

> A thing there was that mattered; a thing, wreathed about with chatter, defaced, obscured in her own life, let drop every day in corruption, lies, chatter. This he had preserved. Death was defiance (202).

She can imagine how a man like Sir William Bradshaw, obscurely evil, "capable of some indescribable outrage—forcing your soul" (203), could drive a young man to protect himself through death. Here the word "forcing" distinctly has the connotations of rape, and Septimus' death scene, in which he jumps out the window to avoid the relentless bearing down on him of the doctors, suggests a melodrama in which the virginal girl leaps off a cliff rather than submit to a sexual assault.

I think it no accident that Mrs. Dalloway's first name is the same as that of Richardson's heroine Clarissa Harlowe. In that saga of procrastinated rape, Clarissa struggles to maintain her sexual integrity against an aggressor she cannot help but find attractive; violated, she dies. If Holmes and Bradshaw play Lovelace to Septimus' Clarissa, Peter Walsh is more truly Clarissa Dalloway's Lovelace. Constantly fingering his pocket knife, he is vaguely menacing, aggressive: "with Peter everything had to be shared; everything gone into" (10). She rejected Peter and chose to marry Richard Dalloway, "for in marriage a little licence, a little independence there must be between people living together day in and day out in the same house; which Richard gave her, and she him" (10). Walsh sees with all the clarity and bitterness of a rejected man that there is something fundamentally untouched and untouchable in Clarissa; what she esteems as "the privacy of the soul," the need to maintain even in the closest of relationships a protective space around oneself ("a solitude; even between husband and wife a gulf"), he considers "the death of the soul" (66), a fatal timidity and hardness in her.

Few writers have discussed a woman's reluctance to love without implying that this reluctance was neurotic. We assume so readily that in love and sex one finds satisfaction, and the more passionate the love, the more satisfying. But Chaucer, with his usual tact and sanity, has Criseyde pause for a moment before embroiling herself with Troilus to wonder what she needs this for. Love, even when one has nothing more important to do than pick flowers in the garden, can be, it seems, a nuisance.

Systematically, and in the interest of her own integrity, Mrs. Dalloway rejected the possibility of intense passion in her life by her choice of a husband. She knows what she has missed. Peter would have tried to bring to life that central wooden core, and part of her regrets not having allowed him to do this: "If I had married him," she thinks, "this gaiety would have been mine all day!" But instead, "it was all over for her. The sheet was stretched and the bed narrow. She had gone up into the tower alone and left them blackberrying in the sun" (52). She is doomed to the independence she has chosen, and it is wrong to miss the regret she feels, but equally wrong to see her choice as any less courageous than to have accepted Peter's offer of potential intensity. One might say that Clarissa Harlowe could have saved herself a lot of pain and perhaps allowed herself some pleasure by giving in to Lovelace, but this is not Richardson's point; it is equally beside the point with *Mrs. Dalloway* to accept Peter Walsh's view that Clarissa should have married him and that in refusing to, she proved her frigidity. One of Woolf's concerns in this novel is the strategic value of frigidity, its use in preserving a woman's sense of autonomy and selfhood.

To leap from words like "autonomy" and "integrity" to the specifically sexual "frigidity" in discussing *Mrs. Dalloway* is not so daring as it seems, for in her delicate way Woolf suggests sex at many points. Peter calls Clarissa cold, wooden, and impenetrable (68). She is repeatedly compared to, or compares herself to, a nun, "cloistered, exempt" (134). We are reminded often of her attic room, the narrow bed where she sleeps alone, or sits up reading.

> And really she preferred to read of the retreat from Moscow. He knew it. So the room was an attic; the bed narrow; and lying there reading, for she slept badly, she could not dispel a virginity preserved through childbirth which clung to her like a sheet (35–36).

Even her choice of reading matter (the retreat from Moscow) suggests her enjoyment of the pattern of aggressors repelled, of a city resisting takeover by a foreign tyrant and triumphing partly by sheer will to maintain its integrity and partly because of the coldness of its winters.

Yet Clarissa is not triumphant about her own unconquerability. She thinks of moments, at Clieveden, at Constantinople, and again and again when "through some contraction of this cold spirit" (36) she failed Richard. She knows something is missing in her and that she is missing something in life, "something central which permeated; something warm which broke up surfaces and rippled the cold contact of man and woman, or of women together" (36). With women, sometimes, she can achieve moments in which the barriers go down and emotional contact is made, but she is wary of men, as she is wary of love and religion (139).

When fear of domination is gone, as it seems to be gone between Clarissa and certain women—Sally Seton, for one—
souls can touch. But "against such moments" are contrasted
"the bed and Baron Marbot and the candle half-burnt"
(36–37). Physical or spiritual, her frigidity is to Clarissa herself a high price to pay for her independence, but whatever
creativity she commands rests on that narrow bed, that attic
room, that tight-stretched sheet.

I have been presenting Clarissa Dalloway, along with her
dark nemesis, Septimus Smith, as a composite portrait of the
artist—in the buoyant society woman and the terrified ex-
soldier Virginia Woolf reveals some of the "tides" of her own
emotional life. But if *Mrs. Dalloway* is principally a celebration—a celebration of life and the creative imagination—it is
hard to ignore the fact that its heroine, while she is stoical,
energetic, and in her way creative, is also narrow, snobbish,
and somewhat superficial.

> She had a sense of comedy that was really exquisite, but
> she needed people, always people, to bring it out, with
> the inevitable result that she frittered her time away,
> lunching, dining, giving these incessant parties of hers,
> talking nonsense, saying things she didn't mean, blunt-
> ing the edge of her mind, losing her discrimination (87).

This harsh view is Peter Walsh's and may be partially discounted: naturally he would belittle the woman who rejected him. Yet even Peter Walsh cannot match the distaste
for Mrs. Dalloway which Virginia Woolf sporadically venti-
lates in her diaries: "The doubtful point is, I think, the character of Mrs. Dalloway. It may be too stiff, too glittering and
tinselly."[23] "I want to bring in the despicableness of people
like Ott. I want to give the slipperiness of the soul."[24] One
night she decided momentarily to give the book up because
she found Clarissa too shallow.

Then I invented her memories. But I think some distaste
for her persisted. Yet, again, that was true to my feeling
for Kitty, and one must dislike people in art without its
mattering.[25]

This passage bears some examination: that she dislikes
Clarissa bothers her. She tries to justify and deepen the character by inventing her past, giving her more substance
through memories; the dislike persists; she tries to justify it
on the grounds of truth to her feelings—that was, after all,
how she felt about Kitty Maxse, the ostensible "model" for
Clarissa. An exhortation follows: "One must dislike people in
art without its mattering." What strikes me is how uncomfortable Woolf is with her own disaffection. The effort is all
towards liking Clarissa—the excuses, for her failure to do so.
In life it was easy enough for her to dislike Kitty Maxse, so
that I can't help feeling there was another person involved
for whom dislike, disaffection, would be harder for Woolf to
admit.

I have argued earlier on biographical grounds that
Woolf's ambivalence towards Mrs. Dalloway touches on a
profound ambivalence about her mother. I turn now to the
text to show how it supports such a speculation.

Mrs. Dalloway has one child, a daughter, Elizabeth.
Beautiful, on the verge of maturity, she enters the novel
three times, twice briefly and once for an extended appearance, but in all, she is not a major figure in the book. Entering the drawing room during Clarissa's chat with Peter
Walsh, she is patronized by her mother: "Here is my Elizabeth" (53). That is her first appearance. Then she goes to the
Stores with her tutor, Miss Kilman, who passionately hates
Mrs. Dalloway. Eventually, against Miss Kilman's wishes,
Elizabeth leaves her, riding a bus down the Strand and ru-
minating on London and her future in a stream-of-con-
sciousness monologue strikingly like her mother's. Her third

appearance is at the party. Her presence is significant, for Miss Kilman did not want her to go to the party; it represents a triumph for Clarissa in her struggle with Kilman for Elizabeth's allegiance. But at the party we see Elizabeth only with her father, to whom she is attached, it is clear, much more than to her mother. The two brief bracketing episodes, in other words, suggest the distance between mother and daughter: you would not call this a close and loving relationship. Indeed, trying to think about Mrs. Dalloway and her daughter after closing the book, one is likely to come up with a blank. What one does remember is the struggle between Mrs. Dalloway and Miss Kilman over Elizabeth, for whenever Mrs. Dalloway herself thinks of her daughter, she thinks almost immediately of the odious Kilman.

Miss Kilman is a recognizable type in Virginia Woolf's novels: the old maid. Her ancestors were Miss Allan of *The Voyage Out* and Mary Datchet of *Night and Day;* after her will come Lily Briscoe and Miss La Trobe. But in this slightly desiccated company, Kilman stands out as singularly repulsive, fanatical, coercive, destructive. Her Dickensian name points the finger at her as much as anything else. As a type, we might call her the masculine woman, aggressive, embittered by what she does not have. But what is her particular function in this novel?

Kilman serves to express an undiluted, unambivalent hatred of Mrs. Dalloway. "Degradingly poor," she hates Clarissa for being rich, for having what she does not have, beauty, grace, and leisure. She envies her femininity. Beside Mrs. Dalloway, graceful and lovely, Kilman feels lumpish and clumsy. "She should have been in a factory; behind a counter; Mrs. Dalloway and all the other fine ladies!" (137). Her hatred of Mrs. Dalloway is connected with a more general "grudge against the world" which she turned to religion to cure. But the calm religion gives her is illusory—the rage persists underneath:

Fool! Simpleton! You who have known neither sorrow nor pleasure; who have trifled your life away! And there rose in her an overmastering desire to overcome her; to unmask her. If she could have felled her it would have eased her. But it was not the body; it was the soul and its mockery that she wished to subdue; make feel her mastery. If only she could make her weep; could ruin her; humiliate her; bring her to her knees crying, You are right! (138).

We are dealing here, I think, only tangentially with class hatred and class struggle; the envy of Mrs. Dalloway's wealth masks a deeper envy, an envy of her power as a woman.

In this struggle Elizabeth is the pawn. The superbly realized scene in which Elizabeth and Miss Kilman take tea together at the Stores focuses the tensions. Miss Kilman prolongs their outing as long as possible, stuffing herself with food, her only pleasure. Elizabeth sits obediently, accommodatingly, but finds it close inside; she wants to get away.

"Are you going to the party to-night?" Miss Kilman said. Elizabeth supposed she was going; her mother wanted her to go. She must not let parties absorb her, Miss Kilman said, fingering the last two inches of a chocolate éclair.

She did not much like parties, Elizabeth said. Miss Kilman opened her mouth, slightly projected her chin, and swallowed down the last inches of the chocolate éclair, then wiped her fingers, and washed the tea round in her cup.

She was about to split asunder, she felt. The agony was so terrific. If she could grasp her, if she could clasp her, if she could make her hers absolutely and for ever and then die; that was all she wanted. But to sit here, unable to think of anything to say; to see Elizabeth turning against her; to be felt repulsive even by her—it was too much; she could not stand it. The thick fingers curled inwards.

"I never go to parties," said Miss Kilman, just to keep Elizabeth from going. "People don't ask me to parties" (145).

"Like some dumb creature" brought up to a gate for an unknown purpose, Elizabeth Dalloway sits silent, waiting for Miss Kilman to continue. "Don't quite forget me," says Miss Kilman, acknowledging defeat.

> She had gone. Miss Kilman sat at the marble table among the éclairs, stricken once, twice, thrice by shocks of suffering. She had gone. Mrs. Dalloway had triumphed. Elizabeth had gone. Beauty had gone; youth had gone (146).

Mrs. Dalloway's triumph is clear enough, but the reasons for it are obscure: her power over her daughter is unexplored, and in this crucial scene, which tests Elizabeth's allegiance, she merely says she doesn't much care for parties, sits dumb, and then chooses her mother. The emphasis is on Miss Kilman, and the portrait of her stuffing herself with éclairs—I will say nothing about her choice of pastry—is utterly and surrealistically repellent, suggesting her ravenous demand for love.

In an earlier draft of the novel, the conflict between Mrs. Dalloway and Miss Kilman is presented as an inner struggle, something going on inside Elizabeth's consciousness:

> How they hated each other! That was Elizabeth's feeling. She simply wanted to run away and leave them, because it was so painful. And Miss Kilman looked so plain; so big; so shabby. Her mother looked so elegant, so supercilious. And she could see both sides; and she felt she was being torn apart, because her mother and her friend hated each other.[26]

As often in Woolf's process of writing and rewriting a novel, the earlier version, which is more revealing from an autobiographical point of view, is cut. If nothing else, this passage suggests how little we really know about Elizabeth's emotional dynamics: attraction for her mother is one side of her, sympathy for Miss Kilman—and by extension, contempt for her mother—is another. The struggle between love and hate for her mother is "painful"—she feels she is being "torn apart." This earlier draft supports my intuition that Miss Kilman exists in the novel to give voice to that part of the daughter which hates her mother passionately, hates her for being trivial, purposeless, resents her for being unfairly blessed.

If the implicit tension between Elizabeth and her mother is undeveloped in *Mrs. Dalloway,* the nature of the tension will be clearer, I would suggest, in *To the Lighthouse,* in which Lily Briscoe is alternately attracted to and repelled by Mrs. Ramsay. Independent, slightly crotchety, Lily Briscoe subsumes Miss Kilman temperamentally and Elizabeth positionally, that is to say, she adopts a filial role in relation to Mrs. Ramsay. But in the later book the venom is gone. In writing *Mrs. Dalloway,* I suggest, Virginia Woolf still hates the part of herself which hates her mother too much to give it a fair hearing. She labels it Kilman—that way lies death— and dismisses it as repulsive.

Woolf's friends saw no connection between the intellectual and writer they knew and the fashionable society woman she portrayed. Strachey, as I have mentioned, assumed that such a woman as Mrs. Dalloway was a natural butt of satire and couldn't understand why the book was so ambiguous. His comments about Woolf's ambivalence are acute and point to something fundamental in the work, although we need not agree with him that this ambivalence constitutes a flaw and may in fact see it as a source of much of the novel's fascination. Mrs. Dalloway represents for Woolf the path not taken, and, like many untaken paths, this one can look very appealing to the person who has chosen another way. Here, as

*Virginia Woolf in the twenties.*

in *To the Lighthouse,* Woolf tries to make the two paths meet, to bridge the gap between her own activities and the more usual activities of women of her class by trying to present the efforts of hostesses as versions of artistic creation.

Although Clarissa may seem too privileged to be thought of as typical, I believe she represents Woolf's attempt to portray average humanity, with its potential for both triviality and transcendence, and *Mrs. Dalloway* may be seen as Woolf's answer to *Ulysses*, a book she valued highly but could not help finding vulgar. If Leopold Bloom, cuckold, advertising canvasser, Jew, is Joyce's Everyman, Clarissa Dalloway, society hostess, establishment ornament, sexual coward, is Woolf's. As *Ulysses* moves towards a fragile communion between Bloom and Stephen Dedalus, sensualist and intellectual, practical man of business and artist, father and son, so *Mrs. Dalloway* moves towards an even more tenuous communion between Clarissa, worldly, stoical, sane, and Septimus Warren Smith, shell-shocked war veteran, news of whose suicide reaches Clarissa in the midst of her party. As Bloom and Dedalus are both parts of Joyce, Mrs. Dalloway and Smith represent conflicting aspects of Woolf, the impulse towards life and the impulse towards death, the effort to create order and meaning, the urge to despair in isolation. The novel reveals a deep sense of division and a hope for unification—it recalls Woolf's personal mythology in which she sees herself repeatedly moving back and forth between two worlds, satisfied with neither.

Its feminine point of view makes *Mrs. Dalloway* a personal milestone. In presenting Everyman as a woman, Woolf released for the first time in her career her full creative energy: "It seems to leave me plunged deep in the richest strata of my mind. I can write and write and write now: the happiest feeling in the world."[27]

# 8

# To the Lighthouse

She finished *Mrs. Dalloway* in January of 1925, and four months later the idea for *To the Lighthouse* came to her with astonishing clarity:

> This is going to be fairly short; to have father's character done complete in it; and mother's; and St. Ives; and childhood; and all the usual things I try to put in—life, death, etc. But the centre is father's character, sitting in a boat, reciting We perished, each alone, while he crushes a dying mackerel.[1]

*To the Lighthouse* is Woolf's most directly autobiographical novel. St. Ives of her childhood becomes the Hebrides, and Leslie and Julia Stephen are transmuted into the magnificently realized characters Mr. and Mrs. Ramsay: Mr. Ramsay, that bold mind bound to a quivering ego, so vigorous and austere in his pursuit of truth, so pathetically dependent on his wife (and women in general) for emotional support and reassurance; and Mrs. Ramsay, that gracious and beautiful exemplar of self-sacrificing femininity, who gains immense power precisely because of her self-abnegation and her gift for making other people pleased with themselves. But Woolf's autobiographical venture in *To the Lighthouse* goes deeper than portraying these important figures of her past. By introducing as a complex observer of the Ramsays' marriage the touchy, somewhat defensive spinster and aspiring artist Lily Briscoe, Woolf finds the way to express her continued ambivalence toward her parents and her sense of the threat they posed to her identity. The novel becomes her subtlest and most revealing exploration of autonomy, the most charged for her of all issues of identity—of the giving necessary to marriage and the not-giving necessary to art; of the fine line which separates the autonomy necessary for achievement of any sort from egotism pure and simple. For a woman, these issues have a particular urgency, because our cultural tradition has so long and so strenuously discouraged in women a strong and assertive sense of self. So Woolf, setting out to write about her parents and her past, comes inevitably to confront the central anxiety of her life. Can one be both a woman, as women have been culturally defined, and an artist?

*A Room of One's Own,* published two years after *To the Lighthouse,* was written in much the same frame of mind. When Woolf says in that brilliant essay on women and creativity that in order to write one must have five hundred pounds and a room of one's own, she is speaking as much of psychology and the psychological basis of artistic achievement as of economics. Creativity can scarcely exist without a substantial sense of self and a conviction, at least for the moment one is writing, that what one can produce is worthwhile: this is the implication of the metaphorical room and income. Woolf suggests that such confidence is at least partially instilled in a young Englishman of the upper classes by the wealth poured into universities to dignify the molding of his mind; the sumptuous dinners of roasts and delicacies are compared to the fare of the women's colleges—gravy soup and prunes. Gold plate and Persian rugs may seem trivial in the life of the mind, but they are instruments by which a society nurtures the privileged among its young. Woolf lingers over the physical luxuries of Oxbridge in *A Room of One's Own* not in materialistic envy, but in envy of the buoyancy of ego such pampering produces.

This buoyancy can easily merge into unpleasant egotism, and, in either form, she tends to regard it as a male prerogative. A demanding, tiresome visitor provokes this exclamation, for example:

> And the egotism of men surprises and shocks me even now. Is there a woman of my acquaintance who could sit in my armchair from 3 to 6.30 without the semblance of a suspicion that I may be busy, or tired, or bored; and so sitting could talk, grumbling and grudging, of her difficulties, worries; then eat chocolates, then read a book, and go at last, apparently self-complacent and wrapped in a kind of blubber of misty self-salutation? Not the girls at Newnham or Girton. They are far too spry; far too disciplined. None of that self-confidence is their lot.[2]

Notice the combination of exasperation and envy: the man's egotism is messy, distasteful, yet it is a manifestation of that self-confidence which is his peculiar privilege as a man. (Not all men are so bursting with self-confidence, of course; we are again in the realm of mythology.)

To Virginia Woolf, self-confidence did not come easily. One of her triumphs as a novelist is that she made this tenuousness of self the basis of her artistic vision and of new literary modes—the replacement, for example, of the narrator or a Jamesian central consciousness by an authorial presence more diffused—thus coming by her own personal route to participate in the early-twentieth-century revolution in the form of the novel. Part of her importance as a feminist is that she offered cultural and social explanations for this psychological handicap, which she perceived was not hers alone, but that of many women. The inhibition of a woman's sense of independent worth and identity she saw as the product of her education (or lack of it), family life, and professional opportunities. This is the story she tells most explicitly in her polemical writings, but also, if less insistently, in much of her fiction. She turned to feminism because patriarchal Victorian society had crippled her own sense of humanity and dignity. With no very robust ego, with no conviction of her own genius (compare some male writers of her time—Hemingway, Lawrence, Joyce, for example), she managed to create some splendid and original fiction, but the cost in suffering was high.

The imaginary creature who embodied everything damaging for a woman writer Virginia Woolf called "the angel in the house." I have mentioned her briefly before, but now I would like to discuss her more thoroughly. In "Professions for Women" Woolf describes this creature, and how she had to do battle with her and kill her before she could write. "She was intensely sympathetic. She was immensely charming. She was utterly unselfish. She excelled in the difficult arts of family life. She sacrificed herself daily. . . . She was so constituted that she never had a mind or a wish of her own, but preferred to sympathize always with the minds and wishes of others." She is, in short, in more than one sense, a perfectly selfless being, whose only purpose is to please, flatter, and smooth the way for others, particularly men. She is deadly to a woman writer because she whispers in her ear, " 'You are writing about a book that has been written by a man. Be sympathetic; be tender; flatter; deceive; use all the arts and wiles of our sex. Never let anybody guess you have a mind of your own. Above all, be pure.' "[3] And so the angel corrupts a woman's honesty and undermines her independence, whether the woman is trying to write the truth about another writer's work or about life itself.

The angel in the house, as Woolf sees it, is a role, inherited from the Victorians, to which women are socialized. "You who come of a younger and happier generation may not have heard of her," she writes, but "in those days—the last of Queen Victoria—every house had its Angel." She borrowed the name from Coventry Patmore's poem in praise of domestic bliss, but one need only think of the usual Dickens heroine to see what she means. David Copperfield's Agnes is a perfect embodiment of the type; always "pointing upward," to remind David of his heavenly home, she serves selflessly as David's spiritual inspiration. The Victorian conception of women relied heavily on the idea that moral and spiritual matters were the province of women and that however debased and brutal men might become from the dirty business of making money, women were free—indeed required—to resist the slow contagion of commerce and to remain the embodiments of moral perfection.[4] A woman was expected to live out an imitation of Christ, sacrificing her own desires to the needs of her husband and children.

This image of the pelican woman, feeding her brood with her own vital substance, dominated Victorian conceptions of the female role, and it was a phantom of this selfless creature who appeared before Virginia Woolf as she sat trying to write her first reviews and whom she had to kill before she could write. "I turned upon her and caught her by the throat. I did my best to kill her. My excuse, if I were to be had up in a court of law, would be that I acted in self-defence. Had I not killed her she would have killed me. She would have plucked the heart out of my writing." Whimsical, of course, and yet that mortal struggle with a phantom woman seems a disturbing fantasy when you realize that the sketch of the angel in the house (sympathetic, charming, self-sacrificing, excelling in family life) could also serve as a sketch of Mrs. Ramsay and of the real woman on whom Mrs. Ramsay was based. For Virginia Woolf, becoming an artist involved the rejection of a powerful model of femininity, one culturally endorsed and, more importantly, embodied exquisitely in her own mother. This rejection, fierce and determined one moment, ambivalent and guilt-ridden the next, underlies and animates the elegant lyricism of *To the Lighthouse*.

Usually in discussions of Woolf's family background her father receives the most attention, if only because he was a prominent figure on the Victorian literary scene, because we can read his critical writings and compare them to his daughter's, because, being a man, he led a public life that was recordable. And there is no doubt that, intellectually, Leslie Stephen had great influence on his daughter. Her essay about him in *The Captain's Death Bed* pays tribute to an intellectual mentor.

But the public praise for her father's modesty, vigor of mind, and intellectual honesty contrasts strikingly with Woolf's portrait of him as the self-torturing, self-pitying, tyrannical killjoy of *To the Lighthouse*, Mr. Ramsay. This more intimate portrait can be substantiated by the record of his private life which Leslie wrote for his children in "The Mausoleum Book," a record, among other things, of his exasperating domestic tyrannies. For despite his worship of Julia, he treated her somewhat as a servant, someone who should be constantly available, constantly supportive, constantly working to order his life. Hard on all the women who cared for him, he combined a theoretical veneration of women with actual condescension and harassment, demanding a total dedication to his own needs. No wonder that on the anniversary of her father's birth in 1928 Virginia Woolf noted the occasion, but noted too, with relief, that he was dead. "He would have been 96, 96, yes, today; and could have been 96, like other people one has known: but mercifully was not. His life would have entirely ended mine. What would have happened? No writing, no books;—inconceivable."⁵ Had he lived, Leslie would have destroyed his daughter's sense of independent self and hence, in her view, her ability to write.

This remarkable outburst about her father in the diary serves as a gloss on the scene in Part III of *To the Lighthouse* in which Lily Briscoe, painting on the lawn, is interrupted by the approach of Mr. Ramsay, whose unspoken demand for sympathy makes it impossible for her to continue working.

> Let him be fifty feet away, let him not even speak to you, let him not even see you, he permeated, he prevailed, he imposed himself. He changed everything. She could not see the colour; she could not see the lines; even with his back turned to her, she could only think, But he'll be down on me in a moment, demanding—something she felt she could not give him.⁶

What he wants is simply attention, affection, for Lily to convince him again of his importance and success. "Greedy, distraught," he will not give up without it, until Lily thinks, "it would be simpler then to have it over. Surely, she could imitate from recollection the glow, the rhapsody, the self-surrender, she had seen on so many women's faces (on Mrs. Ramsay's, for instance) when on some occasion like this they blazed up . . . into a rapture of sympathy" (224). But Lily, both by constitution and by choice not the self-sacrificing woman Mrs. Ramsay was, cannot force herself to bow before Mr. Ramsay's demands. His response to her coldness is "such a groan that any other woman in the whole world would have done something, said something—all except myself, thought Lily . . . who am not a woman, but a peevish, ill-tempered, dried-up old maid, presumably" (226).

Who would expect such sympathy from a man—from the poet Mr. Carmichael, for example? For a woman, however, expectations are different, and Lily, knowing most people would think her a peevish old maid for her coldness to Mr. Ramsay, ends by suspecting it herself.

> A woman, she had provoked this horror; a woman, she should have known how to deal with it. It was immensely to her discredit, sexually, to stand there dumb. . . . His immense self-pity, his demand for sympathy poured and spread itself in pools at her feet, and all she did, miserable sinner that she was, was to draw her skirts a little closer round her ankles, lest she should get wet (228).

Through Lily, Virginia Woolf asserts the artist's need for self-containment, the need to refuse service to someone else's ego, but she also suggests the fear that in doing so (in refusing to play a role like the one Mrs. Ramsay played to Mr. Ramsay and Mrs. Stephen had played to Mr. Stephen), the woman artist might be losing her sexuality.

The sequel to the confrontation between Lily and Mr. Ramsay suggests the nature of Virginia Woolf's retrospective emotional settlement with her father. Lily and Mr. Ramsay have reached an impasse, when suddenly over something entirely trivial it breaks: she chances to admire his boots. Now Mr. Ramsay prides himself on his boots, but essentially they are outside the realm of the personal, having nothing to do with the immediate relationship between himself and Lily; they are safe. On such grounds the two can come together, and, indirectly, without compromising herself, she can give him the admiration he needs. "They had reached, she felt, a sunny island where peace dwelt, sanity reigned and the sun for ever shone, the blessed island of good boots. Her heart warmed to him" (230). This is a spontaneous movement of affection, to be compared with her forced effort to "be nice" to Charles Tansley at the dinner party, an effort which undercut her integrity and made her feel that relations between men and women must inevitably be insincere (139). Here, Lily has enacted her resistance to Mr. Ramsay, and so can feel affection for him. Between Lily and Mr. Ramsay, between Virginia Woolf and her father, one has a sense of catharsis, of things having been worked out. "I used to think of him and mother daily," she wrote a year after *To the Lighthouse* was published, "but writing the *Lighthouse* laid them in my mind. And now he comes back sometimes, but differently. (I believe this to be true—that I was obsessed by them both, unhealthily; and writing of them was a necessary act.) He comes back now more as a contemporary." For a woman with a Stracheyan hatred of Victorianism to call him "more a contemporary" is equivalent to saying her feelings about him were no longer charged—they had reached the blessed island of good boots, where a man can be appreciated as a writer and thinker alone. "I must read him some day," she notes, all passion spent.[7]

The statements in her diary about her father and the statements in "Professions for Women" about the angel in the house—by extension, her mother—echo each other eerily: "His life would have entirely ended mine." "Had I not killed her she would have killed me." "What would have happened? No writing, no books." "She would have plucked the heart out of my writing." In both cases it is not so much her parents she must deny as a certain feminine role they sought, or she felt they sought, to impose on her.[8] Indeed, to succeed as a writer Woolf found it necessary to model herself largely on her father, adopting his compulsive methods of work, and rather laboriously acquiring a sense of self that ran the risk of becoming the "masculine" egotism she hated. Of the two relationships, however, I will continue to suggest that the one with her mother was the more significant in Virginia Woolf's psychic life—none the less so because of Julia's existence in Woolf's mind as a phantom model based

*The Stephen family, between 1890 and 1895, from a snapshot in Stella Duckworth's album. Virginia at lower right, leaning on Vanessa.*

partly on her childhood memories, partly on Leslie Stephen's idealization of his wife in "The Mausoleum Book," and partly on her own idealization of her sister, Vanessa Bell.

In developing a certain hardness and independence, Woolf felt herself turning away from her mother's model in a way she did not like. The attraction of that model is revealed in her attitude toward Vanessa Bell, who, although an artist herself, tends to appear in Virginia Woolf's mythology as a maternal figure, the one who inherited their mother's mantle and took the domestic path Virginia herself avoided. Typically, Woolf records in her diary the fear that she is getting too self-absorbed, too wrapped up in her own work, and immediately compares herself in this respect to her sister:

Now with middle age drawing on and age ahead it is important to be severe on such faults. So easily might I become a harebrained egotistic woman, exacting compliments, arrogant, narrow, withered. Nessa's children (I always measure myself against her and find her much the largest, most humane of the two of us), think of her now with an admiration that has no envy in it; . . . and how proud I am of her triumphant winning of all our battles; as she takes her way so nonchalantly, modestly, almost anonymously, past the goal, with her children round her.[9]

Between the lines we may see self-congratulation as well as self-reproach, but the dichotomy of roles is clear: on the one hand, the modest angelic woman who wafts through life with her children about her; on the other, the self-absorbed artist encased in the bubble of her dreams.

Woolf's letters to her sister reveal her sometimes quite conscious jealousy of Vanessa and illustrate the opposed roles she saw herself and her sister fulfilling. In 1926 she visits an exhibit of Vanessa's paintings and resents (or professes to resent) how good she finds them: Vanessa has the children; by rights the fame should belong to her, Virginia. She would have liked people to say that she had all the talent of the two, whereas Vanessa was merely a domestic body; unfortunately, after this exhibit, they will never say that. This train of thought is no less revealing if we assume that it is merely part of a graceful compliment. Another symptom of her jealousy of Vanessa is the frequency with which she feels impelled to defend the rigors of her own art and contrast it to the easy life of painters, who, for example, do not have to come to terms with the humanity of the dreary ladies of South Kensington, as the novelist does. The story goes that Virginia got into the habit of writing standing up when someone remarked that Vanessa had a harder time of it than she did, having to stand at an easel while Virginia could sit in a chair to read and write. The competition between them so pervades Woolf's view of herself that even her lesbian sympathies become a way of setting herself off from her sister. Vanessa, she writes, chooses impossible men as friends. It must be that Vanessa is magically affected by the male sex and sees splendors in men hidden to her; on the other hand, she, Virginia, can perceive the charm of her own sex in a way that will remain closed to her sister.

One can understand some of Virginia's fears, for there is an ease and largeness of gesture in Vanessa wholly lacking in her sister. People admired Virginia; they adored Vanessa. Her children, her lovers, her unconventional ménage, her frequent stays abroad give the impression of more fullness, certainly more movement, more activity, more attachments, in her life than in Virginia's. Virginia's existence, by contrast, seemed entirely cerebral: she wrote, she walked, she lived rather quietly. Understandably, Virginia was obsessed by the idea that her sister thought she led a dreary and respectable life. She could imagine her saying "Look at me now—only sixpence a year—lovers—Paris—life—love—art—excitement. God! I must be off!" and this would leave her in tears.[10] She could imagine Vanessa and Duncan Grant visiting her house and making fun of her decorations.

So Virginia was delighted when Vanessa liked *To the Lighthouse;* she had thought she could never win her sister's approval. Vanessa saw in Mrs. Ramsay "an amazing portrait" of their mother, and on reading the book she "found the rising of the dead almost painful."[11] Virginia, in reply, acknowledges her pleasure at the praise but professes bewilderment about how she had achieved such a likeness. Could a child have understood Julia Stephen? She supposes their mother had "cut a great figure" on her mind when it was just awakening and had little experience of life. But wouldn't such an image, born of loss, be a sham, idealized beyond recognition? "Probably," she writes, "there is a great deal of you in Mrs. Ramsay; though I think, in fact, you and mother are very different in my mind."[12] But then, she wonders, why does she attach so much importance to what Vanessa thinks of her? Perhaps the most striking thing about the charged and complex relationship between the sisters is that Vanessa has evidently assumed for Woolf some of the psychic status of her mother. The two women, mother and sister, were partially conflated, and their prime connection (for Vanessa Bell's bohemian existence differed vastly from her mother's staid, late-Victorian life) was their maternal character, their willingness to sacrifice themselves—and, to Virginia's great irritation in Vanessa's case, everyone else—to their children ("You would fry us all to cinders to give Angelica a day's pleasure").[13]

At the time of writing *To the Lighthouse*, Woolf had come to feel about maternity the way her sister felt about marriage, that is, philosophically opposed to it. Of the two relationships, motherhood seemed to her decidedly the more destructive, involving as it does profound instincts, deep and unscrupulous passions, whereas marriage was (in her view) at least potentially rational. (We might notice, parenthetically, that years have not changed Woolf's view of marriage as an emotionally tepid relationship, at its best a kind of enlightened companionship, supportive of industry and passion directed at other ends.) Occasional comments in her diary about children and about herself as a mother elaborate her mythology of choice. "And yet oddly enough," she writes at the age of forty-five, after admiring Vanessa's children, "I scarcely want children of my own now. This insatiable desire to write something before I die, this ravaging sense of the shortness and feverishness of life, make me cling . . . to my one anchor. I don't like the physicalness of having children of one's own."[14] Between children of the mind and children of the body she was clear as to which she wanted, but now and then one detects regret. In 1929, for example, in a moment of total despair, she writes, "There is nothing—nothing for any of us. Work, reading, writing are all disguises; and relations with people. Yes, even having children would be useless."[15]

On days of exhilaration, however, when writing was going well, it would be: "Children are nothing to this." The tension between the role she had chosen and the role she felt she had to reject was constant, and although she wrote several pieces to show why it was difficult for a woman to be an artist, I suspect she also worried about whether it was possible for an artist to be a woman.[16]

In *To the Lighthouse* Lily Briscoe, torn between her work and her attraction to Mrs. Ramsay's life, serves to focus, although not to resolve, I would argue, Woolf's ambivalence about her mother. Characteristically, Lily sees Mrs. Ramsay's life, that is, marriage, children, a dedication to the weaving of relationships between people, as an attack on her selfhood, a "dilution," a "degradation"; she will "put the tree further in the middle" (128), will devote herself to art instead. Nevertheless, Lily's response to Mrs. Ramsay's unwavering message—"they all must marry" and "an unmarried woman has missed the best of life"—is less than resolute: "She liked to be alone; she liked to be herself; she was not made for that"; and yet what she has in her life seems "so little, so virginal, against the other" (77). She compares Mrs. Ramsay's "abundance" with her own "poverty of spirit," and of course we recall how, in refusing to feign an unfelt sympathy for Mr. Ramsay, she comes to question her own femininity.

This conflict in Lily between two ways of life—dedication to self, being alone and working, as opposed to dedication to others—is no static weighing of abstract alternatives, no medieval debate between virginity and married life, nor could it have been such for Woolf. It is a highly charged emotional issue, pursued largely beneath the level of conscious thought. The following passage reveals something of the dynamics of the ambivalence, suggesting that at the very moment of creation, at the moment of greatest self-assertion, the psychological recoil is also greatest and Lily is most tempted to give up her effort and, in her own words, "to fling herself at Mrs. Ramsay's knee."

It was in that moment's flight between the picture and her canvas that the demons set on her who often brought her to the verge of tears and made this passage from conception to work as dreadful as any down a dark passage for a child. Such she often felt herself—struggling against terrific odds to maintain her courage; to say: "But this is what I see; this is what I see," and so to clasp some miserable remnant of her vision to her breast, which a thousand forces did their best to pluck from her. And it was then too, in that chill and windy way, as she began to paint, that there forced themselves upon her other things, her own inadequacy, her insignificance, keeping house for her father off the Brompton Road, and had much ado to control her impulse to fling herself (thank Heaven she had always resisted so far) at Mrs. Ramsay's knee and say to her—but what could one say to her? "I'm in love with you?" No, that was not true. "I'm in love with this all," waving her hand at the hedge, at the house, at the children (32).

Clearly, this concerns more than a choice between marriage and solitude; it suggests a fundamental ambivalence between a desire for self-definition and a desire for self-surrender, an almost childlike yearning for dependency.

To imitate someone is a way of possessing them: Mrs. Ramsay's way of life is closely connected with Mrs. Ramsay's affection, and we can sense in this passage the fear that in rejecting one, the self-assertive woman cuts herself off from the other. In rejecting her mother's model, in becoming a writer and killing the angel in the house, Virginia Woolf must surely have suffered in more ways than one. In addition to doubting her sexual identity, it would seem that she also felt painfully tempted, a lost child in a dark passage, to give up the effort of creation in exchange for maternal love and protection.

A rhythm of assertion and dependence was tragically in evidence in her life. Leonard Woolf has given us a valuable account of Virginia Woolf's illness in *Beginning Again,* listing four periods of insanity. The first followed the death of her mother and the second, the death of her father. The later ones, as Leonard points out, coincided roughly with completions of manuscripts—in 1913 after *The Voyage Out* was accepted for publication and in 1941 while she was polishing *Between the Acts;* furthermore, a comment in her diary in 1934 upon completion of the first draft of *The Years* reveals other periods of danger—that she was in "the same misery" after *The Waves,* and that after *To the Lighthouse* she was "nearer suicide, seriously, than since 1913."[17] Leonard Woolf attributes these attacks to "an almost pathological hypersensitiveness to criticism, so that she suffered an ever increasingly agonizing nervous apprehension as she got nearer and nearer to the end of her book and the throwing of it and herself to the critics."[18]

Publication repeated and magnified that simple situation which so terrified Virginia Woolf—being looked at. We recall that being photographed was agony for her and sitting for a portrait bust almost brought on a nervous breakdown. So revealing her soul in a book made for tremendous anxiety. People might say there was nothing there; she might bare her soul only to be told she had none. It is as though, having engaged in the enormously aggressive act of writing a book, she became overwhelmed by fears of her own emptiness, sterility, nullity. To put it in the terms I have been using, having denied her mother (or, more precisely, her mother's model) and having asserted herself strongly, she felt panic and a need to "fling herself at Mrs. Ramsay's knee," to become a child, dependent and protected. Many writers, of course, suffer from a kind of postpartum depression after finishing a book; what distinguishes Woolf's attacks is their intensity. For even when mild, her attacks, according to the treatment prescribed, rendered her helpless and reduced her to a situation very like infancy. She was required to stay in bed, needed constant nursing care, and, because of her refusal to eat at such times, she had to be fed by others. These periods of illness and the perpetual fear of them turned her husband into a kind of mother, always watching over her safety, and the fear that her fragile mental and physical constitution would not support the strain of maternity kept her from becoming a mother herself and taking care, rather than being taken care of.[19]

Without discounting either the genetic tendency toward some form of insanity which seems to have run through the Stephen family, or the possibly pathogenic effect of childhood experiences, I want to suggest that there was some connection between the outbreaks of Woolf's illness and her feeling that in being a writer she was doing something her family and society did not fundamentally support. A crude summary of the chain of causality might go like this: everyone loved her mother (and after her mother's death, her sister, so read "sister" interchangeably for "mother" in what follows). To be loved she must be like her mother. Committing herself to children of the mind over children of the body, art over people, is not being like her mother. Therefore, after producing each work of art, she feels excessively unlovable; having reasserted her difference from her mother, she fears people will ignore or reject her and needs excessive reassurance that she is loved and protected. While this particular psychic pattern is, I believe, Virginia Woolf's, the problem for women of achievement is no doubt general. George Eliot, another writer whose books were her children, with her pathetic susceptibility to attention was perhaps responding in her own way to similar pressures.

In *To the Lighthouse* Woolf dramatizes the working out of a way in which she can see herself as her mother's heir while still rejecting the model of womanhood she presents. She does this by conceptualizing Mrs. Ramsay as an artist, transforming the angel in the house, who had been for the Victorians an ethical ideal, into a portrait of the artist. Mrs. Ramsay is an artist working in human emotion and human relationships, but essentially she is engaged in "making of the moment something permanent (as in another sphere Lily herself tried to make of the moment something permanent)"

(241). As an artist her triumph is the dinner party in Part I, a *tour de force* in which she converts base emotions into gold filigree and weaves relationships between chaotic and recalcitrant masses. Even from an ordinary scene on the beach, with Lily and Charles Tansley squabbling, Mrs. Ramsay manages to create order and beauty. "She brought together this and that and then this, and so made out of that miserable silliness and spite" something which survived complete, a scene which "stayed in the mind affecting one almost like a work of art" (240).

If the dinner party is Mrs. Ramsay's triumph, it is also Virginia Woolf's triumph, for she of course created it in words—emotional minuets, enchanting hostess, *bœuf en daube*, and all. It is the finest section of the novel, and for the time she was working on it, Woolf must have felt the thrill not only of successful creation, but also of complete identification: Mrs. Ramsay's work of art was hers.

For the most part, however, the rhythm of ambivalence, of attraction and rejection, dominates the book, channeled through Lily, who can accept Mrs. Ramsay as a fellow-artist but wants to reject the preconditions of her art, the cultural formulae by which she works—that people must marry and have children, that women must sacrifice themselves in order to nourish men's egos, that men must need them to do so.

> Mockingly she seemed to see her there at the end of the corridor of years saying, of all incongruous things, "Marry, marry!" . . . And one would have to say to her, It has all gone against your wishes. They're happy like that; I'm happy like this. Life has changed completely. At that all her being, even her beauty, became for a moment, dusty and out of date (260).

But no sooner has Lily dismissed Mrs. Ramsay as old-fashioned than the old yearning returns:

To want and not to have, sent all up her body a hardness, a hollowness, a strain. And then to want and not to
have—to want and want—how that wrung the heart,
and wrung it again and again! Oh, Mrs. Ramsay! she
called out silently, . . . as if to abuse her for having
gone, and then having gone, come back again. It had
seemed so safe, thinking of her. Ghost, air, nothingness, a
thing you could play with easily and safely any time of
day or night, she had been that, and then suddenly she
put her hand out and wrung the heart thus (266).

Passages like this one were probably what Woolf had in mind
when she feared that people would find her novel sentimental. That almost inarticulate yearning, that unresolved ache
to have Mrs. Ramsay in the present even though she has been
irrevocably relegated to the past, that is where the author's
deepest feeling in *To the Lighthouse* lies. Here clearly is a
ghost that has not been laid to rest, and a relationship that
has not reached the island of good boots.

Readers of the novel, particularly men, are understandably attracted to Mrs. Ramsay—Julia Stephen goes on
in her fictional incarnation making people fall in love with
her—but to stop with simply loving her is not to experience
all that the novel asks you to. The novel asks you, I think, to
see her from Lily's point of view, to feel divided by love for
her and the need to reject her, to feel the love as a kind of
pull towards one identity, and to experience the pain and
guilt of separation almost more than love. More particularly,
if you are a woman, the novel makes you question how you
can be a woman without being Mrs. Ramsay. If you are determined not to be Mrs. Ramsay, if you resolve to draw your
skirts tighter about you as the pool of Mr. Ramsay's self-pity
widens at your feet, it makes you question whether it is not,
after all, poverty of spirit moving you to do so, or whether it
is really the intermittent need for self-containment that art,
or achievement of any sort, demands. *To the Lighthouse*, with
its superficially straightforward contrast of the male and fe-

male modes of Mr. Ramsay and Mrs. Ramsay, raises more questions than it answers about feminine identity.

Virginia Woolf had to pay an enormous psychic price for the privilege of writing. She was proud of the number of works she managed to write, and well she might have been, for every book was wrested from an enemy within, the angel in the house she never completely succeeded in killing. Perhaps because the mother she loved so perfectly embodied the Victorian ideal of womanhood, perhaps because no other image of womanhood was available, some part of Woolf judged herself by the standard she tried consciously to reject. The martyr of stereotypes she was trying to destroy, she nevertheless succeeded in illuminating in her fiction—preeminently in *To the Lighthouse*—the tensions and fears that can afflict a creative woman.

In writing this novel she did what she set out to do: she captured her father's character in words, and her mother's, and the ambiance of her childhood summers at St. Ives. Doing this, she felt released. Woolf, who usually struggled over every sentence, wrote this novel with unusual ease, and when she was done she felt freed from the ghosts of her parents, liberated from her bondage to the past. Yet at her most autobiographical and personal, Woolf writes the novel that, of all her work, is the most universal. Trying to recreate her past, she touches on a universal pool of fears and longings; *The Waves*, which strives so hard for universality, ends up being obscure and irritatingly subjective. Like one of Gertrude Stein's more abstract pieces, in an attempt to transcend the personal, it creates a lyric monotony into which few readers are willing to penetrate. But in writing *To the Lighthouse* part of Woolf's exorcism of her personal ghosts was to see them as cultural artifacts, monuments not only of personal history but of the history of us all. This specificity and historical perspective help raise *To the Lighthouse* from autobiography to the more general relevance of great fiction, and insofar as Victorian ideals of masculinity and femininity persist in many of us, the conflict she explores transcends the historical moment she began recording. Whether the novel truly released her from her bondage to the past, as she so much wanted to believe, is another matter entirely.

9

# V. Sackville-West and Androgyny

The second half of the twenties was Virginia Woolf's greatest period. After *Mrs. Dalloway* came *To the Lighthouse*, then *Orlando*, then *A Room of One's Own*—as a group, the most successful and invigorating of all her works. No accident, I think, that this was also the time when Woolf engaged most actively in the kind of feminist activity she considered appropriate, writing about women, considering women in the context of culture. Two excellent pieces on what have become feminist topoi, the essays on Mary Wollstonecraft and Dorothy Wordsworth, date from this period, along with sev-

175

eral other essays on women which appeared in *The Second Common Reader* and *The Moment*.[1] The major works—*Lighthouse, Orlando, A Room of One's Own*—are all in different ways concerned with sex roles, and all in different ways suggest the desirability of an end to rigid designations of what is masculine and what is feminine, an ideal which we might—very cautiously—refer to as androgyny.

Intimately connected with this period is V. Sackville-West, whom Woolf had known since 1922 and with whom she fell in love around 1925. It was a delightful and energizing experience for Virginia, her first great passion, none the less welcome because it came to her in her forties and was inspired by a woman. Indeed, looking back over her youthful romances with women, her lifelong love affair with her sister, her tepid physical response to men, and the obsession with her mother which underlies it all, it seems inevitable that whatever passion she had should be evoked by a woman. Inevitable, too, that Vita should be an aristocrat, with a family history stretching back to the Elizabethan Sackvilles, enlivened by a marriage to a gypsy, tied always to that great house, Knole, which Vita adored and which she was barred from inheriting because she was a woman.

Vita Sackville-West, a woman with the looks of a pedigreed setter, square of line, shaggy of coat, was a poet, novelist, biographer, and horticulturalist. As a writer, she was prolific, but hardly inspired. Her novels (the best of them is *The Edwardians*) appealed to popular taste, however, and she became one of the Hogarth Press's best-selling authors in the twenties. (Her given name was Victoria, her friends called her Vita, and V. Sackville-West was the name under which she wrote.) Her private life is fairly well documented through her extensive correspondence with her husband, parts of which he printed in his collected *Diaries and Letters*[2] and some of which appear in *Portrait of a Marriage*. In these documents, she and her husband sometimes appear to be snobs and anti-Semites, and so, to recapture the charm she projected to people who knew her, I would suggest two ways to view Vita: one is to see her as a gardener, for she was an inspired artist with flowers as she never was with words; the other is to see her through the eyes of Virginia Woolf.

To appreciate Vita, visit if you can the gardens at Sissinghurst, the Tudor castle in Kent which the Nicolsons bought in 1930, when it was little more than a junkyard with a few fine brick towers and walls, and which they turned into one of the most beautiful places in England. They covered the bare walls with vines and climbing roses. They built a series of gardens, spreading back from the central tower, in which Vita's romantic taste for abundance and Harold's classical feeling for structure combined to make a masterpiece. Vita's way with flowers was daring and unorthodox. She planted great masses of the same color, or in the same color range. (There is a breathtaking garden all of white flowers and gray and silver foliage). She allowed roses to grow freely without trimming them back to the roots every year. She under-planted and over-planted. She had spent time in Persia, and her color sense—she loved vibrant color—reminds one of Moslem mosaics. The way she writes about gardening, too, is delightful, for she talks about flowers as though they were people. Her collected articles on gardening are full of loving contemplations of specific flowers and inventive ideas on how to bring out the best in them.[3] One is grateful to people who have created beauty in whatever form, and one responds to loving people; V. Sackville-West loved flowers and she created, at Sissinghurst, something beautiful.

Looking at her through the eyes of Virginia Woolf, we see a wholly unconventional woman with a romantic past, her gestures large and generous, her indifference to propriety supreme. Her intelligence is not up to Virginia's and she writes with a pen of brass. But of what importance is that? Virginia had intelligence and talent enough for both of them. More importantly, Vita, like her gardens, was well-rooted and luxuriant of growth. A woman of supreme competency, able "to take the floor in any company, to visit Chatsworth, to control silver, servants, chow dogs." Virginia admired her for being a mother—despite her coldness to her children—for "being in short (what I have never been) a real woman."[4] Not the least of her appeal was that Vita lavished on her the maternal protection which Virginia had insight enough to realize was what she had always most wanted from everyone close to her.

Vita was forthright about her homosexuality, and the story of her remarkable marriage to Harold Nicolson, who was also homosexual, has been told by their son, making use of the Nicolsons' diaries and letters and of the memoir Vita wrote about her affair with Violet Keppel Trefusis, with whom, leaving her husband and family, she eloped to France. The two husbands came after the women and managed to return them to their families, in Vita's case, happily so, for she and Harold, though often apart, though frequently engaged in affairs with other people, remained close and indispensable to one another. When Vita met Virginia Woolf, the affair with Violet Trefusis was in the past, but she must have told Virginia about it and about the times, in London and in Paris, when she had dressed as a man to squire Violet about. She was, by her own account, remarkably successful in her imposture, walking down Piccadilly smoking a cigarette, buying a newspaper from a boy who called her "sir," taking a lodging-house room for the night with Violet, whom she told the landlady was her wife, penetrating even Knole in her disguise. Later, in Paris, she practically lived in the role, her hands and face browned, her head bandaged to imitate a veteran of the war. Violet called her Julian, and "Julian" and Violet strolled the boulevards, sat in cafés, went dancing; Vita had never felt so free in her life. "I never," she wrote, "appreciated anything so much as living like that with my tongue perpetually in my cheek, and in defiance of every policeman I passed."[5] Virginia was no doubt dazzled by these stories of sexual adventure and freedom—the kind of life she so much envied—and Violet turns up in *Orlando* as Sasha, the fascinating and elusive Russian princess, while the lady Orlando, like Vita, disguises herself as a man to enjoy the freedom of London.

One could view Vita's behavior condescendingly, as a forced, even tame piece of aristocratic bohemianism, her lesbianism no more than a chic French import, but she herself felt wracked by what she thought of as a dual personality, one in which masculine and feminine elements preponderated alternately. She wrote the account of her affair with Violet largely in the belief that in the future, the psychology of people like herself would become a matter of interest. "I believe it will be recognized that many more people of my type do exist than under the present-day system of hypocrisy is commonly admitted."[6] No doubt this view of herself as a strange and dubious hybrid of the sexes, more common than conventional thought would allow, was communicated to Virginia, for if it did not inspire it certainly reinforced Virginia's own concern at the time with the dubiety of sex and the arbitrariness of sex roles.[7]

A mock biography, *Orlando* (1928) parodies also unity of identity and unambiguous gender, for it begins with Orlando as a dashing young man at the time of Queen Elizabeth, follows him to Turkey as ambassador in the early seventeenth century, brings him back to England as a woman at the time of the Restoration, and follows her through the eighteenth century, when she is a friend of Pope and Swift, through the nineteenth, in which she responds to the cultural pressure to marry, to the present, at which time she is still in her early thirties. The very titles of the illustrations state the theme of sexual ambiguity: "Orlando as a Boy," "Orlando as Ambassador," "Orlando on her return to England." And when we compare the painting which serves to illustrate Orlando as ambassador with the photograph of V. Sackville-

West which represents Orlando on her return to England, we see little to distinguish their sex beyond the woman's décolletage, the man's goatee and mustache. The Jacobean Sackville, to be sure, has longer hair, but the astonishing physical resemblance between the two seems to transcend both time and sex.

Dedicated to V. Sackville-West, inspired by her character and her family's history, *Orlando* is a fantastically developed and embellished portrait of someone Woolf loves, a man-woman who is as much a family as an individual. Nigel Nicolson describes the book, with some truth, as the "most charming love letter in literature," in which the author explores her friend, "weaves her in and out of the centuries, tosses her from one sex to another, plays with her, dresses her in furs, lace, and emeralds, . . . drops a veil of mist around her, and ends by photographing her in the mud at Long Barn, with dogs, awaiting Virginia's arrival next day."[8]

Woolf herself called it a joke, a writer's holiday.[9] She wrote it very quickly, well within a year, and speed and laughter, gaiety and satire were part of the original design:

> Everything is to be tumbled in pell-mell. It is to be written as I write letters at the top of my speed. . . . My own lyric vein is to be satirized. Everything mocked. And it is to end with three dots . . . so. For the truth is I feel the need of an escapade after these serious poetic experimental books whose form is always so closely considered. I want to kick up my heels and be off.[10]

These high spirits sustained Woolf through the writing of the book. Rarely had she had so much fun, and one feels this in reading *Orlando* and loves it. It was written in a state of exuberance.

Among the many light-hearted impulses which form the creative thrust of this book—the impulse to parody biography, the impulse to portray Vita, the impulse to play with the history of the Sackvilles and of Knole, the impulse to recapitulate and parody the development of English literature

*Vita Sackville-West as "Orlando on her return to England," one of the illustrations in* Orlando *(1928).*

in terms of its styles—we should place (but gently, so as not
to upset the holiday balance of the novel) the impulse to
make a statement about women and creativity. For Orlando
is a writer, carrying along through the centuries the manuscript of an epic poem called "The Oak Tree." It may well be
that Woolf chose the Restoration as the appropriate moment
for Orlando to turn from a man into a woman because that
was the moment in English history when women first began
writing professionally. Of all the centuries, the nineteenth is
the only one which threatens to break Orlando's spirit (indeed it seems to dampen Woolf's spirit in the very process of
imagining it), but even then, by a dextrous compromise with
the spirit of the age, she manages to make peace and to bring
her poem, at long last, to completion. Like V. Sackville-
West's long poem, "The Land," which won the Hawthornden
Prize, "The Oak Tree" is published in the twenties and brings
Orlando, after all those years, recognition as a writer, in the
form of the "Burdett Coutts" Memorial Prize.

Orlando's sex change is the book's pivot, its central jest.
However, *Orlando* is no tragic story of a woman trapped in a
man's body, a man in a woman's. Orlando as a man is perfectly content, does not feel, in the jargon of theorists of androgyny, that he is leaving part of his human potential un-
fulfilled. In the early parts of the book, writing of a male
Orlando, Woolf is at her most fantastic. Letting her imagination race about, she plays with the rich Elizabethan prose
style she loved from her youth, when she read Hakluyt's
*Voyages.* Here we get the description of the frozen Thames,
the carnival on the ice, the romantic Russian princess with
whom Orlando falls in love. When Orlando changes sex, the
book shifts gears slightly. A note of didacticism enters. Sex
becomes problematic. Lapped in Padua silk, she/he cannot
express all of his/her personality. As a man, Orlando never
has to disguise himself as a woman, but as a woman Orlando dresses herself as a man in order to walk through
London alone at night, to talk to prostitutes, to recapture the
freedom and the range of experience she had as a man.

Orlando enters the female sex with the naive wonder of an eighteenth-century traveler returning to England from the land of the Houyhnhnms. No longer, she finds, can she do what she pleases. She must do what pleases men, "be obedient, chaste, scented, and exquisitely apparelled—things which require discipline since they do not come by nature."[11] No longer can she curse, or crack a man over the head, or tell him he lies, or run him through the body with a sword, or wear a coronet, or sit with her peers, or walk in procession, or sentence a man to death, or lead an army, or prance down Whitehall on a charger, or wear seventy-two different medals on her breast. All she can do is pour out tea and ask her guests how they like it: "D'you take sugar? D'you take cream?" As she minces the words, she is horrified to discover what a low opinion she is forming of the opposite sex, to which it was once her pride to belong, not so much because they keep women in subjection as because they are themselves women's fools, performing all those ludicrous actions (marching, fighting, wearing medals) in order to impress women, because the sight of a woman's ankle (in Orlando's metaphor) can make a sailor fall from the masthead. "Ignorant and poor as we are compared to the other sex . . . armoured with every weapon as they are, while they disbar us even from a knowledge of the alphabet . . . still— they fall from the masthead" (145–46).

Orlando discovers, in short, the privileges as well as the penalties of being a woman; she discovers the hidden sources of women's power, discovers how in submissiveness, in the game of resisting and yielding, or refusing to yield, pleasure may be found. In a twist of thought which should be familiar to us now, constructing out of women's disadvantages a basis for their distinction, Orlando concludes that it is better

> to be clothed with poverty and ignorance, which are the dark garments of the female sex; better to leave the rule and discipline of the world to others; better be quit of martial ambition, the love of power, and all other manly

desires if so one may more fully enjoy the most exalted
raptures known to the human spirit, . . . contemplation,
solitude, love" (146).

Orlando's arbitrary catalogue of the exclusive joys of
womanhood will not stand up to a moment's analysis—does
she really mean that men cannot indulge in contemplation,
solitude, or love?—nor were they intended to, for that
wretched hyperbole, "exalted raptures," signals that Woolf is
mocking, and mocking not only men, but these everlasting
distinctions between what is masculine and what is feminine. Because *Orlando* plays as fast and loose with history as
it does with sex, it is peculiarly structured to consider the effect of cultural conditioning on behavior, especially behavior
supposed to be innately male or female. Woolf seems to take
the position that while everyone has potentialities for male
and female behavior, cultural endorsement of one or the
other makes us limit our responses. To give a simple example, Orlando, as a man, felt the impulse to cry but only
allowed himself to cry when he became a woman. "Different
though the sexes are, they intermix. In every human being a
vacillation from one sex to the other takes place, and often it
is only the clothes that keep the male or female likeness,
while underneath the sex is the very opposite of what it is
above" (171–72).

Although it is spotted with such mini-manifestos on the
subjects of sexuality and women's condition, *Orlando*
presents so preeminently a mocking and satirical face that
one feels foolish taking them too seriously. The rapid pace,
the constant changes, the unfailing satire of the book have
the effect of leaving the reader thoroughly and comically
confused as to what sex is. Is it determined by one's drives (to
make war or babies, paintings or soups), or by one's genitals,
or by one's clothes? What do we mean when we say one sex
or the other is uppermost in a person? What do we signify by
talking of a man in a woman's body or a woman in a man's?

Isn't any sort of distinction between male and female charac-
teristics spurious? At the very least, crude?

In 1927, accompanied by Vita, Virginia Woolf went to lecture to some undergraduates at Oxford. The trip combined
business with the pleasure of a jaunt alone with Vita. She
found the young men callow, ignorant of both poetry and fiction, asking innocent questions about Joyce, about whether
Bell and Grant could make a living from decorations, about
whether Tom Eliot was happy with his wife. Her report to
Vanessa is much more concerned with Vita than with the
students,[12] and her lack of involvement with her audience on
this occasion contrasts strikingly with a similar expedition,
in October, 1928, when she went to Cambridge to give a
series of talks to the students of Newnham and Girton, the
women's colleges. It was, of course, a much more important
occasion than the earlier one, for from these talks on women
and fiction developed *A Room of One's Own.* In her diary she
noted that her audience looked "intelligent, eager, poor." "I
blandly tell them to drink wine and have a room of their
own. Why should all the splendour, all the luxury of life be
lavished on the Julians and the Francises?"[13] But bland is
hardly the word for *A Room of One's Own.*

    Virginia Woolf rarely lectured—I count three lectures, to
three different groups of students, between 1919 and
1929—but when she did, the results, revised of course for
publication, tended to be exceptional. She benefited from
knowing her audience. There is a strong sense of an audience
in *A Room of One's Own,* and it is an audience likely to bring
out the best in her. It is talented, but uncertain whether it
can accomplish anything. It is, of course, female. It feels simultaneously privileged and oppressed. It is a version of her
younger self. This audience Woolf addresses in what was apparently her usual speaking voice—elegantly silvery and
ladylike, never leaning hard on any point, yet trenchant.
Above all, jesting, bantering, full of playful irony which seeks

to be answered in kind. She assumes the role of a person of no particular distinction, no claim on their attention except that she has thought long and diligently over the subject assigned to her, "Women and Fiction." She places very little stress on the fact that she is herself a writer of fiction, a great deal on the fact that she is a woman, emphasizing what she has in common with her audience, that they are all women, all outsiders. Addressed to an audience of men, this delightful performance would perhaps be vulgarly seductive—a little too charming. But addressed to women, as it is, its seductiveness has rather a different edge. The tone of the piece is proof of what she had said in *Orlando* with perhaps too much insistence: women can like women. *A Room of One's Own* shows the same concern with restrictions on women, the same concern with creativity, the same concern with sexual polarization as *Orlando*.

Woolf writes about what she knows: how a woman's upbringing and social role impair her ability to produce works of art. One of her great strengths is to know her limitations, not to attempt to speak for everyone. As she said in her introduction to *Life as We Have Known It,* she could not speak for Mrs. Giles of Durham, because she had not stood over a tub and scrubbed the linen. But she had written books. She had struggled with her own feelings of inadequacy, and she knew where they came from. What is amazing to me is that no one had written anything like this book before, nor did anyone for some fifty years after again touch on this crucial subject, the relationship between sex, self-confidence, and creativity.

Most of the book deals with ways in which self-confidence and a sense of independent worth have been bred out of women, making it difficult if not impossible for them to create works of art. Lack of experience, lack of education, sex roles which demand that women stay in the home and put their energies in the service of men—these factors weigh heavily against a woman who wants to write. But then Woolf turns from the original question, "What conditions are necessary for the creation of works of art?"—to which the answer is the metaphorical room and income, signifying independence and solitude—to another question: "What is needed to produce *great* works of art?" She examines *Jane Eyre,* deciding it is a flawed novel because Charlotte Brontë's anger and indignation at her lack of opportunity have made themselves heard. Anger tampered with her integrity. "She left her story, to which her entire devotion was due, to attend to some personal grievance. She remembered that she had been starved of her proper due of experience—she had been made to stagnate in a parsonage mending stockings when she wanted to wander free over the world." [14] No longer disinterested, she has allowed her own personality and her own history to intrude into her fiction. The final obstacle a woman writer has to overcome, it seems, is her own resentment. The great mind, outrageously to mix metaphors, cannot have a chip on its shoulder. But the metaphor Woolf herself chooses to suggest the state of disinterestedness necessary to create great art is characteristically sexual. She adopts Coleridge's notion that great minds, fully creative minds, are "androgynous."

The concept of androgyny is currently receiving a good deal of attention, and for some people it is a utopian ideal, a blending of masculine and feminine elements in the personality so that in every person the full range of his or her impulses is expressed. [15] A more skeptical perspective holds that in such a formulation one idea, the idea of the feminine, is added to another idea, the idea of the masculine—neither idea grounded in anything pre-existing and real—to form an illusory whole which is greater than the sum of its illusory parts. [16] In other words, the skeptical view questions whether there really are masculine and feminine elements which, like hydrogen and oxygen, can be combined. It tends to invoke androgyny to signify cultural opposition to the culturally constructed polarization of sexes.

At first glance, Virginia Woolf would seem to be in the camp of those who believe in masculine and feminine elements as they would in oxygen and hydrogen. Only when a fusion takes place between the male and female parts of the brain, she says, is the mind fully fertilized and able to use all its faculties. "Perhaps a mind that is purely masculine cannot create, any more than a mind that is purely feminine" (148). But I would argue that, in this highly metaphorical treatise, which makes its case by images (five hundred pounds, a room of one's own), this statement about the androgynous mind is the final image, a metaphor which employs sexual terms to signify the transcendence of sex.

When she examines Coleridge's notion of the androgynous mind, she insists first of all that androgyny does not mean simply a redressing of the balance of sexual concern. "Coleridge certainly did not mean, when he said that a great mind is androgynous, that it is a mind that has any special sympathy with women; a mind that takes up their cause or devotes itself to their interpretation" (148). When she speculates on what he did mean, sexual qualities are conspicuously absent. This androgynous mind is no mere union of masculine intellect and feminine intuition, for example, or of masculine assertion and female sympathy. Coleridge meant, "perhaps, that the androgynous mind is resonant and porous; that it transmits emotion without impediment; that it is naturally creative, incandescent and undivided." The emphasis is on ease and spontaneity, on the absence of propaganda and self-justification. Self-assertion is as bad for a woman's art as it is for a man's. "It is fatal for a woman to lay the least stress on any grievance; to plead even with justice any cause; in any way to speak consciously as a woman. And fatal is no figure of speech; for anything written with that conscious bias is doomed. It ceases to be fertilized" (157). The great writer must rise above sex to achieve that fertile disinterestedness which she signifies by the word androgyny.

Shakespeare is the type of the androgynous mind as he

was, to Keats, the supreme exemplar of "negative capability," the ability to remain in doubt, to refrain from making
up one's mind, to enjoy both fair and foul, rich and poor,
high and low, the creation of an Iago as much as the creation
of an Imogen. The "chameleon poet," Keats called him; he
might have said androgynous poet. For what Keats meant by
negative capability and what Woolf meant by the androgynous mind are, I suspect, much the same thing. Keats
exclaimed against poetry "that has a palpable design upon
us—and if we do not agree, seems to put its hand in its
breeches pocket"; he imagines how we would come to hate
the very flowers of the field if they took to exclaiming, "Admire me I am a violet!" [17] So Woolf feels about the self-assertive virility of, for example, Kipling's fiction: "One blushes
. . . as if one had been caught eavesdropping at some purely
masculine orgy" (154). Keats she includes with Shakespeare
in the ranks of the androgynous; Wordsworth is pointedly
excluded.

In an essay written three years before *A Room of One's
Own*, Woolf uses a rather different metaphor to describe that
state of "incandescence," of disinterestedness, which typifies
the creative mind working at the top of its bent. "When a
crack player," she writes, "is in the middle of an exciting
game of baseball he does not stop to wonder whether the audience likes the color of his hair." His entire mind is on the
game.[18] This strangely American image is no accident, for
Woolf is writing on American fiction, and, in seeking to understand the problems of American writers in creating a gen-
uinely expressive native fiction, she is struck by the analogy
between them and that other "underdeveloped" race of
writers, women. The first step in the process of being an
American writer is "not to be English," to abjure mere imitation. But the second step is even more difficult. "For having decided what he is not, he must proceed to discover what
he is." The ensuing stage of acute self-consciousness, often accompanied by bitterness, reminds Woolf of women writers.
Sherwood Anderson and Dreiser, in very different ways, are

unable to forget they are Americans, and one senses assertive pride or bitterness that flaws their work: they are the Charlotte Brontës of this essay. To Woolf, Ring Lardner is an example of a writer who transcends the stage of self-consciousness, playing the game with such intensity that he forgets to wonder what the audience thinks of his hair color, or of the fact that he is American. This transcendence of personality is the third stage in the threefold process Woolf outlines: rejection, self-assertion, transcendence.

The American context for this discussion of the growth of a writer's sense of identity is useful because it counterpoints the discussion in *A Room of One's Own* and illuminates the essential irrelevance of sex to the androgynous ideal. It makes as much sense, or as little, to talk of the necessary marriage of English and American traits in the greatest literature as it does to talk of the marriage of male and female traits. Androgyny is a temporary metaphor, appropriate in the context of an essay on women and fiction, but baseball—the passion with which it is played—serves as well in a discussion of Americans and fiction.

To urge the women in her audience not to write merely as women is a fitting conclusion for her talk. To urge an escape from the personal is a respectable notion, allying Woolf in various ways with Keats, Carlyle, Joyce, and Eliot, although the twentieth century has not come to accept as inevitable the idea that the artist must be free from the taint of personality. It may be that Woolf's best work was done in a certain translucence of spirit: rage, it is true, betrayed her into didacticism, and yet mockery and irritation served her well. She wrote best, as she herself said of her imagined novelist, Mary Carmichael, when she "wrote as a woman, but a woman who has forgotten that she is a woman, so that her pages were full of that curious sexual quality which comes only when sex is unconscious of itself" (140).

In the next phase of Woolf's career, it was harder for her to strike the balance of tranquility.

Throughout 1926 and 1927 Virginia and Vita frequently spent weekends together, either at Long Barn, Vita's impressively planted and much-restored house in Kent, or at Virginia's place in Sussex, Monk's House, which the Woolfs had bought in 1919—an unpretentious cottage fronting the main street of the tiny village of Rodmell, a house of low-ceilinged rooms, with little luxury but with a certain cozy charm, and, at the back, a good view and lovely garden. Sometimes Leonard would go to London on Thursday, and then they could have the whole weekend at Rodmell alone. Virginia was self-conscious about their nights together and concerned about handling Leonard tactfully: she tried to remember, when she went to Long Barn, to invite Leonard to come, too. When the Woolfs stayed with Vita, Leonard would generally leave on Sunday night and Virginia would stay until Monday, but in this situation, too, she tried to act considerately and occasionally made a point of going home with Leonard.

Vita, who fell in love frequently and was experienced in extramarital romances, confessed her love for Virginia frankly to her husband but downplayed the importance in the affair of physical passion. She was afraid of arousing physical feelings in Virginia because of her madness.

> I don't know what effect it would have, you see: it is a fire with which I have no wish to play. I have too much real respect and affection for her. Also she has never lived with anyone except Leonard, which was a terrible failure, and was abandoned quite soon. So all that remains an unknown quantity; and I have got too many dogs not to let them lie when they *are* asleep. . . . Besides, Virginia is not the sort of person one thinks of in that way. There is something incongruous and almost indecent in the idea. I *have* gone to bed with her (twice), but that's all.[19]

As for Virginia, whatever went on in bed, the idea of having a lesbian affair seems to have excited her enormously.

If she was tactful with Leonard, she was downright boastful to Vanessa. She refers to Vita as her lover, she eagerly anticipates the nights alone with her, she twits Vanessa for refusing to respond to Vita's charms.

> You will never succumb to the charms of any of your sex. What an arid garden the world must be for you! What avenues of stone pavements and iron railings. Greatly though I respect the male mind, and adore Duncan (but, thank God, he's hermaphrodite, androgynous, like all great artists) I cannot see that they have a glow worm's worth of charm about them. The scenery of the world takes no lustre from their presence. They add of course immensely to its dignity and safety; but when it comes to a little excitement—![20]

It is, of course, one of the set pieces of their rivalry, one of those topics of continuing semi-jocular debate, women vs. men, writing vs. painting, motherhood vs. marriage. Nonetheless one senses—and the writing of *Orlando* proves—how precious Vita was to her, and how invigorating was the secret (for it was a secret from most of her friends) that she was at last in love.

Some people work best when they are in love, and being in love with V. Sackville-West certainly seems to have fueled Virginia Woolf's imagination. If she did not become, under Vita's influence, a mouthpiece for Sapphism—as she called herself, somewhat extremely, in describing a story about subdued erotic feeling between two women, a music teacher and her student, which ends with the older woman kissing the younger on the lips[21]—she freed herself, in her writing and in her life, of many vestiges of Victorian assumptions about sex, as, in 1927, she rid herself of the long coil of hair she had carried around with her since childhood.[22] In 1928, at the time of the publication of *Orlando*, with its suggestion of sexual unorthodoxy, she found the courage to take a trip to France alone with Vita and to protest the banning of Radclyffe Hall's lesbian novel, *The Well of Loneliness*, both in a letter to the *Nation and Atheneum* and by a personal appearance at Bow Street court.[23] But most importantly, her work of this time is buoyed up by a frank concern and affection for women. Her lesbianism, so much of it a matter of political strategy as well as physical impulse, reinforces her feminism, which was based on her reasoning from personal experience to general condition; and her feminism, thus understood, is the key to her flowering in the late twenties.

> There was a division between her and other people which she attempted—not quite satisfactorily perhaps— to bridge by questions. She enquired of everyone end- lessly about his or her life: of writers how and why they wrote, of a newly married young woman how it felt to be a bride, of a bus conductor where he lived and when he went home, of a charwoman how it felt to scrub floors. Her strength and her limitations were that she didn't really know how it felt to be someone else. What she did know was how it felt to be alone, unique, iso- lated, and since to some extent this is part of a univer- sal experience, to express this was to express what many feel. . . . What bound people together escaped her. What separated them was an object of wonder, delight and despair.[24]

Stephen Spender's acute description captures an important part of Virginia Woolf, her isolation, but it ignores her feminism. It was only through her sense of herself as a woman and her feelings about other women, her sympathy for the limitations on their lives, that she did participate in a communal life, a life beyond the personal. Feminism was her channel for social concern, and to ignore it is to reduce her to the ranks of those who record the flarings up and dyings down of their own wavering egos and nothing more.

# 10

# The Thirties

In 1932 Virginia Woolf was fifty years old. Her reputation as a novelist was so firmly established that critics had begun to fight about the ultimate value of her work. Muriel Bradbrook in *Scrutiny* accused her, in effect, of being a feather brain.[1] Wyndham Lewis, who had satirized Bloomsbury in *The Apes of God* (1930), devoted a chapter to ridiculing Virginia Woolf in *Men Without Art* (1934).[2] But if these attacks were distressing, her allies could be equally unnerving. The first academic studies of Woolf's work were published around 1932 (one French, one German), along with a readable biography by Winifred Holtby.³ Woolf received these books warily. They were danger signals at best, tombstones at the worst. She was obsessed, as she had been for ten years, with growing old, and she was especially concerned about being made a monument before her time.

By the thirties, the general public seemed conditioned to respond to her work at the very least respectfully. *The Waves* (1931) confirmed her reputation as an experimental writer and, although it is a much less vital book than *To the Lighthouse*, was hailed as her masterpiece. *The Years* (1937), perhaps because it was a refreshingly accessible work from a writer reputed to be difficult, turned into her greatest popular success. So, although her writing in the thirties is the weakest of her career, she enjoyed at that time the greatest prestige, the accumulated reward of a lifetime of work. Honors were offered insistently. In 1932 she was asked to deliver the Clark lectures at Cambridge, an honor indeed, for she was the first woman ever asked. "Think of me," she wrote in her diary, "the uneducated child reading books in my room at 22 H.P.G.—now advanced to this glory."⁴ She refused. She was too busy, but she also rather liked the idea of being offered and refusing a position her father had held. She was offered honorary degrees—from Manchester and Liverpool. She refused them, too, declining to be assimilated into a patriarchal educational establishment which, as she continued to feel, had excluded her when she needed it. She was offered royal honors (Companion of Honour) and refused them in the same intransigent spirit. But to stop the process of becoming a public figure was beyond her control. Whether she wanted it or not, she was now part of the establishment, and the woman who had formed her character upon being a rebel against the social and literary conventions of her father's world became in her turn the target of a younger generation of writers and intellectuals. The key issue was the relationship between art and politics, for as fascists gained power in one country after another, as Europe moved towards World War II, events seemed in the grip of forces too powerful to be dealt with by reason. As young men wanted to fight, Bloomsbury pacifism seemed outdated and the art of Virginia Woolf irresponsibly solipsistic.

It must have been in the early thirties that the difference between the older and the younger generations became—along with the difference between writers and painters—a set piece in the conversation of Virginia, Vanessa, and their friends, for when her nephew, Julian Bell, went to Cambridge, Virginia could be sure that another generation was about to come of age. In some ways Julian seemed a reincarnation of Thoby Stephen, naturally magnetic, vigorous, attractive, although Virginia, in her memoir of Julian, confessed she did not like the comparison.[5] Thoby had been pure Stephen; Julian's blood was diluted by the Bells. She acknowledges the snobbishness of this, and acknowledges too the various kinds of jealousy which complicated her relationship with Julian—jealousy that Vanessa should have such a child and also "generation jealousy." For Julian wrote poetry, considered himself a writer, and Virginia did not particularly encourage him. With some justice, she considered his writing sloppy and self-indulgent, but after his death, she wondered how much of her response to his work had been prompted by honesty and how much by jealousy.

If Virginia was wary of her nephew, Julian, despite his great fondness for his aunt and his passionate attachment to his mother, had serious misgivings about the values of the two sisters and their friends. In some ways, it was a perfectly ordinary case of generation gap, but because of the dramatic way in which Julian's later years—and particularly his decision to go to Spain—embody the reaction against Bloomsbury typical of much of his generation, it bears looking into.[6]

Julian grew up in the company of Clive and Vanessa Bell, Roger Fry, Duncan Grant, Leonard and Virginia Woolf, J. M. Keynes, and E. M. Forster. He joked with Virginia, talked politics with Leonard, played chess and talked art with Roger. Still, by the time he reached Cambridge, he had compressed these figures of his childhood and youth into an orthodoxy, Bloomsbury, towards which he felt a violent see-sawing of love and distrust which it seems inadequate to call ambivalence. "Bloomsbury" meant liberalism and the belief that through the application of reason all problems could be solved and the good be made to prevail. It meant the savoring—according to the precepts of G. E. Moore—of certain states of mind. It meant pacifism and a devotion to the arts. While Julian was supremely happy with his family—indeed, nowhere more so—and enjoyed the good life at Charleston, his Marxist logic made him see their leisured cultivation as a privileged anachronism, a fragile remnant of bourgeois capitalism. "I can't see," he wrote to Lytton Strachey's niece, Janie Bussy, "how anyone with a decent intelligence can fail to see the intellectual irrefutability of the general Marxist hypothesis, and how anyone who has had the advantages of bourgeois civilization, pheasant shooting, leisure, the company of Roger [Fry] and Goldie [Goldsworthy Lowes Dickinson], can help seeing that even the best the revolution can offer is fifth-rate by comparison."[7]

Somewhat at loose ends after his departure from Cambridge, where he had stayed beyond the normal time trying for a fellowship, he elected in 1935 to go to China, to be professor of English at Wuhan University. Partly it was an attempt to strike out for himself in a new direction, and secretly he hoped that he might get involved in revolutionary activity. But China did not help to resolve his ambivalences. He turned at least one of his courses, a survey of English literature, into an introduction to Bloomsbury; he saw constant, welcome resemblances between the landscape of China and that of Sussex, between the life of a small provincial faculty and that of Bloomsbury; and by walking, shooting, sailing, and engaging in love affairs which he wrote home about in detail, he tried to reproduce what he liked so much about English country life.

At the same time, in three essays written as a testament to his generation, he codified his position in regard to his past and rationalized a rejection of his parents' values. In these public statements he exaggerated the gap between art and politics, regally preempting the latter realm for himself and his peers: "Like nearly all intellectuals of this generation, we are fundamentally political in thought and action: this more than anything marks the difference between ourselves and our elders."[8] In an essay on Roger Fry, who had recently died, Julian declares Fry's preoccupation with the arts to be inexplicable to his generation. That a man with such intellectual power could find complete satisfaction in a contemplative, disinterested life is hard for Julian to understand. And yet it may be hard for us to understand how a man who goes to the trouble of having a sailboat made to order in the middle of China and looks to the shooting of birds for the preservation of his sanity can regard himself as "fundamentally political in thought and action." In retrospect it seems that the chief difference between Julian's generation and their elders—or perhaps we should rather say Julian, and not make him carry the entire burden of his generation, as he seems willing enough to do—the difference between Julian, then, and his elders is that he preferred to *think* of himself and present himself publicly as fundamentally political.

Julian at this age—he was twenty-eight in 1936—was still a puzzled mixture of what he was by nature and what he wanted himself to be. Take pacifism, the most important of the issues to divide him from his mother. Grant, Strachey, and Garnett were all conscientious objectors in World War I, and Vanessa and Virginia were both pacifists by belief. Julian, raised among pacifists, had been himself a pacifist all through Cambridge; but his pacifism, like that of most of his generation at Cambridge, endured little beyond a large anti-war demonstration in 1933 and gave way to a militant activism that radically altered the atmosphere of the university.⁹ Julian since childhood had loved to play war games and was fascinated by strategy. Writing to his mother, explaining his turn against pacifism, he referred to his "mental kink" of savoring war as an art or a science which he thought might be a "freakish and slightly neurotic reaction" to his pacifist childhood.¹⁰ Neurotic or not, his last essay, written on the way back from China as an open letter to E. M. Forster, is a defense of war and an encomium on the military virtues. While illogical and badly organized, this defense of barbarity is great fun to read, as are all attempts to shock people in their most solemnly held beliefs. To praise soldiers to E. M. Forster was rather like baring one's bottom to Queen Victoria. The essay also proclaims Julian's serious conviction that the good must be fought for and perhaps even forced upon people, that it would not prevail through education and enlightenment.

In 1936 the Spanish Civil War provided a focus for Julian's desire for political action. Here was a chance to put his opinions into practice, not merely to be anti-fascist, but to fight against fascism. (His affair with a Chinese faculty wife had been discovered by her husband, so there were other reasons why it was convenient for him to leave China now.) He resigned his professorship and returned to England to try to convince his mother that fighting in Spain was the right thing for him to do. Their relationship had always been exceptionally close, and Vanessa was distraught at the idea of Julian risking his life in a war, distraught as a mother, opposed as a pacifist. Eventually they compromised: he would go to Spain, but as an ambulance driver, not as a soldier. Nevertheless, soon after his arrival in Spain in July 1937, after sending home a few excited letters ("It's a better life than most I've led"),¹¹ he was killed by the explosion of a bomb. His last coherent words were, "Well, I've always wanted a mistress and a chance to go to war, and now I've had both."[12] At the end of the three-week Brunete campaign, which ended in a stalemate and in which Julian lost his life, half of the British Medical Unit had been killed.

*Journey to the Frontier*, Peter Stansky and William Abrahams' account of the lives of Julian Bell and John Cornford and the paths by which these two young English intellectuals reached the same fate in Spain, investigates with great subtlety and wisdom the complex of motives—personal and psychological drives as well as consciously held beliefs—which impelled Julian to want to fight. Certainly there was some silliness involved. Julian liked activity, so he argued for the superiority of the active life over the contemplative, and shooting pheasants in Sussex seems to modulate rather too flawlessly into shooting fascists in Spain. His knowledge of the intricacies of politics within the anti-fascist forces was crude, and later generations who have had the benefit of reading *Homage to Catalonia*, with its disturbing account of the suppression by the Communist Party of non-Communist elements on the left, like the anarchists, may pity Julian for offering his life in a cause so murky, so far from the clearcut confrontation between popular revolution and fascist dictatorship he imagined. Yet surely, if one can believe in heroism at all, there was heroism in Julian's choice, a courageous belief that if you opposed something, you had to oppose it with your very life. The fascists were taking over Europe. To sit at home and write articles against them to be read only by other English intellectuals seemed an inadequate response. So it would be absurd to say that Julian's political activism was merely a self-defining reaction to the values of his parents' generation. But separate them, set one generation off from the other, it certainly did.

When the news of Julian's death reached England, Vanessa took to her bed, almost out of her mind with grief. To Virginia, it seemed a senseless death. Ultimately, she could not understand what had made Julian go to Spain:

> What made him feel it necessary, knowing as he did how
> it must torture Nessa, to go? . . . He knew that: & yet
> deliberately inflicted this fearful anxiety on her. What
> made him do it? I suppose its a fever in the blood of the
> younger generation which we can't possibly understand.
> I have never known anyone of my generation have that
> feeling about a war. We were all C.O.'s in the Great war.
> And although I understand that this is a "cause," can be
> called the cause of liberty & so on, still my natural reac-
> tion is to fight intellectually: if I were any use, I should
> write against it. . . . The moment force is used, it be-
> comes meaningless & unreal to me. And I daresay he
> would have lived through the active stage, & have found
> some other, administrative work. But that does not ex-
> plain his determination.[13]

Clearly for Woolf the personal commitment (how could he go
when he knew it would torture his mother?) took precedence
over a public commitment (fighting for the "cause of liberty
& so on") which seems nebulous and unreal. She did not understand that this was precisely the point, for insofar as Julian's determination to go to Spain was a gesture, it pro-
claimed the importance of public commitments over private
ones.

The world of letters reflected the change of emphasis from
private values to public ones. George Orwell, writing in
1938, provides an evenhandedly weary overview of the
change in the literary climate from the twenties to the thirties. According to Orwell, the keynote of the twenties writers
is "the tragic sense of life."

> What "purpose" they have is very much up in the air.
> There is no attention to the urgent problems of the mo-
> ment, above all no politics in the narrower sense. Our
> eyes are directed to Rome, to Byzantium, to Montpar-
> nasse, to Mexico, to the Etruscans, to the Subconscious,
> to the solar plexus—to everywhere except the places
> where things are actually happening.[14]

Russia means Dostoevsky and Tolstoy and exiled counts driving taxicabs, not the Revolution. Rome means art galleries, not Blackshirts and Mussolini. These writers (he is talking most particularly of Lawrence and Eliot) see life comprehensively, more so than the writers who succeeded them, but even the best of them can be "convicted of a too Olympian attitude, a too great readiness to wash their hands of the immediate practical problem." Then, between 1930 and 1935, a new group, "Auden and Spender and the rest of them," appears, and "suddenly we have got out of the twilight of the gods into a sort of Boy Scout atmosphere of bare knees and community singing. The typical literary man ceases to be a cultured expatriate with a leaning towards the Church, and becomes an eager-minded schoolboy with a leaning towards Communism." "Serious purpose" replaces "tragic sense of life" as the keynote.[15]

Ultimately, it was through Julian that Virginia Woolf came to know the younger generation of writers ("Spender and the rest of them"), for Julian brought his Cambridge friends home just as Thoby had two decades before. When, in 1931, the Woolfs decided they needed help with the Hogarth Press, they chose Julian's friend John Lehmann to be manager, with the prospect of becoming eventually a partner. At the time, Lehmann was one more of those rosy-cheeked, golden-haired, goodlooking, intelligent, poetry-writing youths that Oxbridge turned out, but he was also exceptionally inventive, sensitive to contemporary literature, sound in judgment. And he had wide contacts. A master anthologizer, he produced in 1932 *New Signatures*, a volume which, by putting together the "Oxford poets"—Auden, Spender, and C. Day Lewis—and the "Cambridge poets,"—including Empson, Eberhart, Julian Bell, and Lehmann himself—and by presenting them as a united front created in the mind of the public a new literary movement.

To this talented young man, both Leonard and Virginia Woolf were, at the time he met them, already legendary. His attitude toward her was one of hero-worship.[16] Whereas at

*Leonard and Virginia Woolf, with their dog, in 1939.*

first he "revered" her, considering her the "sacred centre" of her circle, the most gifted, adored and feared, he came in time to feel less awe-struck affection. She took an interest in his life; she questioned him about his work, his goals. But the feeling of *de haut en bas*, one imagines, was never entirely lost. The relationship with Lehmann went smoothly only so long as he was content to consider himself a literary neophyte sitting at the Woolfs' feet. As the promised partnership became more of a reality, the relationship became so strained that in 1932 Lehmann left, not to return until 1938 when he bought out Virginia's share of the press and became a full partner.[17]

Through Lehmann, Stephen Spender entered the Woolfs' orbit. Writing twenty years later, Spender retains a view of Bloomsbury which was typical of the thirties. First of all, he thought in terms of "Bloomsbury"—he saw a group, not a collection of individuals with different ideas and tastes. Secondly he saw a privileged caste. In describing his entry into this pleasant world, Spender tries not to be harsh:

> In order to produce a few works which seem likely to live, and a great many witty, intelligent, and graceful conversation pieces, they needed to nourish themselves on a diet of the arts, learning, amusement, travel, and good living. They certainly were not malicious exploiters of their fellow men, and they expected less reward than the bureaucratically favoured Soviet writer receives today. At the same time, their standard of "five hundred pounds a year and a room of one's own" . . . made them decidedly unwilling to sacrifice their independence to the cause of the working-class struggle.[18]

The most remarkable thing about Spender's comments—and this is by no means unusual in the thirties—is that "Bloomsbury" is attacked not on aesthetic grounds, for the quality of its work, but on economic grounds, because it makes too much money. That "room of one's own" was to be flung in Woolf's face again and again. Dmitri Mirsky's attack in *The Intelligentsia of Great Britain* (1935) is even more dogmatically Marxist and unites a critique of Bloomsbury capitalism with one of capitalist consciousness in their work: "Being theoreticians of the passive, dividend-drawing and consuming section of the bourgeoisie, they are extremely intrigued by their own minutest inner experiences, and count them an inexhaustible treasure store. . . ."[19] Compared to this, Spender's critique of Bloomsbury seems mild, but it is founded on the same resentment of bourgeois individualism and privilege.

Living in their small country houses, their London flats, full of taste, meeting at week-ends and at small parties, discussing history, literature, gossiping greatly, and producing a few very good stories, they resembled those friends who at the time of the Plague in Florence withdrew into the countryside and told the stories of Boccaccio. Our generation, unable to withdraw into exquisite tale-telling and beautiful scenery, resembled rather the *Sturm und Drang* generation of Goethe's contemporaries, terribly involved in events and oppressed by them.[20]

The problems of unemployment, economic crisis, nascent fascism, and approaching war were hardly unknown and undiscussed in the Woolf household. Leonard was deeply involved in Labour Party politics, and John Maynard Keynes, one of their closest friends, had foreseen as early as 1919 the economic crisis and probable war that would ensue from the settlement of World War I made at Paris.[21] Even Spender concedes that Leonard and Virginia Woolf "were among the very few people in England who had a profound understanding of the state of the world in the 1930's."[22] But in the first flush of popular Marxism and in the process of defining themselves and their distinctive goals, the young writers of the thirties flattened the writers of the twenties (and there is no doubt about it—by this time Virginia Woolf had become a "twenties" writer) into precious technicians, with no roots in contemporary or popular life, sublimely unconcerned with any problems beyond those of their own sensibilities. Thus began, in the crisis-ridden days of the thirties, the myth of Bloomsbury which has lasted until recently.

For Virginia Woolf, there must have been a sense of *déjà vu* about her encounter with the young men of Oxford and Cambridge in the thirties, only the work of alienation performed earlier by sex was now accomplished by the difference in age. Julian's friends were much like Thoby's had been, even if their arrogance was founded on Marxism and their feeling of ties to the working class rather than on Moore's rationalism and the conviction of privilege; and the literary aristocracy—Auden, Spender, Isherwood—was as aggressively homosexual as Strachey had been twenty years before, though not as given to public display of it. Virginia called them the "niminy-piminies—the Stephens and Williams, whose minds are refrigerators, and souls blank paper,"[23] and if Spender thought that Virginia and her friends did nothing but gossip and talk of art, Virginia feared that Spender talked only of Spender.[24]

It might be said that the manifest issue dividing the generations was the relationship between art and politics, but to state it that way is to adopt the viewpoint of the younger generation. Art versus politics was their topos. Spender notes that he and Virginia Woolf did not differ about issues. She hated fascists, sympathized with the Spanish Republicans, held much the same political views as he did. "But she objected to the way in which our writing was put to the service of our views, and she discerned that my generation were 'sold' to the public sometimes more on account of their views than for the merit of their writing."[25] But when we look to Woolf's work, we see that something else is on her mind.

*A Letter to a Young Poet* (1932) and *The Leaning Tower* (1940) are the works in which Woolf launches attacks on the younger generation of writers. In the earlier essay she quotes Auden, Day Lewis, Spender, and Lehmann to show that contemporary poetry tries too hard to include the intractable, essentially unpoetic material of everyday life. It is a mulish argument, and astonishing from the publisher of *The Waste Land*. What she really wants to tell young poets comes at the end of the essay and is, bluntly, "Don't publish." Rip it up, scrap it, hide it—at least until you are thirty. She had come to find distasteful the urge of the young to see their work in print. She would later become conscious of having reached in 1935 a stage of hating personality, desiring anonymity in writers, but in fact this "standpoint," from which the very act of submitting for publication smacked of egocentricity, was evident rather earlier.[26]

*The Leaning Tower* is not really concerned with art and politics in the narrow sense, either, although it, too, vents her irritation at the up-and-coming writers. Briefly, it argues that all art rests on a basis of capital and education, a tower of privilege which places artists above most people. It acknowledges that any writer is a privileged being, set apart from the working class by virtue of the fact that he or she has leisure to write. The more successful the writer, the greater the gap; as Woolf pointed out elsewhere, the successful novelist always moves upward socially, never down. He or she may become sought after by peers and Mayfair hostesses, but will not be asked for dinner by the plumber and his wife.[27] The writers of the thirties, uncomfortable with this privilege, conscious of the social injustice which supports their leisure, but unable to change the social structure, merely take potshots at a bourgeois society which continues to support them. They are self-conscious, and their work is consequently crabbed and constrained.

Behind both these essays lies the assumption, which we first noticed in *A Room of One's Own*, that "consciousness" of any sort is bad for a writer.[28] I call it an assumption, but it is more than that, it is an argument and her principal critical response to the young writers of the thirties, as the definition of the subjective nature of reality had been her response to the parental generation of novelists, Bennett, Wells, and Galsworthy. What had been description in 1929 becomes in the thirties prescription. The great writer must create in a state of transcendent oblivion, what she called in *A Room of One's Own* "incandescence." When the "surface mind" is at work, the "inner mind" from which great art proceeds is paralyzed. So one must still the surface mind. One must imagine oneself in the company of Chaucer, Shakespeare, and Dante, the inheritor of past ages, the source of the future, the momentary embodiment of an enduring tradition.

Threatened by another generation—not her elders, not her peers, but the inheritors, the children—she flees, retreats into the anonymity of tradition, as though to say: you are not really there, or if you are, you should not be. And I am where I belong, with Shakespeare and Chaucer, oblivious, transcendent. What we have here is not a discussion of art and politics, but a flight from public and private identity.

The elevation of what Woolf variously calls "anonymity," "impersonality," and "unconsciousness" to the status of cardinal artistic virtue was a product of the thirties. As advice to a generation of writers at an age inevitably self-conscious and living in an age which demanded awareness of public events, it was as trivial and irrelevant as preaching temperance to starving miners. The flight from the personal also did nothing for her own work.

*The Waves* is a novel many people admire and few people love, though those who love it tend to be eloquent. Its conception is ambitious and, in its way, magnificent: to present six individuals in all their distinctiveness, yet to follow them through the various stages of life, showing the similarities of their movement through existence. The effect is to depict life as an organic process in which each of us participates, individual yet inseparable from the whole of humanity through all time, as a wave is inseparable from the eternal sea, yet distinct and momentary. Descriptive passages following the sun's effect on the landscape through the day mark the different stages of life of the six characters who reveal the innermost structure of their minds in a series of what David Daiches has aptly called "recitatives."[29] These are not interior monologues as we have learned to expect them in Joyce and Faulkner and in Woolf's earlier work, where they are conceived as depicting a temporal flow and seek to follow the movement of the mind from one thing to another. The monologues in *The Waves* seek to define mental spaces, the structures habitually imposed on experience.

They should be compared to a post-impressionist painting like Cézanne's *Mont Ste. Victoire* which doesn't "look like" a mountain so much as it captures the geometric substructure of a mountain. So too *The Waves* tries to present the enduring abstract pattern beneath perception, and it achieves in the process a regal monumentality and dignity.

Woolf attempts in this book a frontal assault on the nature of the novel. She wants to go directly to the sense of mortality, to feelings about life and death, without rooting them in specific deaths, specific losses. Mrs. Ramsay's death in mid-sentence in *To the Lighthouse* affects us because we have the illusion of having known Mrs. Ramsay. But when Percival dies in *The Waves* (Percival is a character present in the novel but not presented—he does not have monologues and serves as the focus for the other six, their common hero) it is hard to feel anything, and it is with some shock that one reads in Woolf's diary about her impulse, upon finishing the novel, to scrawl across it the name of her brother Thoby (who like Percival was magnificent and died young)—so thoroughly has any personal element been erased from the work.

Occasionally, caught up in the rhythms of the book and its exquisitely precise visual images, one feels—does not realize intellectually, but feels, viscerally—the sense of life, time, and change in the way Woolf intended, and it takes one's breath away. But the overall effect is too frequently tedious:

> My daughters shall come here, in other summers; my sons shall turn new fields. Hence we are not raindrops, soon dried by the wind; we make gardens blow and forests roar; we come up differently, for ever and ever. This, then, serves to explain my confidence, my central stability, otherwise so monstrously absurd as I breast the stream of this crowded thoroughfare, making always a passage for myself between people's bodies, taking advantage of safe moments to cross.[30]

That is Susan, the woman rooted most closely to nature. Here is Rhoda, the character most often associated with Woolf herself, who finds reality frighteningly alien:

> I hear the rush of the great grindstone within an inch of my head. Its wind roars in my face. All palpable forms of life have failed me. Unless I can stretch and touch something hard, I shall be blown down the eternal corridors for ever. What, then, can I touch? What brick, what stone? and so draw myself across the enormous gulf into my body safely? (113).

It is beside the point to say that one hears no distinctive voices in *The Waves*, that Rhoda's rhythms are much like Susan's. Woolf was not aiming at such conventional realism. But it is not irrelevant to note that the effect is monotonous. As Woolf described her concept of the book to John Lehmann, "I wanted to eliminate all detail; all fact; and analysis; and myself; and yet not be frigid and rhetorical; and not monotonous."[31] She succeeded in eliminating fact and self, but the price was the monotony and frigidity she feared. Her goal seems curiously negative. She wanted to *eliminate* detail, fact, analysis. But what, if anything, did she want to achieve? Her goal, I think, was "poetry"—but it is a goal which masked a deeper evasion.

E. M. Forster, her chief literary confidante, had been telling her throughout her career that poetry was her distinctive contribution to the novel and her chief strength. Woolf herself tended to agree with this view of her talent, unfortunately; for she was betrayed by her own metaphor—the novel as a poem—and by her notion of poetry, which is disturbingly conventional.[32] It is, in fact, Tennysonian, valuing beauty of sound and mellifluousness above everything. Consequently her eyesight was dim regarding artists whose style was less aggressively elegant than her own. As Diana Trilling has pointed out, Woolf gave D. H. Lawrence a very great compliment when she said of him, intending no compliment, that you never felt in his work he had chosen a word for its beauty in the sentence.[33] Such careless finesse was beyond her. She strove perhaps a little too hard to create beauty and so, in a work like *The Waves*, she presents too unbroken a surface. She is always riffing. There are no rhythmic letups which let you appreciate the highs when they come. It is, one feels, an inability to relax as typical of her life as of her work. Life was messy; life was ugly; care and discipline were constantly required to fashion it into something worthwhile. As she strove to make the novel more poetic, that is, more rhythmic and laden with visual images, she found she could not accommodate what she referred to with distaste as "raw fact."[34]

Poetry and fact had become an irreconcilable dichotomy in Woolf's mind—poetry was noble and beautiful, but draining to produce; fact was drab, mundane, but nourishing, something solid on which the imagination, overtired from producing poetry, could lean. She divided her own works into two categories: on the one hand, serious, poetic novels like *To the Lighthouse* and *The Waves*, on the other hand novels of fact, like *The Years* and *Night and Day*, but *also* sprightly works, *jeux d'esprit* like *Orlando* and *Flush*. The poetry-fact dichotomy is in fact highly subjective shorthand, and what she is really distinguishing between are books in which she feels she is laying herself on the line and books which present a mask, a mask of laughter or a mask of objectivity. It is clear that when she turns to "fact" in the thirties, it is with relief, with a sense of being freed from a burden of personality, as though the "facts" bear the responsibility for the book rather than the writer. But if poetry (or, let us say, lyricism) had earlier been a kind of sluice gate for her deepest feelings, in *The Waves* she seems rather to aspire through lyricism to the state of a golden bird on a gilt bough, as in Yeats's poem, singing beautifully of what is past and passing and to come—the artist removed from nature, wholly anonymous. By the thirties, I would argue, both fact and poetry had become for Woolf escapes from personality, from the self.

*The Years* (1937) is a more readable novel than *The Waves*, though it too ultimately suffers from a scrupulous impartiality, Woolf's refusal to define a central character or to shape a narrative, while heaping upon us the kind of detail that demands such a shape. The book follows the children of Colonel and Mrs. Pargiter from 1880, when they live together in a gloomy Victorian house waiting for their mother to die, to their scattered and various maturities in "the present" (1936), when most of them are still waiting for something to set life into significant motion. Although *The Waves* is "poetic" and *The Years* "factual," the novels resemble each other in showing the effect of time on a group of characters and in their panoramic ambitions. But *The Years* has a historical dimension absent in the earlier novel. The childhood of the young Pargiters is specifically Victorian. In the brilliant opening scenes we see them stifling beneath the weight of conventionalized emotion, enacting roles of mourning when Mrs. Pargiter finally dies, yet secretly relieved. As they grow up, they live in ways unthinkable to their parents. Rose becomes a suffragette and goes to prison. Sarah forms her closest tie with a homosexual. Peggy becomes a doctor. War and the emancipation of women are the two great historical facts of their lives. Ostensibly, there has been progress: life is less bound by artificial conventions than it was in the past. The past, in fact, as one character puts it, was Hell, and in escaping from the house on Abercorn Terrace, by surviving into a present in which women may vote and be doctors and needn't marry, the Pargiter children re-enact Woolf's personal myth of liberation. Yet in another sense, there is no progress whatsoever.

Most family chronicles demonstrate progress or decline—the form invites it. But *The Years*, working against the

bias of its chronological format, demonstrates stasis—stasis
in emotional development. Frustration is the keynote. In the
last chapter, at Delia's party, various characters attempt to
make speeches. The reader expects a summing up, but the
expectation is frustrated. Peggy, for example, can hardly get
beyond "look here," although she wants "to express something that she felt to be very important; about a world in
which people were free."[35] She ends by making a personal
attack on her brother, North: he will marry, have children,
write "little books" to make money, instead of "living differently." That phrase, "living differently," comes to bear a
great weight of significance as North repeats it over and over
to himself. "To live differently." It strikes a chord, but he
can't quite put his vision of the better future into words,
can't say what it would mean to live differently. Nicholas,
another disappointed speechmaker, when prodded, reveals
that he had intended to toast the human race: now in its infancy, may it grow to maturity. But Nicholas himself displays no growth. He talks about the same subjects in 1936
that he talked about in 1918—Napoleon and the psychology
of great men. His understanding has not deepened.

Woolf's stylistic device of concerning her characters
with things they cannot quite define may get out of hand in
*The Years*, striking us as the author's evasion rather than that
of her characters. There is something there, yes, but what is
it? One can't quite say. The *aperçu* is faintly perceived, just
beyond reach. Some children, for example, enter the room
and sing, but no one can understand their words.

> "But it was . . ." Eleanor began. She stopped. What
> was it? . . . Beautiful?" she said, with a note of inter-
> rogation, turning to Maggie.
> "Extraordinarily," said Maggie.
> But Eleanor was not sure they were thinking of the
> same thing (430–31).

This picture of a world of anticlimax, in which kettles don't
boil, sick people don't die, speeches are interrupted and

finally abandoned, and communication is almost always incomplete, generates an atmosphere of drabness and despair. We may find the effect dispiriting, but it is powerfully realized. The years pass, but go nowhere.

The disturbing thing is that the static effect of *The Years,* its pattern of frustrating expectation and embedding the reader in inconclusiveness, seems to stem less from conscious design than from a perilous reticence in the author. The novel is at once highly autobiographical and completely unrevealing.[36] Its time span coincides with the span of Woolf's life (she was born in 1882, the book begins in 1880). Life in Abercorn Terrace is modeled fairly obviously on life at Hyde Park Gate. Certain incidents, such as Delia's fear of not feeling enough when her mother dies, are taken directly from Woolf's life. Kitty's semi-erotic attachment to her tutor, Lucy Craddock, mirrors Virginia's relationship with Janet Case, her Greek teacher. But the overall impression we get from the book is of a tight-lipped refusal to elaborate, so that the past reverberates hollowly. As a child on her way to the candy store, Rose saw a man exposing himself. As an adult, she still remembers it. But to what end? Woolf scrupulously avoids all examination of effect, as though she might be giving herself away by straying from the facts.

Often in *The Years* she speaks in a kind of private code, a shorthand, employing phrases that have great personal resonance, and resonance for us if we have read her diaries and memoirs, but little resonance for the average reader of the novel who cannot bring to it a sense of Woolf's interior demons and dramas. For example, in 1913 Martin goes to visit Crosby, the Pargiters' old servant, now retired. To get away, he pretends he has an engagement elsewhere.

> It was a lie. He had no engagement. One always lies to servants, he thought, looking out of the window. The mean outlines of the Ebury Street houses showed through the falling sleet. Everyone lies, he thought. His father lied—after his death they had found letters from a

woman called Mira tied up in his table-drawer. And he
had seen Mira—a stout respectable lady who wanted
help with her roof. Why had his father lied? What was
the harm of keeping a mistress? And he had lied himself;
about the room off the Fulham Road where he and
Dodge and Erridge used to smoke cheap cigars and tell
smutty stories. It was an abominable system, he thought;
family life; Abercorn Terrace. No wonder the house
would not let. It had one bathroom, and a basement;
and there all those different people had lived, boxed up
together, telling lies (222–23).

This passage, intended as a passionate indictment of the Victorian family system, fails to generate any emotion. We are
bombarded with specifics—Colonel Pargiter's mistress,
Dodge and Erridge, one bathroom and a basement—but the
core of horror is avoided. Certain words, "family life" and in
particular "lies," are supposed to summon up that heavy
weight of hypocritical emotion which Woolf associated with
Victorian family life and the great lie she detested above
all—to pretend there was love when there was none. But the
code is private, so the emotional resonance is private. Assum-
ing that other people have the same responses one has oneself
to key words is a beginning writer's error. We saw how in
*The Voyage Out* Woolf sometimes left autobiographical material underdeveloped for this reason. But she did it in *The
Years* out of a determined resolve to stick to what she called
facts, and not to slip into the more personal element she
called poetry. Thus the curiously drained quality of *The
Years*, which is so powerful, may be seen as a triumph of
craft or a failure of nerve or a little of both.

Various readers have connected the bleakness which
shadows *The Years* with the deaths of Woolf's friends in the
thirties. These began in 1932 with the death of Lytton Strachey. Carrington, in despair, killed herself soon afterward.
Then Goldsworthy Lowes Dickinson died, and in 1934—in
some ways the most devastating loss of all—Roger Fry. Cer-

tainly it was not a buoyant time. By 1935 the exciting romance with Vita was a thing of the past; they were old and
good friends, but the thrill was gone. Instead of love, she had
to contend with death, in the face of which creativity became all the more important and thus all the more difficult.

No book was so hard for Virginia Woolf to write as *The
Years*. She worked it over and over again, almost driving
herself into insanity with diligence (she was close to a total
collapse in 1936). It is the kind of book one writes and the
kind of approach one takes (unrelenting hard work, substi-
tuting doggedness for inspiration) in a state of doubt. The
picture of her at work on the revisions is painful. She would
lie on her bed, make her way to her desk to squeeze out a
sentence or two, and then return to bed again. When she
read the book in proof, she concluded almost with relief that
it must be burned, so agonizing had been the strain of trying
to decide, in the course of the writing, whether the book was
any good. "Now I was no longer Virginia, the genius, but
only a perfectly magnificent yet content—shall I call it
spirit? a body? And very tired. Very old."[37] The crisis of self-
confidence of her early years had recurred. Virginia the genius was an impossible burden to bear. Virginia the failure,
the empty-headed and badly trained, was in some ways easier to live with. Why not let her emerge? Why maintain the
elaborate facade? She seems to have regarded advancing age
as an ally in this process of unmasking and to welcome
it—the end of the parabola, the longed-for conclusion in the
deconstruction of the self.

The literature of the thirties that survives tends to
present the self in conflict with the times, engaging the
times, or trying to engage—with history, with a public
cause—and failing. I think of Orwell's works and lyrics by
Auden and Spender. Significantly, Auden's most popular
poem, the one by which he is known to the greatest number
of "common readers," is "Musée des Beaux Arts," with its
brilliant image of how ordinary life continues placid, undis-

turbed in the face of the most dramatic events and the greatest suffering. Sadly, it was Woolf who abandoned the self in the thirties, responding to the demand for public commitment not with a frank assertion of the value of private experience, but by embracing impersonality and anonymity. For a writer whose greatest impact derives from a private understanding of life's precariousness, the escape from the personal meant cutting herself off from the roots of her art. Had she been less sensitive to her times, more truly Olympian, she would have survived the thirties better. As it was, she exhausted herself in a futile fight against the very principle of self-consciousness.

It will surprise no one, then, if I suggest that her best work from the thirties—best in the sense of most energetic and most provocative—is also her most personal, tapping her persistent rage at "the great Victorian fight between the victims of the patriarchal system and the patriarchs, between the daughters and the fathers"[38] which was, for this daughter, this victim, one of the great fights of her own life. I speak of that part feminist, part pacifist "treatise" (it is hard to know exactly what to call it), *Three Guineas* (1938). Written in the years of the Spanish Civil War, and with a general conflagration on the horizon, it is Woolf's most direct engagement with contemporary problems. In attempting to answer the question, "How can we prevent war?" she surveys the current state of women in England, explores the vestiges of patriarchal mentality, implies that the will to dominate is the same in a Victorian father as in a Hitler and that the battles against the patriarchal state and against fascism are closely allied. Moreover the very desire to make war derives largely from notions of manliness and from the desire to prove oneself a man, for which the old formulations of relationships between the sexes are responsible. Her answer to the threat of war is to educate more women, to help them enter the professions (so that they can have the financial independence to express their views frankly), and to encourage them, even as they gain power and responsibility in the Establishment, to retain the point of view of outsiders, avoiding the ambition and competitiveness which make professional life a hell and which are also the emotions that generate war.

E. M. Forster considered *Three Guineas* the worst of Woolf's books. "In my judgment there is something old-fashioned about this extreme feminism; it dates back to her suffragette youth of the 1910's. . . . By the 1930's she had much less to complain of, and seems to keep on grumbling from habit."[39] But it was Forster who had added fuel to the fire behind *Three Guineas* in 1935 by telling Virginia it was out of the question for women to serve on the London Library Committee.

More disturbing, because it came from one of the women Woolf was presumably addressing, was the scathing review in *Scrutiny* by Q. D. Leavis.[40] Leavis thinks that rather than whining, women must come up to snuff. The onus, as she puts it, is on them to prove they are worthy of further emancipation. As it is the universities are hard put to fill their ten percent quotas without lowering standards. She attacks Woolf on class lines, accusing her of upper-class elitism, without recognizing Woolf's implicit argument—that women constitute a class in themselves, cutting across the class lines in which *Scrutiny* was interested.

*Three Guineas* has irritated many people who see it as a flip and ignorant analysis of war and totalitarianism. Forty years later, we can see the emphasis rather differently. It is, first of all, an irreverent—and courageous—refusal merely to cheer for democracy on the eve of World War II, an insistence on examining the kinds of society England was fighting for and fighting against, to see if there were pernicious similarities. It is a refusal to take seriously the military virtues or pretensions, of which Julian Bell—to take only one personal example—made so much. It is an impudent piece, designed to irritate, for, as always, mockery and impudence seem to Woolf the only healthy responses to masculine pomposity.

Her linkage of patriarchal thinking with war and fascism seemed at the time a far-out hypothesis, but today it remains a question of concern to feminists and cannot be discounted.[41] A more neglected, but equally provocative part of *Three Guineas* is the survey of women's professional status in England twenty years after emancipation, which leads Woolf to fundamental questions about the role of women in society.

Despite having had the vote and the right to enter the professions for twenty years, women were still in 1938 a disadvantaged class, according to Woolf's disturbing account. In education, they still had not achieved full equality. The women's colleges were not members of the universities of Oxford and Cambridge and women graduates had only recently and after a great struggle obtained the right to put B.A. after their names, like men. In the Civil Service, women were under-represented and underpaid, and this was true also throughout most of the professions. Injustices and indignities are cited on every page; the text is full of quotations which make a woman want to laugh—or cry: "It is time the Government insisted upon employers giving work to more men [as opposed to women], thus enabling them to marry the women they cannot now approach" (78). That, from a working man. But from so respected a person as Walter Bagehot:

> I assure you I am not an enemy of women. I am very favourable to their employment as *labourers* or in other *menial* capacity. I have, however, doubts as to the likelihood of their succeeding in business as capitalists. I am sure the nerves of most women would break down under the anxiety, and that most of them are utterly destitute of the disciplined reticence necessary to every sort of cooperation. Two thousand years hence you may have changed it all, but at present women will only flirt with men, and quarrel with one another (233–34).

Rarely since Matthew Arnold has quotation been used to such devastating effect.

Woolf brings to her survey of still-existing inequalities a healthy sense of the property basis of the struggle, viewing resistance to women's entering professions as economic at root. Without being a Marxist, she knew that the notion that women doing this or that was ridiculous rested ultimately on a hard core of property arrangements. If a woman makes a great deal of money as a lawyer or doctor, she ceases to look absurd in the practice of her calling. But the more money women make, the less there is to be made by men. If women work, men may end by looking absurd; if women can make money, men lose power. Sophia Jex-Blake's father, who would not allow his daughter to accept money for the tutoring she did, ostensibly because it would "lower" her, provides Woolf's favorite example of how financial compensation has been withheld from women to insure their dependence. Mr. Barrett's refusal to let Elizabeth marry, from a desire in some way to keep her an invalid, is another example of the subtleties of male dominance, and one which probably had a great deal of personal resonance for Woolf, who felt that her own Victorian father had kept her unnecessarily protected.[42]

But Woolf fears that in order to enter the professions successfully, women may become corrupted by the prevailing jealousy, competitiveness, and love of power, that instead of women taking over the system, the system will take over the women and will erase from them valuable spiritual qualities acquired by the experience of exclusion. The issue is important: are women selling their souls in order to enter the professions on male terms?

> We, daughters of educated men [she uses this term instead of "middle-class" throughout the piece] are between the devil and the deep sea. Behind us lies the patriarchal system; the private house, with its nullity, its immorality, its hypocrisy, its servility. Before us lies the public world, the professional system, with its possessiveness, its jealousy, its pugnacity, its greed. The one shuts us up like slaves in a harem; the other forces us to

circle, like caterpillars head to tail, round and round the mulberry tree, the sacred tree, of property. It is a choice of evils (113).

The lessons imprinted on the female character by years of oppression—how to be poor, how to be chaste of spirit, how to sustain derision, to appreciate freedom from unreal loyalties—should not be forgotten. Try to retain the outlook of the loser even after you have won—that is Woolf's advice to the next generation. In *Three Guineas*, not in *Letter to a Young Poet*, not in her dealings with the younger generation of male writers, we find her powers of nurturance mobilized—by a female audience.

Nothing in the period of Woolf's life from 1930 to 1938 is more striking than the amount of work she expended on *The Years*, and hardly had she finished this appalling task when she took on another, equally dreary, the biography of Roger Fry. Nothing demanded the biography had to be dreary, of course, but Woolf turned it into an exercise, a task to be accomplished by disciplined work, time, and patience, again attempting to substitute sheer work for genius, a genius she feared was no longer there. Famous, ostensibly strong, she felt she had more to hide than ever, worried more, and covered her insecurity by dogged activity. If she could not be great, at least she could be good.

*Three Guineas* was not part of this drudgery; she wanted "violently, . . . persistently, pressingly, compulsorily"[43] to write that book. It was written from her own rage and from the only point of her identity that had not been shaken in the thirties, her femaleness and identification with other women. When it was finished, she feared that the book she had written in such violent passion would not dimple the surface of public response. Also, she was afraid of being autobiographical, that is, of revealing the deep sense of personal hurt which inspired the book. But ultimately the fears were outbalanced by the "relief and peace" she felt.

> Now I am quit of that poison and excitement. Nor is that
> all, for having spit it out, my mind is made up. I need
> never recur or repeat. I am an outsider. I can take my
> way: experiment with my imagination in my own way.[44]

There is no mistaking her relief at finding herself an outsider
again. Writing *Three Guineas* retrieved for her, in her own
eyes, that position of the exile in her own country which age
and fame had threatened to destroy.

The years I have been discussing, roughly 1930 to 1938,
were probably the most difficult of Woolf's adult life, but the
diary entries for 1938 bespeak a weary peace. There is a retrospective quality to them. On November 22, she looks back
over the twenty years since she wrote *Night and Day* and considers the exalted position she reached, and then her "decap-
itation." She remembers the decade in terms of attacks upon
her. First *Scrutiny*. Then Wyndham Lewis. She became
aware of an active opposition. She who used to be praised by
the young and attacked by the elderly was now in the other
camp. Undoubtedly, she tells herself, the reputations of Forster and Eliot stand higher now with the young. "Well? In a
way it is a relief. I'm fundamentally an outsider. I do my best
work and feel most braced with my back to the wall."[45] The
myth of her own demise was restorative. It returned her, sub-
jectively, to a position of weakness, of opposition, and hence,
through some personal transformation, to psychic strength.
The outsider of 1938 no less than the immured maiden of
1903 was energized by the experience of exclusion.

And so she could address a working-class audience in
Brighton in 1940 and say with no affectation whatever that
she and they had a common cause against the Stephens and
Williams of England who would presume with the arrogance
of a university-trained elite to dictate in realms of culture.
"We must become critics because in future we are not going
to leave writing to be done for us by a small class of well-to-
do young men who have only a pinch, a thimbleful of experi-

ence to give us." Self-educated, she sees herself in the same position as her audience and recommends they read and think and write for themselves in order to avoid subjection to a cultural dictatorship.

> Of course—are we not commoners, outsiders?—we shall trample many flowers and bruise much ancient grass. But let us bear in mind a piece of advice that an eminent Victorian who was also an eminent pedestrian once gave to walkers: "Whenever you see a board up with 'Trespassers will be prosecuted,' trespass at once."[46]

The sense of trespass in the realms of light, ingrained from childhood, had become a necessity, the precondition of creative vitality. By writing *Three Guineas* she reminded herself of a truth she needed to function as a writer, that the whole world she lived in was a male preserve with "No Trespassing" signs at its borders, and that, no matter how famous, how established she became, she would always be an outsider.

# 11

# Life
# without a Future

In September 1939, England declared war on Germany and soon found itself in the middle of a disaster for which even the first World War, fought at a distance, had been no preparation. London was bombed, invasion feared, and victory for the Nazis predicted. The world in 1939 made the world of 1914 seem gentlemanly and rational. Who would have thought, in 1914, of killing themselves if the Kaiser's armies invaded England? Yet the Woolfs, the Nicolsons, and Adrian Stephen all made arrangements for suicide should Hitler prevail. Leonard had some idea of what was happening to Jews in Europe. He kept enough gasoline in the garage so they could asphyxiate themselves on automobile fumes. Later Adrian, who had become a physician, supplied them with enough morphine to overdose. The barbarians were at the gates, and if Athenian civilization had gone down before Alexander and Roman civilization before the Goths, there was no reason why English civilization should prove invincible to the Nazis. On the day the Woolfs visited Penshurst, the ancestral home of the family of Sir Philip Sidney and a monument of civilized life, Paris fell to the Germans, and Leonard, for one, was fully aware of the irony. War became part of the Woolfs' daily life. In September 1940 their house in Mecklenburgh Square was severely damaged by bombs, and soon afterwards their old place in Tavistock Square, on which they had still been paying rent, was ruined. Even the Sussex downs were not immune. As Virginia worked on what would be her last novel, *Between the Acts,* the Battle of Britain was being fought in the skies over her Rodmell cottage.

Living daily with the prospect of cataclysmic change, if not the end of civilization, Virginia Woolf produced a novel about the genteel inhabitants of a country house, Pointz Hall, their vague desires, muted frustrations, and about the village pageant performed on their grounds. One must fill in the unspoken threat which helps give the book its poignancy and power. This is civilization—strained marriages, amateur theatricals, the serving of tea. It may not be much, but it had taken a long time to evolve, and it was perhaps about to be lost.

Like all of Woolf's best fiction, *Between the Acts* is energized by a concern for what endures and what is lost in the course of time. The thematic emphasis on permanence and mutability, the Shelleyan belief that the One remains, although the many change and pass, which permeates *Mrs. Dalloway* and in some ways *To the Lighthouse,* underlies Woolf's last book as well. It is the theme of a person who, having suffered

an early and disastrous loss, seeks continually for some way
to mitigate it, and it is also the theme of a person uncomfortable in her individuality, who seeks to lose it in some supra-
personal flow.

The second World War provides a focus for these themes
in *Between the Acts*, as the Great War had, just as subtly, for
*Mrs. Dalloway*. The action of the novel takes place in June of
1939, with Europe about to go to war, but of the major characters only Giles Oliver, the young stockbroker, seems concerned. It enrages him to have to sit politely admiring the
view, sipping coffee, "when the whole of Europe—over
there—was bristling like. . . . He had no command of metaphor. Only the ineffective word 'hedgehog' illustrated his
vision of Europe, bristling with guns, poised with planes."[1]
Having to remain in the audience while others act mobilizes
his fury. "This afternoon he wasn't Giles Oliver come to see
the villagers act their annual pageant; manacled to a rock he
was, and forced passively to behold indescribable horror"
(74). Like the crude village pageant, the inexorable movement to war is a spectacle he must witness while remaining
inactive, feeling impotent, for war, to such as Giles, is a test
of manhood. Other characters, old Mr. Oliver and his sister,
for example, are not bothered by their passive roles:

> "Our part," said Bartholomew, "is to be the audience.
> And a very important part too."
> "Also, we provide the tea," said Mrs. Swithin (73).

The best humor in *Between the Acts* is like this, gently mocking the way, in a traditional society, in which people fall to
parody of themselves.

But let us begin by getting a sense of the parameters of
action in *Between the Acts*. What happens? The Olivers, a
country family, sit one evening discussing a cesspool with
Mr. and Mrs. Haines, their neighbors. Young Mrs. Oliver—
Isa—is attracted to Mr. Haines. Next morning, old Mr. Oliver, on his walk, encounters and terrifies his grandson. Isa

orders fish for lunch. Preparations are begun for the presentation of the annual village pageant that afternoon. Isa is bored with the pageant, bored with her life. Lunch is served. The vivacious and vulgar Mrs. Manresa drops in uninvited with a friend, William Dodge. Giles Oliver comes home from work, displeased to find company at lunch, especially offended at the presence of a homosexual (William). There is tension between Giles and Isa. To smooth the waters, Mrs. Swithin, old Mr. Oliver's sister, gives William a tour of the house. Between them, a moment of sympathy and gratitude. As the pageant begins, Isa looks round for Mr. Haines, and William notes that she is a fellow seeker after faces. Miss La Trobe, the writer-producer, is angry when the intermission dissipates the small quantity of emotion her play has managed to generate in the audience. Mrs. Manresa walks around with Giles during the interval, making him feel less like a spectator in life and more of a participant. Isa takes William to the greenhouse where, suddenly, they confide in one another.

This account, alighting here and there, covers about half the Chekhovian "action" of the novel. One has the feeling of wandering around at a garden party, overhearing scraps of half-unspoken conversation. People meet, talk, move away, but the ebb and flow of feeling which goes on beneath has little to do with that. In this somewhat etiolated world, violent action is rare (a snake is strangling on a toad it has tried to swallow, and Giles crushes them both with his shoe, earning Mrs. Manresa's admiration and his wife's contempt for his bravado). There are moments of sympathy and of antipathy. There is a prevailing isolation. Each character walks about enclosed in his or her own buried life. The old dream about the past, the young dream about the future. Almost all are sleepwalkers in the present. Mrs. Swithin, for example, mentally escapes to a warm Italian past while she helps the cook make sandwiches. "Why's stale bread, she mused, easier to cut than fresh? And so skipped, sidelong, from yeast to alcohol;

so to fermentation; so to inebriation; so to Bacchus; and lay under purple lamps in a vineyard in Italy, as she had often done; while Sands heard the clock tick; saw the cat; noted a fly buzz" (43–44). Only the practical and unimaginative, like Sands the cook, stay rooted in present reality, hearing the clock tick, noticing flies.

*Between the Acts* is densely, obsessively concerned with history, with the passage of time. Even the cesspool discussed in the opening pages has a lineage: it occupies the site of what had been, successively, a Roman road, an Elizabethan manor house, and a wheat field during the Napoleonic wars. Mrs. Swithin is fond of reading *The Outline of History* and of musing on days when rhododendrons grew in Piccadilly, when the continent was undivided and inhabited by mammoths. The image of the mammoths recurs throughout the book, a kind of pentimento, influencing our perception of the enervated, slow civilization of the current inheritors of the earth, who live on a continent evolved in some ways, but still given to periodic fits of primitive violence. The novel's setting is a rural England rich in history, a fascinating palimpsest. The people of the village have lived there, in the persons of their ancestors, for hundreds of years.

Woolf's primary jest in this novel, which is not so much lighthearted as it is strenuously gay, is to encapsulate the flow of English literary history, which had obsessed her since her youth, the only system of knowledge of which she was master, in a village pageant directed by a presumptuous amateur which people attend out of duty. Costumed in dishcloths and scouring pads, the villagers perform parodic versions first of a Shakespearian romance and then of a Restoration comedy. But the parodies are not the point of Miss La Trobe's creation; the point lies in the setting, outdoors, in the midst of trees and fields and cows, with a line of villagers weaving their way through a copse, an image of enduring, elemental human nature, of people seen abstractly, monumentally, on the level of rocks and cows. The ways in which love and hatred are expressed may change according to the literary fashion of the times, but love and hatred remain the basic emotions, so no matter what period piece goes on at center stage, the villagers in the background provide the continuing bass chord of emotion in a vision of life which holds that continuities are crucial, the changes from age to age trivial.

> *Digging and delving we pass . . . . and the Queen and the Watch Tower fall . . . for Agamemnon has ridden away. . . . Clytemnestra is nothing but . . .* (164).

The words trail away in the wind. Miss La Trobe is in despair, because her power of illusion has failed. She had tried to find the compelling voice that would make, let us say, Mrs. Porter forget that her grandfather had been in Gladstone's cabinet and Mr. Eyre his youthful glory as President of the Union—the voice, in other words, which would make them forget their paltry individuality and feel themselves part of a timeless whole.[2] That words like "Clytemnestra," "Agamemnon," "Troy," and "Nineveh," tossed into the wind, are not sufficient to effect this mythic nudge was not apparent to Miss La Trobe, who aspired, with the meager means at her disposal, no less than the authors of the great modernist masterpieces, *Ulysses* and *The Waste Land*, to present contemporary life in the context not just of the historical but of the timeless and mythic. The literary parodies of *Between the Acts* serve the same ironic, historical function as the fragments of past masterpieces shored against ruin in *The Waste Land*, but what myth accomplishes in Eliot's poem is accomplished, fortuitously in La Trobe's pageant, artfully in Woolf's novel, by nature. Just when La Trobe is convinced her illusion has failed and that she cannot evoke the primeval voice she seeks, a cow bellows for its lost calf. Other cows take up the cry and "from cow after cow came the same yearning bellow. The whole world was filled with dumb yearning" (165).

La Trobe, whose artistic efforts must be seen as a comic analogue of Woolf's, caps her presentation of the Elizabethan, Augustan, and Victorian ages, amusing but finally trite, with an interesting attempt to throw the present into the faces of the audience. By withholding the action for ten minutes, she wants to force them to contemplate themselves and the cows and trees around them. But Colonel Mayhew asks irritably, "What's she keeping us waiting for?" (209). Puzzled, vexed, the audience discounts as reality their own discomfort, unhappiness, refusals to meet each other's glances, the swish of the trees, the lowing of the cows, and concludes that the next act has been delayed for some mysterious costume change. A sudden shower saves the moment, in La Trobe's view, but even then, literally drenched in nature, in present-time reality, as she wanted them to be, it is doubtful if the audience is made to feel their relationship to nature or to understand that the present is a moment of repressed awareness in which we wait for something to happen—an arbitrary, unarresting freeze-frame in the march of what is past and passing and to come. Her next attempt to hold the mirror up to nature—literally, to allow the audience to glimpse themselves as "orts, scraps, and fragments" through pieces of mirror held by the cast—falls flat, except for the indomitable Mrs. Manresa, who seizes the moment to repair her lipstick. Only the crudest of La Trobe's artistic strategies succeeds, a symbolic tableau in which Civilization (a wall in ruins) is rebuilt by Human Effort (a man on a ladder). Her audience wants "messages." They can see themselves and the present moment only as part of a morality play.

That Woolf continued to write at all when planes were being shot down around her suggests how desperate was her personal need for order, but what she wrote displays no illusions about the role of art in a world of chaos. Partly because this was her last novel, partly because of its sustained—if ironic—attention to the pageant as art and Miss La Trobe as artist, it is hard not to read *Between the Acts* as Woolf's *Tem-*

*pest*, a *Tempest* written in time of war, her assessment of her own art and her farewell to it. The questions she raises do not concern art's utility—no puritan attack lurks at the back of her mind to be answered—but its efficacy. How does art convey meaning? Does it convey meaning at all? The pageant stirs the audience obscurely, but leaves them more puzzled than satisfied or moved. They try to make sense of it, some thinking it "bosh," some finding it brilliantly clever. The obliging rector presents an interpretation which, although largely accurate, makes the author writhe. The audience seizes upon it. Without an interpretation, they cannot grasp the experience, like people who must read a review before they know what the film they've just seen is "about." Someone says that the author should have come forward at the end to explain what she meant and not have left it to the rector.

> He said she meant we all act. Yes, but whose play? Ah, that's the question! And if we're left asking questions, isn't it a failure as a play? I must say I like to feel sure if I go to the theatre that I've grasped the meaning . . . Or was that, perhaps, what she meant? (233).

All this concern with meaning, and so little with experience and emotion. Poor Miss La Trobe, who was only trying to stir up the simplest feelings. In her earlier years; Woolf had called attention to the tyranny and unreality of the fictional structures such writers as Bennett, Wells, and Galsworthy imposed on experience. The fault seemed in the writers. But now it seems the fault is in the audience which craves such authority, whose passion for interpretation, for pattern, for plot, for certitude, for meaning in experience makes it an easy prey for demagogues and dictators, of whom the Reverend Mr. Streatfield is a comically paltry example.

If we direct our attention away from the pageant and back to the family at Pointz Hall, which was the generative core of the novel, we notice that *Between the Acts* has much in common with *To the Lighthouse*. Formally, they share the tight, classically unified format which Woolf handles so much better than the panoramic sprawl of novels like *The Waves* and *The Years*. Also, both of them depict little islands of domesticity, concern themselves with marriage as much as art. But Isa, the woman of the household, is no Mrs. Ramsay. She loathes "the domestic; the possessive; the maternal" (25). She feels imprisoned by the family, waves vaguely through the window to her children, and yearns for escape with Haines, the gentleman- farmer. She turns for adventure to reading, but unlike Madame Bovary, whom she might otherwise resemble, she doesn't trust fiction, only newspapers. The story of a rape, for example, a woman dragged into a soldiers' barracks, hitting her abductors, strikes her as both real and exciting, more real and certainly more exciting than her placid domestic existence. The repetition, year after year, of the same small-town events—above all, those associated with the pageant—has produced a desperation we feel cannot much longer remain subdued. For her husband she can fitfully summon up affection by invoking the useful cliché, "the father of my children," but the amount of outright hostility in her attitude towards him is striking. Mrs. Ramsay, as a type of femininity, seems ever more dusty and out of date, but whether Isa, abortive in all ways, discontented with her life but unable to bring into being a better one, is any advance over Mrs. Ramsay is another question entirely.

Mrs. Manresa, another type of modern woman, her husband a remote figure in the background who supplies her with money to gad about with young men, bursts onto the scene to displace Isa momentarily as center of attention, and it is she who plays, in a strangely dislocated way, the role of Mrs. Ramsay in *Between the Acts*. Not that she is maternal, warm, supportive. Bizarrely showy, overly made up, absurdly presenting herself as a "wild child of nature," nevertheless she energizes people and brings them together as no one else in Pointz Hall can. Mrs. Ramsay's nurturance has become gaudy flirtatiousness in Mrs. Manresa, but the result is the same: she buoys people up.

> Vulgar she was in her gestures, in her whole person, over-sexed, over-dressed for a picnic. But what a desirable, at least valuable, quality it was—for everybody felt, directly she spoke, "She's said it, she's done it, not I," and could take advantage of the breach of decorum, of the fresh air that blew in, to follow like leaping dolphins in the wake of an ice-breaking vessel. Did she not restore to old Bartholomew his spice islands, his youth? (51–52).

In a novel so sensitive to the pervasive etiolation, the enervation of civilized life, Mrs. Manresa represents movement and energy, however vulgar.

The figure who invites comparison with her is Miss La Trobe, the organizer and writer of the pageant. She too is a mobilizer, a doer, and her perhaps unfeminine fondness for "getting things up" flies in the face of most of the characters' tendency toward languor. La Trobe is Virginia Woolf's last portrait of the artist as woman, and she represents a considerable modification of previous models. If Lily Briscoe was wary of men's domination, Miss La Trobe scorns men altogether and is frankly lesbian. But she seems to find it difficult to get along with women, too. She fought with the actress she lived with. The actress left. Since then La Trobe has been drinking, oppressed by solitude, an outcast in the village. People stop talking when she enters the pub; they call her "bossy." Irritable, obsessed by the fear that her work is a failure, that her vision has not been communicated, La Trobe is hardly a charmer. She has sacrificed perfection of the life for perfection of the work but cannot be sure she has achieved it. What is striking about her is her essential self-confidence. Luck or her actors may be against her, but she never doubts the validity of her vision. To create at all, she must be ruthlessly egoistic, and in this we may see something of Ethel Smyth, the composer, and Woolf's good friend in the thirties, who got so used to battling her way up in a man's field that she had no qualms about breaking into a conductor's dressing room, after he had finished a three-hour performance, to demand that he play her music. Lily Briscoe's hesitancies and conflicts are gone. La Trobe reminds us more of the egotistical Mr. Ramsay than she does of the wistful Lily. And here, too, we must ask, is this an advance?

At the end of the novel Mrs. Swithin, who doesn't believe anything fundamental changes in history, picks up her *Outline* for the last time and reads how England was a swamp, with thick forests covering the land. " 'Prehistoric man,' she read, 'half-human, half-ape, roused himself from his semi-crouching position and raised great stones.' " But progress is problematic. Giles and Isa, alone for the first time that day, are silent, soon to be washed to and fro by emotions beyond their control. "Alone, enmity was bared; also love. Before they slept, they must fight; after they had fought, they would embrace. From that embrace another life might be born" (255–26). The presentation is stark, intentionally elemental. Isa and Giles are no longer suburban sophisticates but abstract, monumental human animals, performing one of the basic acts of their kind, of which there seem to be only two, love and war; and the multi-layered title of the novel may refer, among other things, to the nature of our life, suspended between them.

Written at a turning point in history, *Between the Acts* is concerned with what survives such times and what is transformed. Are we and the Victorians the same people in different clothes? Has anything important changed from the first primeval act of love to the edgy rapprochement of Giles and Isa? Are we caught in an eternal seesaw of love and hate, war and peace? These questions are raised delicately. The answers, if we had to put them into words, would be inane, and we are hardly encouraged to articulate them. The tone of *Between the Acts* is anything but hortatory. No nagging or prophetic voice urges us to action, to answers, to save civilization. On the contrary, the neutrality of Woolf's art is nowhere more exquisitely observed than in this novel, which wholly abstains from prescription. The fine high breeding of rationalism, the kind of rationalism that does not survive in a war—tolerant, amused, fair to everyone—finds perfect expression in *Between the Acts*. I am reminded of another great work of 1939, Renoir's film *Rules of the Game*, which breathes the same spirit, as though to remind people, before the wave of pollution breaks, what clean air is like. Renoir, too, set his eve-of-the-war tragicomedy in a country house, finding in that pastoral haven, in the marshes and fields of Sologne, in the great chateau, in the people gathered for a weekend there, a model of civilized life, with its beauties and its potential for generating its own destruction. Renoir was inspired by Marivaux and Beaumarchais, by eighteenth-century comedies of sexual intrigue, as Woolf's imagination responded to Shakespeare's late romances and the Restoration comedies which she parodies in the pageant. Both had war on their minds but were creatively mobilized by its antithesis, by the most stylized of all literary genres and by the remote order of country house life. Life after the war, whether the war was won or lost, was bound to be radically different: the country house and what it stood for—the flowering of bourgeois civilization—seemed unlikely to survive. In *The Leaning Tower*, written at this time, Woolf predicted the evolution, after the war, of something like a classless society, encouraged by the income tax, which would redistribute wealth, and by technology, which would equalize services. In *Between the Acts*, she alludes to an optimistic editorial in a newspaper: "Homes will be built. Each flat with its refrigerator. . . . Each of us a free man; plates washed by machinery; not an aeroplane to vex us; all liberated; made whole" (213). The deferential society portrayed in *Be-*

*tween the Acts,* in which the villagers refrain from taking tea until Mrs. Manresa leads them in, was about to become a quaint relic, a cultural dinosaur. But Woolf's irony suggests that "liberation" and "wholeness" will not necessarily follow in the wake of the dishwashing machine.

Like much of Woolf's fiction, her last novel is inspired by a kind of nostalgia, an effort to rescue or resurrect a world which is passing or past. But here the effort is to fix in the medium of prose not her personal past—as in, say, *To the Lighthouse,* or *Jacob's Room,* or *Mrs. Dalloway*—but rather a communal past, the life of rural England and the beauty of the countryside. Many times in the thirties she had had occasion to note, as she sat at her study window looking at the hills, the disappearance of that beauty—a beauty she had assumed was immutable and eternal, until cement plants and bungalows defaced the hills in the name of "civilization." In *Between the Acts,* the threat of loss served to isolate a subject which otherwise might have seemed too minimal even for her minimalist sensibility, with the result that she finally wrote the book she had been talking about for much of her life, the wholly plotless novel, the novel without melodrama, in which the dissolution of character is achieved and inwardness so equally diffused throughout the group that *Mrs. Dalloway* and *To the Lighthouse,* with their striking protagonists, seem traditional by comparison. In *Between the Acts,* the individual is replaced by the group as focus of attention. The qualities that make Woolf's work distinctive—the leaching away of authorial presence, the lyric grace, the fragmentariness and richly random development—are more prominent here than ever before. Stylistically, *Between the Acts* is the quintessential Woolf novel.

It is as accomplished a novel as Woolf ever wrote. If it does not seem quite of the stature of *To the Lighthouse,* that is because it is somewhat narrower, more bookish. I myself would prefer less attention devoted to the pageant, which throws the book off balance in the direction of artificiality and exam-book cuteness. Perhaps if Woolf had revised it further, she would have altered the proportions slightly; the changes between the first and second drafts of this book are enormous, and many of them are concerned with eliminating excess bookishness, something Woolf had to guard against in her later years as she did against gratuitous autobiography earlier. The first draft is extremely heavy-handed and plodding; she was working simultaneously on *Roger Fry* and *Three Guineas* when she began *Between the Acts*, and she couldn't really concentrate on the novel. But when she devotes her mind to it, the book takes shape, the elliptical outlines of grace appear, and there suddenly materializes a dazzling Virginia Woolf novel, such as she had not written in almost a decade, with no fading of imaginative power or fictional skill. Woolf was never better at presenting the subtly logical flow of conversation, the collective mental drift of a group of people who move, for example, from the subject of fish for lunch, to the sea, to the absence thereof, to prehistoric times when England was part of the continent, and so, through savages, dentists, and royalty, to the preposterous conclusion, "Marriages with cousins can't be good for the teeth" (39). The luncheon scene in *Between the Acts* invites comparison with the dinner party in *To the Lighthouse*, and doesn't suffer from it. The depiction of how alone people are, even in the middle of a convivial group, is handled as brilliantly—and with a new sadness, because the sacramental quality is gone; there is no ultimate communion. Each of the people at the table is led, by looking at the portrait on the wall, to the heart of silence and left there, alone, until roused to superficial life again by Mrs. Manresa.

I want to emphasize that there is no falling off of powers in *Between the Acts* (if anything, the contrary), because on March 28, 1941, after she had completed the novel but not yet given it its final polishing, Virginia Woolf drowned herself in the River Ouse.

Leonard Woolf, who for close to thirty years had been daily monitoring Virginia's health, was caught more or less by surprise. Until the opening months of 1941, he had no idea there was anything wrong with Virginia, and he did not become seriously alarmed until March 18, ten days before her suicide. In his autobiography, he goes back over that painful time, searching her diary for clues to her depression. In retrospect, some of it seems "ominous." A surrealistic venom enters her descriptions of some lower-class women in Brighton: "Where does the money come from to feed these fat white slugs? Brighton a love corner for slugs." In the fall, when Leonard gave a talk in Brighton, she felt preyed upon by the working-class audience: "I was thinking about vampires. Leeches. Anyone with 500 a year and an education is at once sucked by the leeches. Put L and me into Rodmell pool and we are sucked—sucked—sucked."[3] But these passages, which display a souring of the imagination, would not have seemed so "ominous" if she had lived another ten years. They express the vexation of a cultivated woman forced because of the war to live amongst villagers and other people far below her intellectual level. She was, understandably, bored, more than a little bit irritable. But even in the best of times she had little tolerance for vulgarity and ugliness.

Boredom did not drive her to suicide, neither did the war. Some people are courageous because they cannot imagine ultimate disaster. Not so Virginia Woolf. She imagined what it would be like to die from a bomb. "The scrunching and scrambling, the crushing of my bone shade in on my very active eye and brain: the process of putting out the light—painful? Yes. Terrifying. I suppose so. Then a swoon; a drain; two or three gulps attempting consciousness—then dot dot dot."[4] Yet she faced the dangers of living on the German bombers' route to London and near to the often-bombed Newhaven with a cool courage and even humor: "Will it ever seem strange that L. and I walking on the marsh first look at a bomb crater: then listen to the German drone above: then I take two paces nearer L., prudently deciding that two birds had better be killed with one stone?"[5] She had said, "I don't want to die yet," but living with the prospect of death did not make her hysterical. She continued to write, to cook—although their food supply was pitiably reduced—to play bowls with Leonard, to go for walks.

The bombs, the scarcity of food, the absence of friends in the country may have fueled an underlying tension, but by far the most dangerous circumstance was the completion of *Between the Acts*, for finishing a novel had, throughout her life, been the occasion of terrible depression. Even now, close to sixty years old, the author of eight novels and many other books, revered and famous, she still doubted the worth of what she had written. On March 20 she wrote to John Lehmann, Leonard's partner in the Hogarth Press, to ask for his casting vote on what she referred to as her "so called novel." She herself found it slight and sketchy and thought it would be a mistake to publish it, but Leonard didn't agree.[6] By this time her depression was so advanced that it is hard to know whether it was the product or the cause of her low estimation of her novel.

While she was still at work rewriting the book, on January 26, she noted "a battle against depression . . . routed today (I hope) by clearing out kitchen; by sending the article (a lame one) to *N.S.:* and by breaking into *P.H.* two days, I think, of memoir writing. This trough of despair shall not, I swear, engulf me. The solitude is great. Rodmell life is very small beer. The house is damp. The house is untidy. But there is no alternative."[7] She was determined to fight against it, by turning her mind outward, by keeping busy.

I mark Henry James' sentence: observe perpetually. Observe the oncome of age. Observe greed. Observe my own despondency. By that means it becomes serviceable. Or so I hope. I insist upon spending this time to best advantage. I will go down with my colors flying. This I see verges on introspection; but doesn't quite fall in. Suppose I bought a ticket at the Museum; biked in daily and read history. Suppose I selected one dominant figure in every age and wrote round and about. Occupation is essential.[8]

This was written on March 8, when Leonard was concerned about her, but still not seriously alarmed. His reaction seems entirely appropriate. Despondency, especially in time of war and deprivation, does not seem wholly irrational.

What deceived him was the suddenness of this attack. For years, he had been accustomed to watch for danger signals, and the warning symptoms had always come on slowly and unmistakably: headaches, sleeplessness, inability to concentrate. He had learned that a breakdown could be avoided if she retreated into "hibernation" or a "cocoon of quiescence" when the symptoms appeared. "But this time there were no warning symptoms of this kind. The depression struck her like a sudden blow."[9] On March 18 Leonard noted in his diary in his tight-lipped way that Virginia was "not well," which meant he considered her very bad indeed. He suspects that some time in the week that followed she tried unsuccessfully to kill herself, for he met her one day returning from a walk in the water-meadows in the pouring rain, looking "ill and shaken" and soaking wet. She said she had slipped and fallen in the water. If Leonard's suspicion is right, it would explain the otherwise mysterious fact that of the three suicide notes she left (two to Leonard, one to Vanessa), one is dated Sunday and another Tuesday. March 28, the day on which she died, was a Friday. So either she was contemplating suicide before the day on which she actually killed herself, perhaps had even tried it before, or else—and this seems to me just as likely—she was paying no particular attention to what day of the week it was and, as she sometimes did when quite healthy, carelessly wrote the wrong date.

I want to dwell for a moment on the suicide letters in an effort to reconstruct Virginia Woolf's frame of mind before she took her life. The letter to Vanessa dated "Sunday" and the earlier letter to Leonard, which has no date, are written in the same faint shade of ink and on the same size paper. The later letter to Leonard, dated Tuesday, the one which he found on the mantelpiece, is on a smaller sheet and the ink is darker, as though the pen had been refilled since she wrote the first letters. This is the text of the earlier letter to Leonard:

> Dearest,
> I want to tell you that you have given me complete happiness. No one could have done more than you have done. Please believe that. But I know that I shall never get over this: and I am wasting your life. It is this madness. Nothing anyone says can persuade me. You can work, and you will be much better without me. You see I can't write this even, which shows I am right. All I want to say is that until this disease came on me we were perfectly happy. It was all due to you. No one could have been so good as you have been, from the very first day till now. Everyone knows that.
>
> V.
>
> You will find Roger's letters to Mauron in the writing table drawer in the Lodge. Will you destroy all my papers.[10]

She has carried on in her mind the inevitable dialogue ("Nothing anyone says can persuade me") and has reached her conclusion. Her concern is all that Leonard should not feel guilty for her suicide. In the letter to Vanessa, the same concern for Leonard comes through, but she dwells rather more on the extremity of her own situation. "I feel that I have gone too far this time to come back again. I am certain now that I am going mad again. It is just as it was the first time, I am always hearing voices, and I know I shan't get over it now."[11] She ends with a phrase as typical of genuine suicide notes as are her specific instructions to Leonard. "I have fought against it, but I can't any longer."

At some later time, she wrote another letter to Leonard which incorporated phrases from both her previous lettters.

> Dearest,
>    I feel certain I am going mad again. I feel we can't go through another of those terrible times. And I shan't recover this time. I begin to hear voices, and I can't concentrate. So I am doing what seems the best thing to do. You have given me the greatest possible happiness. You have been in every way all that anyone could be. I don't think two people could have been happier till this terrible disease came. I can't fight any longer. I know that I am spoiling your life, that without me you could work. And you will I know. You see I can't even write properly. I can't read. What I want to say is I owe all the happiness of my life to you. You have been entirely patient with me and incredibly good. I want to say that— everybody knows it. If anybody could have saved me it would have been you. Everything has gone from me but the certainty of your goodness. I can't go on spoiling your life any longer.
>    I don't think two people could have been happier than we have been.
>
>                                        V.[12]

A writer to the last, Virginia Woolf made a draft of and then revised her suicide note. This letter is much more studied than the earlier ones, makes more of an effort to persuade her reader of the gravity of her situation and the lack of blame attaching to Leonard. She is arguing, making a case. She gives evidence ("I begin to hear voices, and I can't concentrate"). Regarded as a literary document, however callous it may seem to so regard it, this letter shows a summoning up of powers rather than a disintegration. If we trust the date on this letter (Tuesday), it was written three days before she actually killed herself.

In any case, what is significant is the fact that she reworked her suicide note—whether days before or, as both

Leonard Woolf and Quentin Bell assume, on the morning of her suicide. It bespeaks discipline, rationality, a concern for those she is leaving behind, pride in herself as a craftsman. These were the things that made her what she was. To prevent their loss, she killed herself. Although the fear of insanity is what drove her to suicide, it appears that the suicide itself was not an act of insanity but a supreme and final attempt at discipline.

Some suicides seem more rational than others—a terminal cancer victim in great pain has a motive for suicide that some people might not grant to a sufferer from an internal delusion, however painful. But the pain of going mad is real, too, and not something one wants to experience twice. To say, as A. Alvarez does, that "Virginia Woolf drowned herself, a victim of her own excessive sensibility,"[13] is to invite comparison with Byron's cruelly flippant suggestion that Keats was killed by a bad review. The woman had suffered—had every reason to expect she would suffer again, and not from sensibility or from bad reviews or from wartime tension but from the invasion of the most precious part of herself, her mind. She knew what she could expect: nightmarish visions of guilt and persecution, her best friends appearing as enemies. Perhaps the only people who can feel what she must have felt, without actually having been insane, are people who have endured hideous drug-induced hallucinations, wishing there was some quick antidote, feeling they would rather be dead than continue in such hell.

On the morning of Virginia's death, Leonard sent off a letter to John Lehmann on the subject of *Between the Acts,* enclosing another from Virginia which must have been written during that week. This letter says she has decided not to publish the novel as it stands. She will revise it, and perhaps they can publish it in the fall. She thinks it would mean a financial loss if published as is, and she doesn't want that. These plans for the future were either an elaborate coverup, or she was at the same time preparing for suicide and hoping that the symptoms of insanity would disappear, and she wouldn't have to go through with it.

Leonard, in his covering note, said she was on the verge of a complete mental breakdown. He knew she was terrified of madness; her thoughts were racing out of control, and a desperate depression had settled on her. He thought she might kill herself at any moment. By Wednesday, March 26, he considered her state as serious as it had been in August 1913, when she had suffered a disintegration which led to a suicide attempt. Leonard was convinced that the way to save her in such a condition was to force her into total quiescence and put her under supervised care. Accordingly, he convinced Virginia to go the next day to consult her physician in Brighton, Octavia Wilburforce. Virginia confessed to Dr. Wilburforce her fears that the past would return, that she would never be able to write again, but insisted she was not seriously ill. The consultation was therapeutic in itself but inconclusive about future handling of the problem. More than anything, Virginia feared that rest cure; and both Dr. Wilburforce and Leonard feared imposing it on her, feared it would precipitate an even graver crisis, while at the same time they considered it her only hope. Unnecessarily, Leonard blamed himself afterward for failing to enforce restraints on Virginia. There are limits to the responsibility one person can take for another's life, and Virginia was determined to control her own fate. If she was going mad again, she would choose the cure.

Louie Mayer, who had been the Woolfs' cook in Rodmell since 1934, knew that the weeks following the completion of a book were bad ones for Virginia. She was exhausted, sometimes had headaches. When Virginia was in this state she would wander into the kitchen, sit down, and forget what she had come to say. Then she would go out to the garden and walk about, as though trying to remember. Louie sometimes saw her bump into trees while she walked. On the morning of March 28, as Louie was tidying up Leonard's study, they both entered the room and Leonard asked if she would give Virginia a duster so she could help clean the room. Since Virginia had never done housework with her before, she was evidently having a bad day, and they thought some physical work would make her feel better. But soon she put down the duster and went away. Later in the morning Louie saw her come down from the sitting room on the second floor and go out to her study in the garden. It was about 11:30 when Louie saw her come back into the house, gather up her coat and walking-stick, and head out to the water-meadows through the garden gate.

At one o'clock, when Louie rang the bell for lunch, Leonard went up to the sitting room and found the suicide note on the mantelpiece. He ran to the kitchen to tell Louie that he feared his wife had tried to kill herself. Then he raced to the river, where he found her walking stick in the mud on the bank. Louie fetched the gardener, who ran for the village policeman, and together they searched the river and the water-meadows until it was dark.

Her body was not found for weeks, until some children out walking along the river near Lewes saw it washed up against the bank. A policeman came to inform Leonard. "He said that there were heavy stones in the pockets of her jacket and she must have put them there and then walked straight down into the river. And that," wrote Louie Mayer, "was terrible. It was the most terrible thing I have ever known." [14]

On April 18, Leonard went to the Newhaven mortuary to identify her body. On April 21 she was cremated in Brighton. Leonard had thought that the cavatina from Beethoven's B-flat Quartet, opus 130, should be played at one's cremation, but when the time came to make arrangements for the funeral, he could not bring himself to discuss Beethoven's cavatina. When the doors of the crematorium opened and the coffin slid forward, Leonard heard, to his surprise, the music of the Blessed Spirits from Gluck's *Or-*

*The river Ouse, near Rodmell.*

*pheo.* Later he played the cavatina for himself. He buried her ashes under a tree in the garden.

People have been tempted to see Virginia Woolf's method of self-slaughter as symbolic. David Daiches, for example, imagines her uniting herself with the flux of experience, which had so concerned her in her writing, as she disappeared into the flowing, tidal waters of the Ouse.[15] This seems forced. We should remind ourselves that the river was available, as a bottle of sleeping pills had been available in 1913, and that if Woolf had succeeded in killing herself then, as she very nearly did, few would have seen it as anything other than a simple, painless method of death. Nevertheless, drowning *is* suggestive. The sea is suggestive. And before Woolf tried to kill herself by veronal, she had tried it, in 1904, by jumping out of a window. If one recurrent image in her writing is the room, suggesting the security and limitations of individual consciousness, the other is water, particularly the sea, suggesting a unity with all life either beyond or beneath individual consciousness—the world without a self, in which individuality is dissolved in the eternal rhythms of collective life.[16] If the room betokens a wary, beleaguered ego, the ocean suggests escape into the impersonal, a comforting and protective element—the kind of escape she was obsessed with throughout the thirties. Her earliest memories were of her mother and the water outside her window. In her beginnings was her end.

# Portrait:
# A Woman of Letters

Although photographs show her invariably elegant, wearing clothes on her long lean frame with negligent grace, Virginia Woolf always felt shabby and unattractive. She was not comfortable in life. Things that other people do easily, without thinking, such as going to a store to buy a dress, could be difficult for her, sometimes insurmountably so. She had to construct normal gestures painfully. In some ways, her greatest personal triumphs were in the realm of the absolutely ordinary, like hiring a governess for her sister's children. Performing such an act, she felt she had successfully impersonated what she never believed she was, a real woman.

Her husband treated her, and she usually treated herself, like a finely tuned mechanism constantly in danger of flying apart. If she stepped too hard on any point, if she worked too hard or slept too little, got angry or jostled routine, the nitro-glycerine inside her brain would explode. From childhood she had been fearful, afraid of provoking disasters, and disasters had come. Her mother had died, then Stella, and then, at a time of confused feelings about him, her father. The magical associations of childhood, according to which one's evil thoughts can themselves cause disaster, never left her, so magical prohibitions marked out her path through adult life. If she revealed herself, allowed people to see her as she really was, terrible things would happen, either to herself or others. People would jeer at her and she would go mad, or someone would die. She could not speak openly of her feelings. She envied those, like Ethel Smyth, who could, and yet so ter-rified was she of open conflict that she preferred to lose a friend rather than endure a "scene."

Hatred, love, and fear were transmuted into faintly ma-licious banter. Irony and ladylike manners served as cos-metics for the soul. So much energy went into self-conceal-ment and the construction of a charming facade that little was left for imaginative sympathy. Like many people who are acutely responsive to other people's reactions to them, she was sensitive to nuances of gesture and appearance, but of people's deeper drives her perception was dim. She com-pensated in her novels by making character of secondary im-portance, by diffusing her own lyrical response to life throughout. In her personal life she compensated by being an intrepid asker of questions. How does it feel to wake up in the morning on a Tuscan farm? How, exactly, does a scientist extract protein from minced liver? She had a hunger for precise information; it was her way of getting to know other people. But almost everyone who mentions this habit of hers mentions also their sense of the alienation behind it. She questioned, because she felt cut off from the world of fact. Iris Origo has described her as an insect beating against a pane of glass to get to a light on the other side. David Cecil thought she was like a beautiful mermaid, who would swim up out of the sea to have a look at the rest of us—remote, but very curious. Alix Strachey said she always looked as though she were surprised to find herself there.[1] Her bodily existence *was* a surprise, and not always a pleasant one.

People who knew her frequently describe her as like a fairy-tale princess, otherworldly, so elegant of build, with such deep-set eyes, so wraithlike, so distinguished, and so fragile. (In most of her posed photographs, she and her photographers have seemed to collaborate to emphasize this delicacy and other worldliness.) When she rubbed her hands by the fire, you could almost see through them. But what made her one of the most enchanting people in the world to be with was her wit and imagination. She was always "taking off," talking about the most unexpected subjects or developing some absurd premise into a spectacularly baroque verbal edifice. Since people were not quite real to her, she often made them up—to their faces, and to their astonishment. Once she had pried loose from them a nugget of fact, she went on to coat it, to engulf it in her own imaginative wave. It did not seem to occur to her that people might object to serving as fodder for her fantasies. She was far from being a comfortable and kindly presence—people who demand to be amused, who demand of themselves that they be amusing, rarely are—but few seemed to mind. One looked for kindliness elsewhere; one turned to Virginia for imaginative delight. Children, those excellent judges of adult vivacity, always looked forward to her visits. She was, in conversation, a fantasist, an inventor, a teller of tales, not a scrupulous intellectual. Wild, spontaneous, abundant, her talk seemed to come from the same part of her mind as the racing thoughts of her madness and the inspired frenzy of her writing. When she laughed so hard at something she had said that tears came to her eyes, Leonard would begin to look concerned.

Beneath that high-strung inventiveness was a soul that guzzled affection. As a child, she would ask her sister, "Do you like me better than . . . ?" naming a list of friends and relatives. As a woman in her fifties she played the same game, explaining to the puzzled object of her questions that the response she wanted was not sober self-questioning and scrupulous honesty but emotional extravagance. Her own set was tight-lipped. Vanessa, for example, could never adequately respond to her sister's declarations of love which she realized constituted demands for a return in kind. To satisfy her need, as imperative in its way as a junkie's, Virginia turned to women of a different sort, to women who had retained the knack of expressing simple affection, to hostesses like Ottoline Morrell and Sybil Colefax, who flattered her self-esteem as an artist, and to downright, emphatic, unself-conscious women like V. Sackville-West and Ethel Smyth, who were not embarrassed to talk about their feelings and whose feelings for Virginia were gratifyingly exuberant. But even when she obtained the enormous infusions of affection and esteem that she required, the effects soon wore off, for she did not have that irrational, unshakable sense of her own worth which, when it is found at all, is found in people who have been extravagantly wanted and loved as children and which such lucky people carry through life. No amount of external approval can make up for that feeling. For Woolf, certainly, the honors, the fame, and the money she eventually won for herself did not make up for it.

As she got more famous, she felt no more secure. The gap between her private feelings and her public position was perhaps the most enduring feature of her inner world, stretching back to earliest childhood. The kind of mother everyone thinks of as perfect frequently doesn't give enough love to one particularly needy little soul, which may be one

*Virginia Woolf, 1939.*

of the reasons that in later years, Virginia treasured every reference to her mother's malice, any description painting a moustache on that madonna. Love was the first deceit—that she loved and that she was loved. Other deceits were to follow, real and imagined. Her socially impeccable half-brother behaved indecently to her. Lonely and needy in her deepest self, she was forced to play the charming youngest daughter in a big happy family. It was a betrayal of her real self. It was false in every way, because as she knew well, life was a matter of unsatisfied longings, pain, and guilt. By her teens, Virginia had developed a fairly complete dual identity. Her real self read books, wrote, lived in a private world of the mind. Her false self, centered on her body, with which her real self felt little connection, got dressed in seed pearls and silk, served tea, and made polite conversation.

R. D. Laing's brilliant description of the schizoid personality in *The Divided Self* [2] must be mentioned here, although in suggesting that Woolf's inner world was of the type described by Laing, my intent is not clinical and certainly not judgmental. I merely want to indicate the mental ground in which her art flourished and to suggest why it took the distinctive forms it did. The states of being Laing describes many of us will have experienced. Madness is to him an exaggeration, a chaotic and imprisoning caricature, of an alienation not limited to the mad. The personality he calls schizoid does not experience itself as a unified whole but is split in two fundamental ways, in its relation to the world, from which it feels separate, and in its relation to itself; for it is divided into two or more selves, a real self, which must remain hidden, and a false self, which must interact with the world the real self does not trust. The threshold of security is so low for such a person that everything outside seems a threat. The false self goes through the motions of compliance to the demands of that threatening world—embodied in father, mother, husband, or whoever—but eventually, accumulated hatred against that person, who has come to be seen as a tyrant, pours out. Love threatens loss of self, so that such people are reluctant to love. Their essential defense against the loss of self they so much fear is to pretend that no self exists, to be anonymous or incognito, or to pretend to have no body. A schizoid organization need not degenerate into chaos; it is capable of creativity. Indeed, since love is so difficult for such a person, life threatens to be meaningless without some creative work. But of course, once that work is finished, the hidden self is embodied and liable to the hostile gaze of the world outside.

Woolf noticed much of this in herself but explained it in her own way. She thought her insanity was inherited, and so, to some extent, it may have been, a genetic predisposition aggravated by the circumstances of early childhood. She also thought she had inherited a fear of men which modulated into a disgust with sex, and that seems highly *un*likely. But if she ignored the potential importance of her earliest years in explaining her inner makeup, she didn't ignore the effects on her self-esteem of social conditioning, of the treatment accorded women, while she was growing up. The "ontological insecurity" Laing evokes is not a problem only of women, but in Woolf's mind the perils of identity were intimately connected with her femaleness. She saw how the self-confidence of men was systematically nurtured by British society whereas women's was almost as systematically attacked. She became sensitive to the minuets of ego in a group and quick to notice coercion and manipulation in any form. Much of what was hostile in the outside world she identified as patriarchal. Many of her personal experiences—such as her social and sexual bullying by George Duckworth—made sense to her as expressions of patriarchal high-handedness. Feminism was her only acceptable way of stating publicly the sense of oppression and persecution she suffered from. Since some of the oppression she noted was real, feminism became the point at which her private fears and fantasies touched on public issues. For her, it served a therapeutic function. It was the only perspective she had on her life which allowed her to see herself as part of a group whose problems could be traced to common sources.

Superimposed on the class structure as usually defined, she saw a much simpler grid of power—insiders and outsiders. Women, along with the poor, were outsiders in England, and to be born female partially offset the advantages of being born to money and privilege, for although wealth might be counted on to bring freedom to young men, to young women it seemed to bring only greater restrictions on their experience and mobility in the name of protection and good breeding. This had been her own experience, and she assumed it was general for what she called in *Three Guineas* "the daughters of educated men." Because the family's education fund had been devoted to her brothers, she felt she had been deprived of the best training and the widest experience of life, had missed out on discussing Plato casually, before a fire, with her intellectual equals, as she had missed out on the kind of experience that can be gained by walking through a city alone at night. She imagined herself a kind of maiden enchanted by the evil power of patriarchy; outside her tower lay the world, but like the Lady of Shalott, she could view it only indirectly, through the medium of books. It is the romantic myth of the isolation of the artist with a feminist twist—she is locked in the palace of art because she is a well-born woman.

As a young woman, it took her a long time to convince herself that difference of style did not mean inferiority, that she had her own voice, unique, feminine, worth attending to. The Immured Maiden became the Outsider, who derived strength and distinction from exclusion. Nothing is more striking in her career than the crazy seesaw between two very different kinds of works, works of genuine originality and works of academic discipline. She wrote radically individual novels like *Mrs. Dalloway*, *To the Lighthouse*, *The Waves*, *Between the Acts*, and parts of *The Voyage Out*, but she also repeatedly—one might almost say compulsively—turned out books in which there was as little of herself invested as possible: *Night and Day, The Years,* and the biography of Roger Fry, massive, time-consuming, exhausting exercises in self-suppression. Writing style, identity, and madness were perilously interconnected. When she felt threatened, she clung to the novel of fact and traditional form. She wrote *Night and Day,* for example, while the idea for her new style was taking shape, but she postponed the excitement and the terror of innovation and stuck to her academic task because she had just been insane (from 1913 to 1915) and feared becoming insane again. The traditional novel was her magical antidote.[3] At such times she relapsed into the Immured Maiden, writing to fit some imaginary paternal standard of reality and fiction, renouncing her terror-filled individuality.

Her political consciousness—and feminism was her only true politics—ebbed and flowed, and there is a striking correspondence between its heights and times of her good work. Her writing was at its best in the twenties when her feminism was firmest. It faltered in the thirties under the onslaught of the very different notions of what constituted politics of the young men of the left. Losing her feminist perspective, she lost confidence in herself. It was the personal faith which gave her the courage to write authentically, without warping her talent to suit phantom models of validity. Writing *Three Guineas,* as I see it, enabled her to write *Between the Acts,* one last novel in her own voice and style.

"My terror of real life has always kept me in a nunnery,"[4] she wrote to Ethel Smyth in 1930, when they were relatively new friends and Virginia was explaining herself. Unlike Ethel, the eccentric composer who was unafraid to compare the slow movement of a symphony to the movement of her own bowels, Virginia was a sexual coward—so goes her confession. When she got married, her brains went up in fireworks, and although she was nearly crippled by the fierce discipline of madness, she went on to discover in it almost everything she wrote about. While other versions of her life emphasized the way in which her development had been stunted by particular men or by patriarchal attitudes more generally, this version emphasizes fear, cowardice, and the uses of madness, and any just portrait of her inner world must keep in balance both these pressures, the psychic and the social, without losing sight of the fact that, despite everything, she was a creative, productive, and vital person who made life yield up its fruits.

Writing had been her refuge as a child. She escaped from the emotional turmoil and fitful hypocrisy of downstairs life at Hyde Park Gate to the quiet of her own room, where the authentic life could be lived, the life of the mind. Some girls play at dressing up, copying their mothers; she played at letters, copying her father, until that play became art and the chief justification of her life. The presentation of her work remained throughout her life a source of anxiety, as it was when she and Vanessa left a copy of the *Hyde Park Gate News* next to their mother's chair, for there was always the possibility that approval would not be forthcoming. But if presentation was hazardous, the act of writing was always bracing. Art provided the way of reconciling personal contradictions into harmonious wholes, of fitting, let us say, Septimus Warren Smith and Mrs. Dalloway into the same book. It was a way to make use of her internal sense of division. Moreover, for a person terrified of so much of the world outside her, writing books offered a way of retiring from the world without abandoning the hope of communication—without, that is, retiring into a world so private she was actually insane. Leonard Woolf, along with many others, saw that there was a close connection between her madness and the sources of her creativity, but it is equally true that her creativity was her principal stay against madness.[5]

Finishing a book was dangerous, not just because of the

imminence of presentation and self-revelation. If she was not already working on another book, her underlying guilt and anxiety came to the surface, no longer kept in control by the sheer activity of writing. Or perhaps she was simply exhausted from the effort. She became irritable and melancholy. She felt her mind was bobbing like a cork on the ocean. Absorbed in her work, she lived an underwater existence; she resented interruptions which hauled her, like an indignant fish, to the surface. When she set to work, she would light a cigarette, take her writing board on her knees, and let herself down, like a diver, she said, into the sentence she had written the day before. After some twenty minutes she would see a light in the ocean depths and stealthily approach, flinging a sentence like a net over some sea pearl which was likely to slip away, and which, brought to the surface, might not look anything like what it had underwater.[6] Very little of her imaginative effort went into scene-building or dramatic constructs. An image, a picture (like that of her father sitting in the boat at St. Ives) or an experimental notion (like the mid-section of *To the Lighthouse*) would flash into her mind, often when she was walking, and from then on the business of writing consisted of fitting words onto the backs of rhythms. These subaqueous pursuits were her greatest excitements in life.

Whether she was in her study writing, or walking the Sussex downs, or strolling about the streets of London, she had a capacity for total absorption in her work. Louie Mayer, when she first started work at Rodmell, was startled to hear her talking to herself, asking questions and answering them, as she took her morning bath in the room over the kitchen. She was trying out the sentences that had come to her the night before. Rest consisted of varying her literary activity, turning from fiction to criticism or from criticism to fiction, taking a break for memoirs from time to time, and perpetually making time for correspondence and her journal. If writing articles was like tying up her mind into brown paper parcels, tying up parcels seemed seductively simple when she was writing fiction. But when she was doing journalism, she would long to fly free in fiction once more. This wasn't mere contrariness; it was a finely supervised monitoring of her own psychic states, the exercise of conscious will providing an antidote for her more subterranean (or submarine) creativity, and vice versa. Reading, too, presented itself as a psychic exercise, and not just a way of taking in information —it was a state which consisted, she said, in the total elimination of the ego, providing a disembodied and trance-like rapture.[7] There is, you will note, something sensual in this characterization of reading, as there was in Woolf's enjoyment of literary activity in general. Until the last drafts of a work, when she went back over the manuscript with the impersonal mediation of a typewriter (going over the same page three and four times), she was a longhand writer, sensitive to the texture of the paper, to the flow of ink, to the feel of the pen nibs, about which she was very particular.

Even her hobby was bookish, if you can call bookish or a hobby a business which made money and which turned her variously into a salesperson and shipping clerk. Later in life Virginia invented the story that the Hogarth Press was started so she could have freedom to write what she pleased, but although it eventually gave her this freedom, that is not why it was founded. Its original function was largely therapeutic, to keep Virginia's mind off her mind by involving her in the physical labor of setting up type, running off sheets, and binding up books. But after printing a distinguished list of little books, including *Kew Gardens* and *The Waste Land*, the operation outgrew the Woolfs' basement. The printing was given out, but the Woolfs continued to run the editorial side of the press as a cottage industry. Virginia turned from setting type to reading manuscripts and dealing with authors, manual occupation gave way inevitably to mental, and the would-be printers turned publishers.

She had known great writers in her childhood, with the

result that literary greatness seemed a thing of the past, just as mountains one sees as a child remain in the memory higher and more majestic than any seen in later years. Greatness was someone who came to tea in a frock coat and to whom your parents introduced you. Though she was the center of the literary life of London, she was never again to be conscious of greatness as in the days when Henry James or George Meredith walked through the door of the house in Hyde Park Gate. She was a bad judge of her contemporaries partly because of familiarity. T. S. Eliot was "Tom," with his dotty wife and his overdone American manners. She came, over the years, to love him very much, and, in literature, his rhythm, his vision of London, and his sense of transitions and timing all influenced hers. Nevertheless, she was far from being in awe of his achievement. He was one of the best poets of the age (the others, to her mind, were Yeats and de la Mare), but they were all frail reeds compared to the great poets of the past. The contemporary writer who had influenced her most was E. M. Forster, but that was in her early years, and by 1930 she had come to see his work as immature, impeded, diminished. Typically, she perceived the work as a reflection of the man, who was son, daughter, sister, and husband to his aged mother with whom he lived, the two of them like a pair of mice in a nest. Of the great British writers alive in her lifetime, her awe was reserved for Thomas Hardy, a survivor from the past, a friend of her father's.

Snobbery, too, prevented her from realizing what a heroic literary age she lived in. She could not really appreciate Joyce (and she tried hard to, because Eliot admired his work so much) because of his earthiness, which she considered ill-bred obscenity (a limitation of vision she shared with Edith Wharton), and she realized much too late the stature of D. H. Lawrence, alienated from him by his working-class origins and also by John Middleton Murry's approval.

Contemporaries, moreover, provoked an unhealthy sort

of rivalry. They were doing the same thing she was, but—as she put it—on a different railway track.[8] It was distracting. She had to remind herself that "East Coker" could be good and her own work, different as it was, could also be good. With French writers, she was on safer ground. They were from a different country, wrote in a different tradition. So she could read Colette and Proust with pleasure, while Mansfield and Joyce produced anxiety and irritation. Tolstoy, so distant from her in time, geography, and by virtue of his background, could evoke her strongest admiration. Although she lived among writers, read new books constantly for review and for the press, her eyes were partially closed to them, and her deepest nourishment continued to come from the literature of the past and from her own experience.

As publisher, journalist, essayist, novelist, polemicist, and diarist, Virginia Woolf's literary endeavors matched her father's in heroic energy and achievement, and at some point she must have realized that.

She was almost sixty years old when she died, a fact that always startles me, for I imagine her dying young. Because of illness, her career was a belated one, but long before the age at which Woolf killed herself in an incipient depressive state, Balzac and Dickens had killed themselves through manic overactivity. For Virginia Woolf, because of the careful guardianship of her husband, it was easier to slip off and drown herself than it would have been to kill herself by overwork.

It was typical of Leonard Woolf's conscientious concern for Virginia that he should conceive the notion of getting her involved in printing to keep her from unhealthy involvement in her own imagination. After the massive mental breakdown which so inauspiciously began their married life, he daily kept track of her health, metering work and play. When she caught cold, he moved her bed for her and dressed her in his dressing gown. He never complained. A rationalist saint, and yet, as any reader of his autobiography is aware, a man of almost numbing common sense. It hardly seems fair to blame Leonard for fussiness in his treatment of Virginia— a person tends to get the treatment she expects, and she might not have survived as long as she did without his watchful care and protection—and yet perhaps he was overly protective. A lovely story, perhaps apocryphal, but nonetheless expressive, relates that when a cow wandered into the field adjacent to Virginia's bedroom and stuck its head through her window, Leonard bought the field, so that this event, which had startled but also amused Virginia, might not recur.[9]

The doctors they consulted about Virginia's illness were "nerve specialists," and they called what she suffered from neurasthenia—fatigued nerves—but what they meant they could not say. (Neurasthenia no longer seems a useful medical term and has disappeared with the stereopticon.) Although the Woolfs were aware of psychoanalysis and indulged in discussing each other's flaws in the light of psychoanalysis, Virginia did not consider turning to an analyst for therapy, probably because she conceived of her illness as one of the nervous system and not of the psyche. Under Leonard's supervision, her life was rigidly structured to avoid the fatigue which, in the view of her doctors, provoked her insanity. She wrote only three hours a day, from ten to one, although she spent much of the afternoon revising or typing up what she had written in the morning, also thinking about what she would write the next day. She rarely stayed up past eleven, and social life, which she liked as the other pole of her solitude, in the same systole-diastole way she liked everything else, was strictly rationed. At the least sign of fatigue or headache she had to stop work and take to her bed. Louie Mayer was astonished at the way every hour was accounted for in the Woolfs' routine. Regular, disciplined, Virginia took little time off on weekends and gave herself only two-week vacations, although their moving back and forth between London and the country was a perpetual tonic. Illness was her unscheduled, unchosen rest from her labors. Whole months dropped out of her life, months which healthier, more fortunate people might spend swimming or sunning in the south, but which she spent in bed, in paroxysms of fear and self-hatred.

She never blamed her poor health for the limitations on her life. Nevertheless, if she envied her brothers their Oxbridge experience, she envied her sister her children and lovers. She envied Katherine Mansfield her travel and adventures. She envied Vita her disregard for convention. Thinking of Colette, who had danced in music halls, made her feel dowdy. We have to remember that if Woolf was confined to a life of letters, of mediated experience, other women of her time were not. There was, in fact, more to it than the evil power of patriarchy, but her physical and mental frailty played a restrictive part she chose never to incorporate in the myth of her own life. Her tendency to madness was acknowledged, but only as a nuisance one had to cope with, rather like chronic hay fever. If this was self-deception, it was a useful, strategic self-deception which enabled her to live a productive life. One can't fight—or couldn't in the years before the war—a metabolic predisposition to psychosis. Far from considering her madness the source of her deprivations, she considered it her chief compensation, giving her access to an underworld of experience even more remote from the tea tables of Britain than were the dance halls of France or the brothels of Germany. It was her ticket to chaos, her passport out of the stranglehold of ordinary perception. As his epilepsy was for Dostoevsky, her madness was for Woolf a quasi-religious experience, which released her from the realm of the merely rational and initiated her into the sources of awe.

I would give a great deal to know what her hallucinations in madness were like. When the Devil appeared to

Virginia Woolf, what shape did he take? In addition to the passages in *The Voyage Out* and *Mrs. Dalloway* to which I have already called attention, there are glimpses, frustratingly meager. The doctors and nurses were in a conspiracy against her. Her mother was in the bedroom talking to her. The birds sang to her in Greek. King Edward shouted obscenities, naked in the rhododendrons.

Doctors and nurses engaged in persecution, using magical, scientific, or secret means to interfere with one's body and mind, is a typical delusion of mental patients, but surely only Virginia Woolf in her madness heard the birds singing in Greek. It seems a benign enough delusion, almost comical, yet we know it must have appeared to Woolf sinister, threatening, and horrific. Were the Greek-speaking birds a kind of cabal, a cultural set, a Cambridge-educated aviary from which she was excluded and which was mocking her? With the king, the very symbol of patriarchal authority, the potential for threat—the threat of male lust and male power—is clearer. It seems that the obsession with patriarchal tyranny which gave shape and meaning to her conscious life penetrated her underlife as well. But what was her mother saying on that horrible morning in 1915 when Virginia suddenly saw her by her bedside and began a nonstop response? Was she accusing her of having wished her death? Was Virginia defending herself? We know that to avoid hearing these voices, Virginia Woolf structured her life and finally killed herself.

Yet madness taught her to know the self, in alienation and in terror, and it taught her to observe, with sensuous apprehension, the passing moment, unconnected to other moments, leading nowhere, but ballooning palpably into a space to be explored. If time becomes architectonic in the modern novel, it often does in hallucinations as well, and in this way, as in so many others, Woolf came by a unique route, based on her own experience, to join in the artistic revolution early in this century. Without glamorizing her madness, we may say that it was a more valuable education than the one she so much regretted.

If Woolf's life and work have relevance to many who are not manic-depressives born to culture and terrified of life, it is because she was not as unique as she often thought and sometimes feared she was, because her fears speak to other people's fears, because her sense of life's important points, its delights and crises, corresponds with theirs, because she speaks for a class and not for herself alone, and finally because she successfully transformed her life into a life of letters which anyone may read.

# Chronology

1882   Virginia Stephen born.

1883   Adrian Stephen born.

c. 1888   Gerald Duckworth shows sexual interest in Virginia.

1895   Julia Stephen dies. Virginia's first mental breakdown follows.

1897   Stella Duckworth marries Jack Hills in April and dies in July.

1899   Thoby Stephen enters Cambridge. Virginia studies Greek with Janet Case.

1904   Death of Leslie Stephen. Sexual attention

from George Duckworth. Virginia's second breakdown; she attempts to kill herself by jumping from window. Virginia, Vanessa, Thoby, and Adrian Stephen move to 46 Gordon Square, Bloomsbury. Virginia's first publication, an unsigned review in *The Guardian.*

1905   Thoby's Cambridge friends start coming to 46 Gordon Square on Thursday evenings—the beginning of "Bloomsbury." Virginia teaching at Morley College.

1906   Virginia and her sister and brothers visit Greece. Thoby and Vanessa become ill. Thoby dies.

1907   Vanessa marries Clive Bell. Virginia and Adrian move to 29 Fitzroy Square. Virginia begins working on *The Voyage Out.*

1908   Virginia involved in flirtation with brother-in-law.

1909   Lytton Strachey proposes, is accepted, retracts his offer. Virginia meets Ottoline Morrell.

1910   The Dreadnought Hoax.

1911   Virginia enters into cooperative living arrangement with J. M. Keynes, Duncan Grant, Leonard Woolf, and Adrian at 38 Brunswick Square.

1912   In January Leonard Woolf proposes to Virginia, and in May she agrees to marry him. They are married in August.

1913   Virginia completes *The Voyage Out,* which is accepted for publication by Gerald Duckworth. Virginia increasingly depressed and disturbed. Attempts to kill herself in September.

1914   World War I begins. Virginia seems to be recovering, but it is merely a lull between two bouts of insanity.

1915   Manic phase of breakdown. Virginia is violent and hostile to nurses. Woolfs move into Hogarth House, Richmond.

1916   Virginia returns to normal.

1917   Beginning of the Hogarth Press, whose first publication is Virginia's *The Mark on the Wall*. Virginia writes reviews for the *Times Literary Supplement*. Begins writing her diary.

1918   Strachey's *Eminent Victorians* published. Virginia working on *Night and Day*.

1919   *Night and Day* published by Duckworth. *Kew Gardens* published by the Hogarth Press. The Woolfs also publish this year T. S. Eliot's *Poems*. The manuscript of *Ulysses* has been offered them by Harriet Weaver, but the printers refuse to handle it. The Woolfs buy Monk's House in Rodmell, Sussex.

1920   *Monday or Tuesday*.

1922   *Jacob's Room*. Virginia meets Vita Sackville-West. Begins work on what will become *Mrs. Dalloway*.

1924   Woolfs move to 52 Tavistock Square. *Mr. Bennett and Mrs. Brown*.

1925   Publication of *Mrs. Dalloway* and *The Common Reader*. Beginning of romance with Vita Sackville-West. Virginia starts work on *To the Lighthouse* immediately after finishing *Mrs. Dalloway*.

1927   Spending a lot of time with Vita. *To the Lighthouse* published. Virginia begins thinking of *Orlando*, originally to be called *The Jessamy Brides* and more directly concerned with lesbianism.

1928   *Orlando* published, dedicated to Vita. Virginia delivers the talks which will become *A Room of One's Own*.

1929   *A Room of One's Own* published. Virginia thinking about early version of *The Waves*, called *The Moths*.

1930   Virginia meets Ethel Smyth, the composer and elderly eccentric who will pursue her unrelentingly for the next few years.

1931   John Lehmann hired for the Hogarth Press. Publication of *The Waves*.

1932   Death of Lytton Strachey followed by Carrington's

suicide. *Letter to a Young Poet* published, also *The Second Common Reader*. Virginia begins thinking about *The Years*, originally *The Pargiters*. First academic studies of her work published. Attacked by *Scrutiny* and others. Offered honors. Has become a member of the establishment and a target.

1933  *Flush*. Working on *The Years*.

1936  After three years of writing, Virginia sends manuscript of *The Years* to the printer, then begins an extensive and tedious correction of proofs. Beginning of Spanish Civil War. *Three Guineas* undertaken.

1937  *The Years* published, a popular success. Julian Bell goes to Spain as an ambulance driver and is killed.

1938  War with Germany seems imminent. *Three Guineas* published. Virginia working on biography of Roger Fry and thinking about *Between the Acts*, originally *Pointz Hall*.

1939  The Woolfs live in Rodmell and come to London only for visits. Their London residence is now 37 Mecklenburgh Square.

1940  Publication of *Roger Fry*. Battle of Britain. 52 Tavistock Square and 37 Mecklenburgh Square both bombed.

1941  Virginia polishing *Between the Acts*. Commits suicide in March.

# Notes

## 1 St. Ives and Kensington

1. See Noel Annan, *Leslie Stephen: His Thought and Character in Relation to His Time* (Cambridge: Harvard University Press, 1952).

2. This chapter relies heavily on "A Sketch of the Past," in *Moments of Being*.

3. See "Professions for Women," in Virginia Woolf, *Collected Essays*, 4 vols. (New York: Harcourt, Brace & World, 1967), II, 287–88.

4. Virginia's memoirs place George's aggressions around 1904, although it's possible they had started earlier and Leonard Woolf believed they dated from much earlier indeed—around 1895, just after Julia's death. See Bell, I, 44n.

5. See Virginia Woolf's introductory essay about Julia Margaret Cameron in *Victorian Photographs of Famous Men and Fair Women,* ed. Tristram Powell (Boston: David R. Godine, 1973), p. 14. This is a reissue of a volume of Cameron's photographs originally published by the Hogarth Press in 1926, with introductions by Woolf and Roger Fry.

6. Vanessa Bell, *Notes on Virginia's Childhood* (New York: Frank Hallman, 1974), unpaged.

7. *Moments of Being,* pp. 94–95.

8. Autobiographical fragment, written 1940, beginning "The tea table was the centre of Victorian family life," Berg Collection, New York Public Library.

9. *Moments of Being,* p. 71.

10. *Ibid.,* p. 80.

11. *Ibid.,* p. 81.

12. She was reading Freud in 1939–40, the same period at which she was writing "A Sketch of the Past." See *A Writer's Diary,* ed. Leonard Woolf (London: The Hogarth Press, 1969), pp. 322, 326. The Hogarth Press was Freud's English publisher, but that does not mean Virginia necessarily read Freud's works as they were published. When Freud moved to Hampstead at the start of World War II, the Woolfs went to visit him. Freud gave Virginia Woolf a narcissus (which need not have been meant as a comment on her character).

14. "Reminiscences," in *ibid.,* p. 54.

15. "22 Hyde Park Gate," in *ibid.,* p. 148.

16. *Ibid.,* p. 155.

17. "Thoughts on Social Success," in 1903 Diary, Berg Collection.

18. "An Artistic Party," 1903 Diary. For an interesting analogue to Woolf's experience, see Diana Holman-Hunt's memoir, *My Grandmothers and I* (New York: Norton, 1961), which tells of her dual Victorian heritage: one grandmother was the wife of a retired K.C., the other was the widow of the pre-Raphaelite painter.

19. A first version of *Freshwater* was written in 1923; the final version was written and performed in 1935. Vanessa Bell played Mrs. Cameron and Leonard Woolf played her husband.

20. "Old Bloomsbury," in *Moments of Being,* pp. 160–61.

21. Autobiographical fragment, 1940, "The tea table . . .," Berg Collection.

## 2   Bloomsbury

1. "Old Bloomsbury," in *Moments of Being*, p. 162.

2. *Sowing: An Autobiography of the Years 1880–1904* (London: The Hogarth Press, 1970), pp. 197–99.

3. Quoted by R. F. Harrod, *The Life of John Maynard Keynes* (London: Macmillan, 1951), pp. 71–72.

4. J. K. Johnstone's *The Bloomsbury Group* (London: Secker & Warburg, 1954) is perhaps the most notable example.

5. "Leslie Stephen," in *Collected Essays*, IV, 79.

6. *The Letters of Virginia Woolf, Vol. I (1888–1912)*, ed. Nigel Nicolson and Joanne Trautman (New York: Harcourt Brace Jovanovich, 1975), p. 77.

7. *Moments of Being*, p. 168.

8. *Horizon*, III, 18 (June 1941), 405. This essay is reprinted in *The Bloomsbury Group: A Collection of Memoirs, Commentary, and Criticism*, ed. S. P. Rosenbaum (Toronto and Buffalo: University of Toronto Press, 1975).

9. VW to Vanessa Bell, 29 August 1908, *Letters*, I, 364.

10. *Letters*, I, 208.

11. *Moments of Being*, p. 169.

12. Manuscript fragment, 1906, Monk's House Papers, University of Sussex Library (MH/A 13b). Printed by Quentin Bell in *Virginia Woolf: A Biography*, 2 vols. (London: The Hogarth Press, 1972), as Appendix C, vol. I, "Virginia Woolf and the Authors of *Euphrosyne*."

13. *The Common Reader* (London: The Hogarth Press, 1962; first published 1925), p. 11.

14. See Barbara Currier Bell and Carol B. Ohmann, "Virginia Woolf's Criticism: A Polemical Preface," *Critical Inquiry* 1:2 (December 1974), 361–71.

15. *The Voyage Out* (London: Duckworth & Co., 1915), p. 14.

16. Quoted by Bell, *Virginia Woolf*, I, 209.

17. *Letters*, I, 383.

18. *Collected Essays*, IV, 78.

19. *Moments of Being*, pp. 173–74.

20. VW to Vanessa Bell, 25 December 1909, *Letters*, I, 415.

21. *Moments of Being*, p. 177.

22. Review of Quentin Bell's *Virginia Woolf: A Biography* in *The Listener* 87 (15 June 1972), 794–95.

23. "Am I a Snob?" in *Moments of Being*, p. 188.

24. *Virginia Woolf*, I, 99. The story, which has been given the title "Phyllis and Rosamund" in the Monk's House Papers, University of Sussex Library (MH/A 23f), is dated 20–23 June 1906.

## 3  *The Voyage Out*

1. VW to Lytton Strachey, 28 January 1909, *Letters*, I, 381.

2. *The Voyage Out* (London: Duckworth & Co., 1915), p. 34. Future citations of *The Voyage Out* refer to this edition and will be noted by page number in the text.

3. The Berg Collection has two incomplete typed drafts of *The Voyage Out* (labeled "Earlier Typescript" and "Later Typescript," both undated) and an incomplete holograph draft, which is dated 1912. In this chapter, when I discuss an earlier version of the novel, I am generally referring to the "Earlier Typescript," which predates the 1912 holograph.

4. Quoted by Bell, *Virginia Woolf*, I, 210.

5. See *Ibid.*

6. *The Diary of Anaïs Nin, Volume IV* (New York: Harcourt Brace Jovanovich, 1971), pp. 88–89.

7. *Ibid.*, pp. 142, 148.

8. Journal, Florence 1909, Monk's House Papers, University of Sussex Library (MH/A 7).

9. It prefigures, too, something of the spirit in which she would marry Leonard Woolf, but Hewet could not be based on Leonard Woolf, who only entered Virginia's life in a significant way in 1911. For a fuller account of the amatory play between Clive Bell and Virginia, see Bell, *Virginia Woolf*, I, 132–36.

10. So James Naremore characterizes her treatment of sex in *The World Without a Self: Virginia Woolf and the Novel* (New Haven: Yale University Press, 1973), p. 43. See also pp. 42–44, 47–52.

11. The version of their love scene in the Berg Collection Earlier Typescript brings this out clearly:

> "If you were not here," said Rachel, "I should be frightened."
> The silence was now profound.
> "That's not my idea of you," said Hewet.
> "Your idea of me," said Rachel. She stopped and looked at him.

"You've often known me better than I know myself. It's true, I'm not frightened."

"You're the least frightened person I've ever met," said Hewet. "You really want to know."

"Yes," she said. "Everything. Everything."

12. Monk's House Papers, University of Sussex Library (MH/B 9a).

13. Earlier Typescript, Berg Collection.

14. See Bell, *Virginia Woolf*, I, 109.

15. VW to Violet Dickinson, *Letters*, I, 505.

# 4   Lytton Strachey and Leonard Woolf

1. *Virginia Woolf*, I, 129. For more about their relationship, see also I, 128, 141–42. Bell, as usual, is splendid at evoking the psychological complexities of the situation without pretentiousness.

2. Leonard Woolf, "Dying of Love," *New Statesman* 74 (6 October 1967), 438. See also "Ménage à Cinq," *New Statesman* 75 (23 February 1968), 241. These two reviews of Michael Holroyd's biography constitute Woolf's most extensive and candid statement about Lytton Strachey. Cf. his obituary tribute to Strachey which appeared in *The New Statesman* in 1932 and is reprinted in *The Bloomsbury Group*, ed. Rosenbaum, pp. 177–81.

3. *Virginia Woolf and Lytton Strachey: Letters*, pp. 15, 19, 22.

4. In *Bloomsbury* (London: Weidenfeld and Nicolson, 1968), still the best general account of the Bloomsbury group.

5. *A Writer's Diary*, p. 79.

6. Lecture, The Victorian Counter-Culture Conference, Tampa, Florida, March 1974. According to Annan, Strachey's role in the history of British homosexuality was to insist on the implementation and practice of what had been until then largely sentimental theory.

7. Cf. Bertrand Russell's sketch of "O.B." in *Portraits from Memory* (New York: Simon and Schuster, 1956), pp. 60–66.

8. *A Room of One's Own* (London: The Hogarth Press, 1929), p. 81.

9. Diary, 21 December 1925, Berg Collection, quoted by Bell, *Virginia Woolf*, II, 117.

10. Consulting Quentin Bell's chronology of the Woolfs' activities in *Virginia Woolf*, we see that they were continual visitors at Tidmarsh or Ham Spray (Strachey's residences) until 1925. After that, while

they continued to concern themselves about his health and domestic arrangements, they saw him less often, and by 1930 rarely.

11. VW to Molly MacCarthy, *Letters*, I, 492.

12. "Old Bloomsbury," in *Moments of Being*, p. 175.

13. "Ménage à Cinq," *New Statesman* 75 (23 February 1968), 241.

14. VW to Vanessa Bell, 10 August 1908, *Letters*, I, 348.

15. VW to Vanessa Bell, June 1911, *Letters*, I, 466.

16. VW to Vanessa Bell, 22? August 1911, *Letters*, I, 475.

17. Vanessa Bell to Margery Snowden, 10 May 1909, Monk's House Papers, University of Sussex Library, quoted by Bell, *Virginia Woolf*, I, 144.

18. VW to Clive Bell, *Letters*, I, 383.

19. VW to Leonard Woolf, 1 May 1912, *Letters*, I, 496.

20. See Bell, *Virginia Woolf*, II, 6, and Nigel Nicolson, *Portrait of a Marriage* (New York: Atheneum, 1973), p. 206.

21. VW to Leonard Woolf, 1 May 1912, *Letters*, I, 496.

22. VW to Violet Dickinson, June 1912, *Letters*, I, 502.

23. VW to Violet Dickinson, 4 June 1912, *Letters*, I, 500.

24. March 1941, British Museum (BM. 57947), quoted by Bell, *Virginia Woolf*, II, 226. This is the second version of the note Virginia Woolf left her husband at the time of her suicide. Cf. Terence's words when Rachel dies: "No two people have ever been so happy as we have been" (*The Voyage Out*, p. 353).

25. In April 1913 she writes to Violet Dickinson, explaining their stay in Sussex. "We aren't going to have a baby, but we want to have one, and six months in the country or so is said to be necessary first" (*Letters*, II, 23).

26. Bell, *Virginia Woolf*, I, 178.

27. Diary, 18 April 1918, Berg Collection, quoted by Bell, *Virginia Woolf*, II, 36n.

28. *A Writer's Diary*, p. 76.

29. "Middlebrow," *Collected Essays*, II, 198.

30. To some extent this portrayal constitutes the redressing of a balance, for I assume that in the history of English literature, Strachey is a minor figure and Virginia Woolf a major one, and it is time to recognize that she has done more for Bloomsbury than Bloomsbury has done for her. In fact, her Bloomsbury tie, and especially her association with Strachey, did her reputation considerable harm in the middle of her career. T. R. Barnes, writing in *Scru-*

*tiny* in 1933, provides an example of the way in which Woolf's reputation was linked with Strachey's, to her loss: "Strachey is an influence in life as well as in letters; he set a tone which still dominates certain areas of the highbrow world—e.g. that part of Bloomsbury which has a well-known annex in Cambridge. The deterioration and collapse represented by Mrs. Woolf's latest phase (*Orlando, Common Reader 2nd Series, Flush*) is one of the most pernicious effects of this environment." Edwin Muir provides another case in point, illustrating how the response to Strachey's work bled over and distorted the response to hers. Muir views Strachey as a stylist seeking a literary perfection, essentially inhumane, and he moves naturally from thoughts of Strachey to thoughts of Woolf: "It may be that when I write my final essay in this series [*Transition*] I may have to put her down along with Strachey and Garnett among the forces which are imposing a premature and hardening limitation on contemporary literature" (quoted by Michael Holroyd, *Lytton Strachey: A Critical Biography*, 2 vols. [New York: Holt, Rinehart and Winston, 1968], II, 325). For a contemporary example of Bloomsbury fatigue shaping an approach to Woolf, see Elizabeth Hardwick, *Seduction and Betrayal* (New York: Random House, 1974), pp. 125–39.

31. The image is from *To the Lighthouse* (New York: Harcourt, Brace & Company, 1927), p. 59.

# 5   Transitions and Experiments

1. In 1917 and 1919 respectively. The Woolfs had founded the Hogarth Press in 1917, partly as therapy for Virginia. *The Mark on the Wall*, printed with Leonard's *Three Jews*, was its first publication, followed in 1918 by Katherine Mansfield's *Prelude* and in 1919, *inter alia*, by T. S. Eliot's *Poems*. The year 1917 marked a return to activity for Virginia, who had been ill, on and off, from 1913 to 1915. She began again to write reviews for the *Times Literary Supplement* and to write, on a regular basis, that diary which she continued until her death in 1941 and which is in itself one of her major works.

2. *A Writer's Diary*, p. 47.

3. 27 October 1919, *The Letters of Virginia Woolf, Vol. II*

(*1912–1922*), ed. Nigel Nicolson and Joanne Trautman (New York: Harcourt Brace Jovanovich, 1976), p. 393.

4. *Night and Day* is Woolf's most Austen-like novel, and with it, one suspects, she wrote Austen out of her system. In 1919 she remarked in her diary, "I had rather write in my own way of *Four Passionate Snails* than be, as K[atherine] M[ansfield] maintains, Jane Austen over again" (*A Writer's Diary*, p. 22). In 1923 she did a reconsideration of Austen's work for the *Nation and Atheneum* which was incorporated into her essay on Austen in *The Common Reader*. When Woolf speculates about the kind of novels Austen might have gone on to write had she lived longer, they sound like the kind of novels Woolf herself began to write with *Jacob's Room*.

5. See, for example, James Hafley, *The Glass Roof: Virginia Woolf as Novelist* (Berkeley and Los Angeles: University of California Press, 1954), pp. 34–38, and Jean Guiguet, *Virginia Woolf and Her Works*, trans. Jean Stewart (London: The Hogarth Press, 1965), p. 217. Both essentially follow the lead of E. M. Forster who, in his Rede Lecture on Woolf (1941), characterized *Night and Day* as an "exercise in classical realism."

6. VW to Ottoline Morrell, 20 February 1938, Humanities Research Center, University of Texas, Austin.

7. *A Writer's Diary*, p. 47.

8. See *A Writer's Diary*, pp. 20–21.

9. *The Common Reader*, p. 188.

10. *Ibid.*, p. 189.

11. Cf. "Leslie Stephen," in *Collected Essays*, IV, 80: "For, as his tailor remarked when he saw my father walk past his shop up Bond Street, 'There goes a gentleman that wears good clothes without knowing it.'"

12. "Wanted: A New Self-Image for Women," in *The Woman in America*, ed. R. J. Lifton (Boston: Houghton Mifflin, 1965), pp. 173–92.

13. Alan Friedman, *The Turn of the Novel: The Transition to Modern Fiction* (New York: Oxford University Press, 1966), and Frank Kermode, *The Sense of an Ending: Studies in the Theory of Fiction* (New York: Oxford University Press, 1967).

14. The photograph is reproduced in this volume courtesy of Professor and Mrs. Quentin Bell. See also Adrian Stephen, *The "Dreadnought" Hoax* (London: The Hogarth Press, 1936).

15. *Monday or Tuesday* (New York: Harcourt Brace, 1921), p. 108.

16. *Ibid.*, p. 39.

17. The elliptical prose style of *Jacob's Room* and its recurring tone of fatigue show the influence on Woolf, I would suggest, of Eliot's early poetry. The following passage, for example, in both imagery and tone, recalls "Prufrock": "And everywhere we go wires and tubes surround us to carry the voices that try to penetrate before the last card is dealt and the days are over. 'Try to penetrate,' for as we lift the cup, shake the hand, express the hope, something whispers, Is this all? Can I never know, share, be certain? Am I doomed all my days to write letters, send voices, which fall upon the teatable, fade upon the passage, making appointments, while life dwindles, to come and dine?" *Jacob's Room* (London: The Hogarth Press, 1971, first published in 1922), p. 92.

18. *Jacob's Room*, pp. 70–71.

19. *A Writer's Diary*, p. 23.

20. *Ibid.*, p. 78.

21. *Ibid.*, p. 28.

# 6   The Love of Women

1. See *Virginia Woolf*, I, 80n.

2. *A Writer's Diary*, p. 78.

3. *Ibid.*, p. 224.

4. See Martha Wolfenstein, "How is Mourning Possible?" in *Psychoanalytic Study of the Child* 21 (1966), 93–123; also, Jeanne Lampl-de Groot, "On Adolescence," *Psychoanalytic Study of the Child* 15 (1960), 95–102.

5. Interview with Vanessa Bell, quoted in BBC, "A Portrait of Virginia Woolf" (1956), Houghton Library, Harvard University, Cambridge, Mass., pp. 3–4.

6. "The Mausoleum Book," British Museum (BM. Add. 57920), p. 44.

7. *Beginning Again: An Autobiography of the Years 1911–1918* (London: The Hogarth Press, 1968), p. 163.

8. *Ibid.*, pp. 79, 80.

9. The technical name for this symptom, the refusal to eat to the point of self-starvation, is *anorexia nervosa*. It is almost invariably a female problem. One school of thought connects it with a disturbed relationship to the mother. Another school associates it with an ex-

aggerated need for autonomy. Both explanations are suggestive in connection with Virginia Woolf. See John Sours, "Anorexia Nervosa," in *Adolescence,* ed. Gerald Caplan and Serge Lebovici (New York: Basic Books, 1969).

10. *Letters,* I, 83, 198.

11. *Letters,* I, 79.

12. *Letters,* I, 246, 244.

13. *Letters,* I, 69–70. "Katie" is Katherine Thynne. The editors of the letters point out that Virginia had never been to Paris and mistakenly assume she means by the Venus to refer to some Parisienne. But cf. *Letters,* I, 72: "Thoby might really stand nude with Katie in the Louvre."

14. "The Mausoleum Book," British Museum (BM. Add. 57920).

15. Fragment of a memoir read to the Memoir Club, Berg Collection. This is a draft of "Am I a Snob?" printed in *Moments of Being.*

16. 1903 Diary, Berg Collection.

17. VW to Violet Dickinson, 3 June 1907, *Letters,* I, 297.

18. VW to Vanessa Bell, 22 May 1927, Berg Collection.

19. *World Within World: The Autobiography of Stephen Spender* (London: Hamish Hamilton, 1951), p. 184.

20. "Am I a Snob?" in *Moments of Being,* pp. 185–86. For a fictionalized version of this lunch with Lady Bath, see the account of Jacob's lunch with Lady Rocksbier in *Jacob's Room,* pp. 98–99.

21. *Moments of Being,* p. 190.

22. Ralph Partridge, describing Woolf in social situations at the age of thirty-six, noted that she was particularly hard on "young women with any intellectual pretensions." Pretty girls, who wanted only to attract men physically, were spared her snubs, "but it was *lèse majesté* for a girl to think herself clever enough to talk to Virginia as an equal." BBC, "Portrait of Virginia Woolf," p. 14.

23. VW to Violet Dickinson, 28 December 1903, *Letters,* I, 119. Cf. Woolf's own later comment to Ethel Smyth that in her set she is never praised and never loved openly (VW to ES, 1932, Berg Collection).

24. VW to Ottoline Morrell, [10 August? 1922], *Letters,* II, 542. "I have written two chapters of my Garsington novel, you'll be glad to hear." According to her diary, Woolf had completed the first two "chapters" of *Mrs. Dalloway* ("Mrs. Dalloway in Bond Street" and "The Prime Minister") by October 21, 1922.

# 7  Mrs. Dalloway

1. *A Writer's Diary*, pp. 48–49, 46.

2. *Jacob's Room* holograph notebook, Berg Collection.

3. Reuben Brower explains superbly some of *Mrs. Dalloway's* effect through a close reading of the prose. See "Something Central Which Permeated: Virginia Woolf and *Mrs. Dalloway*" in *The Fields of Light* (New York: Oxford University Press, 1951), pp. 123–57.

4. *Mrs. Dalloway* (London: The Hogarth Press, 1963, first published 1925). Future citations refer to this edition and will be noted by page number in the text.

5. *A Writer's Diary*, p. 56.

6. Pertinent, perhaps, is Judith Bardwick's distinction between masculine motives for achievement and feminine motives for affiliation. See *Psychology of Women: A Study of Bio-Cultural Conflicts* (New York: Harper & Row, 1971), pp. 156–58. Students of creativity are beginning to catch up with the idea (implicit in *Mrs. Dalloway* and *To the Lighthouse*) that creativity need not always express itself in the form of poems, novels, and paintings. Abraham Maslow, for example, asserts that a first-rate soup is more creative than a second-rate painting. See *Toward a Psychology of Being* (New York: Van Nostrand, second edition, 1968), pp. 135–45.

7. *World Within World*, p. 154.

8. "Mrs. Dalloway in Bond Street," in *Mrs. Dalloway's Party: A Short Story Sequence*, ed. Stella McNichol (London: The Hogarth Press, 1973), p. 25.

9. 1903 Diary, Berg Collection.

10. *A Writer's Diary*, p. 44.

11. See Bell, *Virginia Woolf*, II, 87.

12. *Jacob's Room* holograph notebook, Berg Collection.

13. *Ibid.*

14. *Ibid.*

15. *The Common Reader*, p. 193.

16. See *Creativity and Psychological Health* (Princeton: Van Nostrand, 1963).

17. *A Writer's Diary*, p. 58.

18. VW to E. M. Forster, 21 January 1922, *Letters*, II, 499.

19. *Creativity and Psychological Health*, p. 249.

20. Holograph, Berg Collection.

21. Hillis Miller notes the same trait in Clarissa in his superb essay,

"Virginia Woolf's All Souls' Day: The Omniscient Narrator in *Mrs. Dalloway,*" in *The Shaken Realist: Essays in Modern Literature in Honor of Frederick J. Hoffman,* ed. Melvin Friedman and John B. Vickery (Baton Rouge: Louisiana State University Press, 1970), pp. 100–27.

22. *Beginning Again,* p. 76.

23. *A Writer's Diary,* p. 61.

24. *Ibid.,* p. 55.

25. *Ibid.,* p. 79.

26. *Mrs. Dalloway* holograph, British Museum (BM. Add. 51044–46), II, 65.

27. *A Writer's Diary,* p. 69. For the influence of Joyce on Woolf at this time, see Guiguet, *Virginia Woolf and Her Works,* especially pp. 240–45. Woolf was reading *Ulysses* in the spring of 1922 when *Mrs. Dalloway* began taking shape, at first "amused, stimulated, charmed" by the book, but then "puzzled, bored, irritated and disillusioned by a queasy undergraduate scratching his pimples" (*A Writer's Diary,* p. 48).

## 8   *To the Lighthouse*

1. *A Writer's Diary,* pp. 76–77.

2. *Ibid.,* pp. 137–38.

3. *Collected Essays,* II, 285.

4. See Walter E. Houghton, *The Victorian Frame of Mind* (New Haven: Yale University Press, 1957), pp. 348–53.

5. *A Writer's Diary,* p. 138.

6. *To the Lighthouse* (New York: Harcourt, Brace & Co., 1927), p. 223. All future citations refer to this edition and will be given by page number in the text.

7. *A Writer's Diary,* p. 138.

8. See Frank Baldanza, "To the Lighthouse Again," *PMLA* 70 (1955), pp. 548–52.

9. *A Writer's Diary,* p. 120.

10. VW to Vanessa Bell, 20 February 1922, *Letters,* II, 506.

11. *A Writer's Diary,* p. 107.

12. VW to Vanessa Bell, 25 May 1927, Berg Collection.

13. VW to Vanessa Bell, 21 April 1927, Berg Collection.

14. *A Writer's Diary,* p. 119.

15. *Ibid.,* p. 144.

16. In *The Children of the Dream* (New York: Macmillan, 1969), Bruno Bettelheim, discussing the pioneer kibbutzniks of Israel, another group of people who sought, like the Bloomsbury set, to be innovative about sexual roles and family arrangements, notes a psychological reaction among the women similar to Virginia Woolf's. Not wanting to have children, or wanting them on very different terms from their mothers, the Israeli pioneer women felt themselves as "ungiving" and suffered from a sense of "unworthiness and betrayal." Though ready in practice to cast off the role of their mothers, psychologically they remained ensnared by it (pp. 28–31).

17. *A Writer's Diary*, p. 229.

18. *Beginning Again*, p. 149. See also pp. 76–82. Leonard's account omits the breakdown after her father's death and substitutes one in childhood which is not otherwise documented. The dates of her breakdowns were 1895, 1904, 1913, and 1941. In disconnecting the sources of her earlier breakdowns from the sources of the later ones, Leonard may have flattened the picture of his wife's insanity, but he succeeded in locating her most vulnerable times as an adult.

19. Before their marriage in 1912, both the Woolfs were eager for children, although on Virginia's part this eagerness may have resulted partly from a desire to join in the normal great events of existence rather than from a strong maternal urge. Leonard, however, feared maternity would be too much of a strain on Virginia, for whom even the slightest strain seemed disastrous. He consulted Sir George Savage, her mental specialist, and upon finding his advice ("Do her a world of good, my dear fellow; do her a world of good!") worldly and superficial, consulted other specialists, who agreed that it would be too much of a strain. By that advice they abided. It is impossible to know whether the distaste for the physicality of having her own children which Virginia later expressed was a rationalization for her inability to have them or whether the Woolfs may have set out to prove she could not have children because in some way she did not want them. *See Beginning Again*, p. 82.

# 9   V. Sackville-West and Androgyny

1. Another important feminist essay closely related to the works of this period is her introduction to *Life as We Have Known It* (London: The Hogarth Press, 1931), a collection of personal testimonies

by members of the Women's Co-operative Guild, a working-class organization—itself a fascinating volume. Woolf's introduction, later reprinted as "Memories of a Working Women's Guild," (*Collected Essays*, IV, 134–48) confronts with her usual candor the differences between her experience and that of the working women. Woolf's own pained recognition of the class-bound nature of her work always undercuts one's impulse to condemn her as mandarin.

2. Harold Nicolson, *Diaries and Letters*, 3 vols. (New York: Atheneum, 1966–68).

3. See *V. Sackville-West's Garden Book* (London: Michael Joseph, 1968), a collection of gardening columns published in the *Observer* between 1947 and 1961.

4. Diary, Berg Collection, 21 December 1925, quoted by Bell, *Virginia Woolf*, II, 118.

5. See Nigel Nicolson, *Portrait of a Marriage* (New York: Atheneum, 1973), pp. 109–11, 116–17. Dressing as men was a favorite pastime of fashionable Parisian lesbians at the time, according to Colette. See *The Pure and the Impure* (translated by Herma Briffault; New York: Farrar, Straus & Giroux, 1967) for her account of the sexual underground.

6. *Portrait of a Marriage*, p. 106.

7. In 1926 the Hogarth Press published a collection of Julia Margaret Cameron's photographs prefaced with a biographical essay by Virginia Woolf and another on Cameron's work by Roger Fry. Read as a unified volume, both pictures and text of *Victorian Photographs of Famous Men and Fair Women* constitute a statement of Victorian assumptions about sex roles and a critique of them, and while it is not usually considered part of Woolf's canon, the volume may be profitably grouped with her other works of the twenties, especially *To the Lighthouse*.

8. *Portrait of a Marriage*, pp. 200–203. Nicolson also notes that *Orlando* was a great gift to Vita, accomplishing for her what birth could not, that is, identifying her permanently with Knole. For an excellent discussion of *Orlando* as a parody of conventional biographies, see Leon Edel, *Literary Biography* (Garden City, N.Y.: Doubleday, 1959), pp. 134–45.

9. *A Writer's Diary*, p. 124.

10. *Ibid.*, p. 105. Woolf describes here a project called "The Jessamy Brides," which anticipates *Orlando* stylistically, though the story

she outlines is somewhat different, there being two ladies involved and "sapphism is to be suggested."

11. *Orlando: A Biography* (London: The Hogarth Press, 1928), p. 143. Future citations refer to this edition and will be noted by page number in the text.

12. VW to Vanessa Bell, 15 May 1927, Berg Collection.

13. *A Writer's Diary*, p. 134.

14. *A Room of One's Own* (London: The Hogarth Press, 1929), p. 110. Future citations refer to this edition and will be noted by page number in the text.

15. See Carolyn Heilbrun, *Toward a Recognition of Androgyny* (New York: Knopf, 1973), and Nancy Topping Bazin, *Virginia Woolf and the Androgynous Vision* (New Brunswick, N.J.: Rutgers University Press, 1973). *Women's Studies* has devoted an entire issue to the subject of androgyny, 2:2 (1974). See also Herbert Marder, *Feminism and Art: A Study of Virginia Woolf* (Chicago: University of Chicago Press, 1968).

16. Catharine Stimpson, "The Androgyne and the Homosexual," *Women's Studies* 2:2 (1974), 242.

17. *The Letters of John Keats*, ed. Hyder Rollins, 2 vols. (Cambridge: Harvard University Press, 1958), I, 224.

18. "American Fiction," in *Collected Essays*, II, 117.

19. V. Sackville-West to Harold Nicolson, 17 August 1926, quoted in *Portrait of a Marriage*, p. 206.

20. VW to Vanessa Bell, 22 May 1927, Berg Collection. For the other references to Vita see VW to Vanessa Bell, 18 February 1927, 13 June 1926, 15 May 1927, Berg Collection. In the reference to Duncan Grant, it is clear that occasionally Woolf does equate androgyny with bisexuality. What is most interesting to me, however, is that Grant should be her example of the androgynous artist and not Lytton Strachey, who was, of course, exclusively homosexual.

21. "Moments of Being. 'Slater's Pins Have No Points,' " in *A Haunted House and Other Short Stories* (New York: Harcourt, Brace, 1944), pp. 103–11.

22. This, by the way, over Vita's protests, and to the vexation, too, of Vanessa and Angelica Bell.

23. The letter, published 8 September 1928, was co-signed by E. M. Forster.

24. *World Within World;* p. 156.

## 10   The Thirties

1. "Notes on the Style of Mrs. Woolf," *Scrutiny* 1:1 (1932), 33–38. In 1938 she would refer to this article as the one in which *Scrutiny* "found her out" (*A Writer's Diary*, p. 308). It hurt her more than any of the subsequent attacks because it accused her of failings that she suspected in herself, notably that she used feminine charm to cover an absence of thought, achieved delicacy of perception at the price, in Bradbrook's words, of "cerebral etiolation."

2. Her diary for March 16, 1935, refers to three recent "severe swingeings," of which Lewis's was one. The others were by Frank Swinnerton in *The Georgian Literary Scene* and Dmitri Mirsky in *The Intelligentsia of Great Britain*. See *A Writer's Diary*, p. 240, and *The Bloomsbury Group*, ed. Rosenbaum, pp. 332–34 and 381–87, for a sampling of these controversies.

3. Winifred Holtby, *Virginia Woolf* (London: Wishart & Co., 1932); Ingebord Badenhaussen, *Die Sprache Virginia Woolf's: Ein Betrag zur Stilistik des modernen englischen Romans* (Marburg, 1931); Floris Delattre, *Le Roman psychologique de Virginia Woolf* (Paris: J. Vrin, 1932).

4. 29 February 1932, Berg Collection.

5. This memoir, written two weeks after Julian's death in July 1937, is published, in large part, by Quentin Bell as Appendix C in *Virginia Woolf*, II, 255–59. The MS, entitled "Reminiscences of Julian," is in the University of Sussex Library (MH/A8).

6. Peter Stansky and William Abrahams have done this brilliantly in *Journey to the Frontier: Julian Bell and John Cornford—Their Lives and the 1930s* (London: Constable, 1966). I am greatly indebted to their work.

7. Julian Bell, *Essays, Poems and Letters* (London: The Hogarth Press, 1938), p. 111.

8. *Ibid.*, p. 259.

9. See *Journey to the Frontier*, pp. 105–6.

10. *Essays, Poems and Letters*, p. 167.

11. *Ibid.*, p. 192.

12. *Journey to the Frontier*, p. 412.

13. Appendix C, in Bell, *Virginia Woolf*, II, 258–59.

14. "Inside the Whale," in *Inside the Whale and Other Essays* (London: Penguin, 1957), p. 27. Notice that in 1938 the subconscious and

the solar plexus could still be regarded as places where nothing was happening. In revisionist accounts of the thirties, such as Christopher Isherwood's *Christopher and His Kind* (New York: Farrar, Straus & Giroux, 1976), sex is retroactively reinstated as an important subject. Apparently something *was* happening in the solar plexus.

15. *Ibid.*, pp. 29–30.

16. John Lehmann, *In My Own Time: Memoirs of a Literary Life* (Boston: Little, Brown & Co., 1969), pp. 110–11.

17. Leonard Woolf gives his version of John Lehmann's early association with the Hogarth Press in *Downhill All the Way: An Autobiography of the Years 1919–1939* (New York: Harcourt, Brace & World, 1967), pp. 172–77.

18. *World Within World*, p. 141.

19. Quoted in *The Bloomsbury Group*, ed. Rosenbaum, p. 384.

20. *World Within World*, p. 159.

21. See *The Economic Consequences of the Peace* (New York: Harcourt, Brace and Howe, 1920).

22. *World Within World*, p. 154.

23. VW to Ottoline Morrell, 31 December 1933, Humanities Research Center, University of Texas.

24. VW to Ottoline Morrell, 19 December 1933, Humanities Research Center, University of Texas.

25. *World Within World*, p. 158.

26. See Appendix C in Bell, *Virginia Woolf*, II, 257. Written in 1937, her statement dates the emergence of her new attitude two years before, that is, in 1935.

27. "The Niece of an Earl," *Collected Essays*, I, 222.

28. See also "The Narrow Bridge of Art" (1927), in *Collected Essays*, II, 218–29.

29. *Virginia Woolf* (New York: New Directions, 1963), p. 105.

30. *The Waves* (London: The Hogarth Press, 1972), p. 82. Future citations refer to this edition and will be noted by page number in the text.

31. VW to John Lehmann, 17 September 1931, Humanities Research Center, University of Texas, quoted by John Lehmann in *Virginia Woolf and Her World* (London: Thames and Hudson, 1975), p. 79.

32. See Reuben Brower, "The Novel as Poem: Virginia Woolf Ex-

ploring a Critical Metaphor," in Morton Bloomfield, ed., *The Interpretation of Narrative*, Harvard English Studies, I (Cambridge: Harvard University Press, 1970), pp. 229–47.

33. "Virginia Woolf: A Special Instance," in *Claremont Essays* (London: Secker and Warburg, 1965), p. 92.

34. "A Letter to a Young Poet," *Collected Essays*, II, 190.

35. *The Years* (London: The Hogarth Press, 1937), p. 390. Future citations refer to this edition and will be noted by page number in the text.

36. Mitchell Leaska speculates on the material repressed in "Virginia Woolf, the Pargeter: A Reading of *The Years*," in *Bulletin of the New York Public Library* 80:2 (Winter, 1977), 172–210.

37. *A Writer's Diary*, p. 271.

38. *Three Guineas* (London: The Hogarth Press, 1938), p. 97. Future citations refer to this edition and will be noted by page number in the text.

39. The Rede Lecture (1941), in *Two Cheers for Democracy* (New York: Harcourt, Brace & World, 1942), pp. 242–58.

40. "Caterpillars of the Commonwealth Unite!" *Scrutiny* 7:2 (September 1938), 203–14. Interestingly, Leavis also manages to get in a dig at Woolf for not having children. This was another aspect of the perception of Woolf, in the thirties, as an incomplete, rarified person; for popular Freudianism (companion of popular Marxism) in a cruel way seemed to reaffirm the rightness of Victorian domestic obligations just as women were beginning to work themselves out of them. (See Holtby, *Virginia Woolf*, pp. 29–30.) The tyranny of the "complete" and "normal" life cycle was harsh. Erikson had not yet pointed out that there are different ways of being generative.

41. At least one other innovative and imaginative woman, writing close to the time when Woolf wrote *Three Guineas*, thought that the problem with contemporary Europe was "too much fathering." See Gertrude Stein, *Everybody's Autobiography* (New York: Vintage Books, 1973; first published 1936), p. 133.

42. *Flush* (1933), Woolf's mock-biography of Elizabeth Barrett Browning's dog, is really the story of Elizabeth's escape from her father's tyranny, and echoes Woolf's own myth of liberation. The Victorian lady who fled from the repressive atmosphere of Wimpole Street to happiness in Italy had much in common with the immured maiden freed from patriarchal Kensington by moving to

Bloomsbury. The role of Robert Browning was played in Woolf's life by her sister.

43. *A Writer's Diary*, p. 288.

44. *Ibid.*, p. 292.

45. *Ibid.*, p. 308.

46. "The Leaning Tower," *Collected Essays*, II, 181.

## 11   Life without a Future

1. *Between the Acts* (London: The Hogarth Press, 1969), p. 66. Further citations refer to this edition and will be noted by page number in the text. My understanding of *Between the Acts* has been particularly informed by Avrom Fleishman's chapter on that novel in *Virginia Woolf: A Critical Reading* (Baltimore and London: The Johns Hopkins Press, 1975) and by J. Hillis Miller's subtly ironic paper on *Between the Acts*, read at the English Institute, Cambridge, Mass., 1974.

2. The effect sought by Miss La Trobe is clearer in the first draft of the novel: *"Between the Acts*, Earliest Typescript," dated April 2, 1938–July 30, 1939, Berg Collection, p. 173.

3. *The Journey Not the Arrival Matters* (New York: Harcourt, Brace & World, 1970), pp. 89, 77.

4. *A Writer's Diary*, p. 354.

5. *Ibid.*

6. VW to John Lehmann, British Museum (BM. Add. 56234).

7. *A Writer's Diary*, p. 364. *N.S.* is *The New Statesman. P.H.* is *Pointz Hall*, the original title of *Between the Acts*.

8. *A Writer's Diary*, p. 365.

9. *Journey*, p. 79.

10. Quoted by Leonard Woolf, *Journey*, p. 93. The originals of the three suicide notes are in the British Museum.

11. VW to Vanessa Bell, British Museum (BM. 57947).

12. Quoted by Bell, *Virginia Woolf*, II, 226.

13. *The Savage God: A Study of Suicide* (New York: Bantam Books, 1973), p. 228.

14. "Louie Mayer," in *Recollections of Virginia Woolf*, ed. Joan Russell Noble (New York: William Morrow, 1972), p. 161.

15. See *Virginia Woolf*, p. 157.

16. See Naremore, *The World Without a Self*, p. 245.

## Portrait: A Woman of Letters

1. *Recollections of Virginia Woolf*, ed. Noble, pp. 112–13, 125.

2. *The Divided Self: An Existential Study in Sanity and Madness* (New York: Pantheon, 1962).

3. VW to Ethel Smyth, 16 October 1930, Berg Collection.

4. VW to Ethel Smyth, 22 June 1930, Berg Collection.

5. See Anthony Storr, *The Dynamics of Creation* (New York: Atheneum, 1972), especially pp. 40–48 and 79–80.

6. VW to Ethel Smyth, 28 September 1930, Berg Collection.

7. VW to Ethel Smyth, 29 July 1934, Berg Collection.

8. VW to Ethel Smyth, 9 April 1931, Berg Collection.

9. Quentin Bell reports that in his opinion Leonard bought the field in order to prevent its being built upon.

# Index

Titles of VW's works are indexed independent of their author's name. Other works are indexed under author's name.

291